Oracle ADF Faces Cookbook

Over 80 hands-on recipes covering a variety of ADF Faces
components to help you create stunning user experiences

Amr Gawish

BIRMINGHAM - MUMBAI

Oracle ADF Faces Cookbook

First published: March 2014

Production Reference: 1190314

Published by Packt Publishing Ltd.
Livery Place
35 Livery Street
Birmingham B3 2PB, UK.

ISBN 978-1-84968-922-9

www.packtpub.com

Cover Image by Mahmoud Ismail Abdellatief Gawish (gawish_photography@hotmail.com)

Credits

Author

Amr Gawish

Reviewers

Matteo Formica

Mauro Flores Guevara

Victor Jabur

Daniel Ribeiro

Bejoy Thomas

Commissioning Editor

Stephanie Moss

Acquisition Editors

James Jones

Erol Staveley

Content Development Editor

Ankita Shashi

Technical Editors

Rosmy George

Veena Pagare

Manal Pednekar

Anand Singh

Copy Editors

Alisha Aranha

Roshni Banerjee

Gladson Monteiro

Adithi Shetty

Project Coordinator

Priyanka Goel

Proofreaders

Christopher Smith

Joel T. Johnson

Indexer

Priya Subramani

Graphics

Ronak Dhruv

Production Coordinator

Nitesh Thakur

Cover Work

Nitesh Thakur

About the Author

Amr Gawish began his career at the age of 18, working as a web designer before entering college. He is very passionate about technology and always tries to push the limits of the technologies he uses.

He completed his bachelor's degree in Math and Computer Sciences from Al-Azhar University in Egypt and is currently persuing his master's at the University of Liverpool. He is currently employed as an Oracle Fusion Middleware consultant and is certified in Java SE 7, Oracle ADF, WebCenter Portal, and Oracle SOA Suite. He has worked with all these products and the rest of the Oracle middleware stack for more than six years.

He has also gained a fair amount of experience in various other topics such as Gamification, Scala programming, and Akka and is currently working on microcontroller programming with Raspberry Pi and Arduino and robotics.

You can learn more about him by visiting his website, `www.amr-gawish.com`, or follow him on Twitter (`@agawish`).

He is currently working with infoMENTUM (`www.infomentum.com`), which is an Oracle Platinum Partner; a leading company in Oracle Fusion Middleware; and the first company to specialize in WebCenter (both content and portal), Oracle SOA, ADF, and Java in the EMEA region.

Acknowledgments

Thank you Ne'ma, my beautiful wife, for always being there for me and supporting me every step of the way.

Thank you Aisha for always bringing a smile to my face.

Thanks dad, mom, and Mahmoud (@Mahmoud_iGawish) for always being there for me.

Thanks infoMENTUM, especially Dan Shepherd, Vikram Setia (@vikramsetia), Marta Monteiro (@martamonteiro), Mauro Flores (@maurofloresg), and all my colleagues for the continuous support and encouragement.

Thanks to all the book reviewers for their hard work. I'm really glad to be supported by such a good team.

Thanks Packt Publishing for this great opportunity, and special thanks to Priyanka Goel and Ankita Shashi for all the guidance and support.

About the Reviewers

Matteo Formica is an Oracle Fusion Middleware specialist with more than seven years' experience in consulting, software design, and development. After completing his master's degree in Computer Science in 2006, he was involved in Forensic Security and High Energy Physics academic projects. During his years with Oracle, he worked with the most popular Java and JEE frameworks and was exposed to the main products of the Fusion Middleware stack. Here, he acquired considerable experience with ADF Framework, data integration, and SOA Suite, by joining projects in different market sectors. Upon relocating from Rome to London in 2010, he joined Sopra Group, where he honed his Java and JEE skills. More recently he joined InfoMENTUM, an Oracle Platinum Partner mainly focused on ECM and WebCenter. Since becoming part of this skilled and innovative team, he has continuously sought to master ADF Framework and WebCenter Portal by joining key projects, and he has recently become an ADF and WebCenter Portal Certified Implementation Specialist.

Thanks to Amr Gawish for giving me this great opportunity, and for his invaluable support in my everyday job. Thanks also to my past and present colleagues for helping me in my professional growth and for making me become what I am today. Finally, thanks to Caz for her help and support.

Mauro Flores Guevara is a WebCenter/ADF specialist and solution architect with 12 years of experience in IT. During this time, he has worked with different technologies such as ADF, PHP, Java, C#, Portals, and among others and is currently certified in the Oracle Fusion Middleware stack. In Mexico, he and the company he worked for had the opportunity to be one of the first teams to deliver an Oracle WebCenter implementation in Latin America.

He is passionate about martial arts and has been trained in it for more than 16 years. He started an academy of self defense (Lima Lama) in 2006 and has been teaching since then.

He now has the opportunity to work with one of the best Oracle partners in the UK when it comes to Oracle WebCenter and Oracle ADF, where he works with high-skilled colleagues. The link to his blog is `http://middlewareforhumans.com`.

I would like to thank Amr Gawish for letting me be a part of this experience, Yannick Ongena for his mentorship, my family for their trust, and my wife for her support and patience.

Victor Jabur currently works as a solutions architect in a large Brazilian retail company. Since 2007, he has been working with Oracle SOA products and has worked in several large-sized Brazilian companies in various segments such as electronic payment services, insurance, and construction. He has also participated in a project for the Port of Santos, one of the main Brazilian ports, among others. He is a Bachelor of Information Systems at University of São Paulo (USP), and is passionate about technology and software development. He lives in São Paulo with his wife Juliana and her daughter Larissa, constituting a very united family, blessed by God. He maintains a blog at `www.victorjabur.com`, which seeks to share knowledge and help people around the world because he believes that the world can become a better place when people help each other.

Daniel Ribeiro is passionate about technology, his son Allan, his girlfriend Patricia Fujioka, family, sports, nature, and science.

Formed in technical software development in 1997 by COTEMIG, he has worked in large companies in the financial sector, telecom, and IT consultancy, always focusing on software architecture.

Daniel has a special son (cromosomopatia on the 13th chromosome, never before mapped), 13 years of age, whom he has been responsible for since the second year of his life. Without the help and patience of his wonderful girlfriend, his work would not have been possible.

Bejoy Thomas is an Oracle Middleware consultant with more than nine years of experience in IT. He is specialized in system integration design and development using Oracle middleware products such as WebCenter, IDM, SOA Suite, and BPM Suite. He is a WebCenter Portal Certified Implementation Specialist and has been working in various WebCenter portals and SOA projects since 2008. He is currently working in the UK for infoMENTUM limited.

He holds a BE in Computer Science and Engineering from University of Calicut, India. He is also the cofounder of an e-commerce startup based in India (www.bluelilys.com).

www.PacktPub.com

Support files, eBooks, discount offers and more

You might want to visit www.PacktPub.com for support files and downloads related to your book.

Did you know that Packt offers eBook versions of every book published, with PDF and ePub files available? You can upgrade to the eBook version at www.PacktPub.com and as a print book customer, you are entitled to a discount on the eBook copy. Get in touch with us at service@packtpub.com for more details.

At www.PacktPub.com, you can also read a collection of free technical articles, sign up for a range of free newsletters and receive exclusive discounts and offers on Packt books and eBooks.

http://PacktLib.PacktPub.com

Do you need instant solutions to your IT questions? PacktLib is Packt's online digital book library. Here, you can access, read and search across Packt's entire library of books.

Why Subscribe?

- ▶ Fully searchable across every book published by Packt
- ▶ Copy and paste, print and bookmark content
- ▶ On demand and accessible via web browser

Free Access for Packt account holders

If you have an account with Packt at www.PacktPub.com, you can use this to access PacktLib today and view nine entirely free books. Simply use your login credentials for immediate access.

Instant Updates on New Packt Books

Get notified! Find out when new books are published by following @PacktEnterprise on Twitter, or the *Packt Enterprise* Facebook page.

Table of Contents

Preface

Oracle ADF Faces is the view/controller part of the Oracle ADF end-to-end framework. ADF Faces has more than 150 Ajax-enabled components that help developers to rapidly build applications that are robust, reactive, and easy to use.

In this book, we will learn how to deal with the different features of the ADF Faces framework. In the first part of the book, we will learn how to install JDeveloper and ADF, create a simple Oracle ADF application, present data in different ways using ADF Faces components, and use common ADF components such as inputs, menus, toolbars, and more.

In the second part of the book, we will understand how to create a unified template for ADF Faces applications, apply different skinning techniques, and use different visualization components and graphs.

In the last part of the book, we will learn how to use partial page rendering and different ADF Faces events; create reactive applications using polling, push, and WebSockets; add validation and conversion for different ADF Faces inputs; and create different ADF Faces resources for reuse. Finally, we will discuss some best practices, tips, and advice on how to scale and tune your ADF Faces application.

What this book covers

Chapter 1, Building Your ADF Faces Environment from the Ground Up, provides the necessary steps to build your environment and install different software to work with ADF Faces.

Chapter 2, Getting Started with ADF Faces and JDeveloper, focuses on getting you started with a simple ADF application and showing you how to deal with JDeveloper IDE.

Chapter 3, Presenting Data Using ADF Faces, shows different ways to present business service data with highlights over i18n and l10n.

Chapter 4, Using Common ADF Faces Components, describes how to work with the common ADF Faces components.

Chapter 5, Beautifying the Application Layout for Great User Experience, provides different techniques of creating great looking application by creating templates and skins, and by using advanced skinning techniques.

Chapter 6, Enriching User Experience with Visualization Components, explains how to work with different ADF Faces Visualization components to create great dashboards.

Chapter 7, Handling Events and Partial Page Rendering, describes how to use partial page rendering and different ADF events. It also provides an explanation of how to create great reactive applications by understanding how to use polling, push, and work with WebSockets.

Chapter 8, Validating and Converting Inputs, explains how to provide conversion and validation for different input components to insure the validity of the data returned to the service layer.

Chapter 9, Building Your Application for Reuse, shows how to create different resources for reuse, such as task flow templates, declarative components, contextual events, and how to package your application for reuse.

Chapter 10, Scaling Your ADF Faces Application, provides multiple tips and advice of how to scale your application and tune its performance.

What you need for this book

To make sure you can work with the recipes in this book, the following software will be required:

- **JDK**: Java SE Development Kit 7u45 or newer
- **Oracle Database**: Oracle 10g or newer
- **Oracle JDeveloper**: Oracle JDeveloper 12c (12.1.2.0.0) or newer
- **Miscellaneous tools**: Scout App (0.7.1) or newer

Who this book is for

If you are an ADF developer who wants to harness the powers of Oracle ADF Faces to create exceptional user interfaces and reactive applications, this book will provide you with the recipes needed to just do that. Readers of this book need to know little or none about Oracle ADF Faces, but should be comfortable with the development of Java applications, Java EE frameworks, and JSF. This book is also for ADF developers who know Oracle ADF Faces but want to know what's new in Oracle ADF Faces 12c.

Conventions

In this book, you will find a number of styles of text that distinguish between different kinds of information. Here are some examples of these styles, and an explanation of their meaning.

Code words in text, database table names, folder names, filenames, file extensions, pathnames, dummy URLs, user input, and Twitter handles are shown as follows: "Open the `jdev\bin\jdev.conf` path under the `jdeveloper` directory."

A block of code is set as follows:

```
# optimize the JVM for strings / text editing
AddVMOption -XX:+UseStringCache
AddVMOption -XX:+OptimizeStringConcat
AddVMOption -XX:+UseCompressedStrings
```

When we wish to draw your attention to a particular part of a code block, the relevant lines or items are set in bold:

```
builder.append("AdfPage.PAGE.showMessages
  (component.getClientId());");
builder.append("component.focus();");
erks.addScript(context, builder.toString());
```

Any command-line input or output is written as follows:

```
PATH=%JAVA_HOME%\bin;
```

New terms and **important words** are shown in bold. Words that you see on the screen, in menus or dialog boxes for example, appear in the text like this: "Click on **Finish** after you finish and you will have the entire book's Git repository locally."

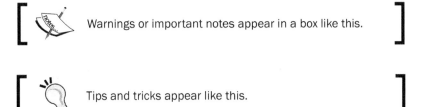

Warnings or important notes appear in a box like this.

Tips and tricks appear like this.

Reader feedback

Feedback from our readers is always welcome. Let us know what you think about this book—what you liked or may have disliked. Reader feedback is important for us to develop titles that you really get the most out of.

To send us general feedback, simply send an e-mail to `feedback@packtpub.com`, and mention the book title via the subject of your message.

If there is a topic that you have expertise in and you are interested in either writing or contributing to a book, see our author guide on `www.packtpub.com/authors`.

Customer support

Now that you are the proud owner of a Packt book, we have a number of things to help you to get the most from your purchase.

Downloading the example code

You can download the example code files for all Packt books you have purchased from your account at `http://www.packtpub.com`. You can also download the files from GitHub at `https://github.com/agawish/ADF-Faces-Cookbook/archive/master.zip`. If you purchased this book elsewhere, you can visit `http://www.packtpub.com/support` and register to have the files e-mailed directly to you.

Downloading the color images of this book

We also provide you a PDF file that has color images of the screenshots/diagrams used in this book. The color images will help you better understand the changes in the output. You can download this file from `https://www.packtpub.com/sites/default/files/downloads/9229EN_Images.pdf`.

Errata

Although we have taken every care to ensure the accuracy of our content, mistakes do happen. If you find a mistake in one of our books—maybe a mistake in the text or the code—we would be grateful if you would report this to us. By doing so, you can save other readers from frustration and help us improve subsequent versions of this book. If you find any errata, please report them by visiting `http://www.packtpub.com/submit-errata`, selecting your book, clicking on the **errata submission form** link, and entering the details of your errata. Once your errata are verified, your submission will be accepted and the errata will be uploaded on our website, or added to any list of existing errata, under the Errata section of that title. Any existing errata can be viewed by selecting your title from `http://www.packtpub.com/support`.

Piracy

Piracy of copyright material on the Internet is an ongoing problem across all media. At Packt, we take the protection of our copyright and licenses very seriously. If you come across any illegal copies of our works, in any form, on the Internet, please provide us with the location address or website name immediately so that we can pursue a remedy.

Please contact us at `copyright@packtpub.com` with a link to the suspected pirated material.

We appreciate your help in protecting our authors, and our ability to bring you valuable content.

Questions

You can contact us at `questions@packtpub.com` if you are having a problem with any aspect of the book, and we will do our best to address it.

1
Building Your ADF Faces Environment From the Ground Up

In this chapter, we will prepare our development environment and install all the necessary software that we will be using throughout this book. This chapter contains the following recipes:

- ► Preparing and structuring the OS for ADF and JDeveloper
- ► Installing JDK
- ► Exploring different options to install the database
- ► Installing JDeveloper
- ► Tuning JDeveloper
- ► Downloading the book's Git repository

Introduction

Oracle Application Development Framework or **ADF** is the Oracle end-to-end flagship framework to help increase a developer's productivity by providing ready-to-use design patterns and best practices so that the developer needs only to concentrate his/her focus on the business logic rather than focusing on the technology behind it.

With **Oracle JDeveloper** as a cross-platform **Integrated Development Environment** (**IDE**), Oracle ADF and all **Oracle Fusion Middleware** suite products find the IDE that simplifies development and supports all development lifecycle stages.

Oracle ADF framework can also be developed with Eclipse IDE. By installing an Oracle Enterprise pack for Eclipse, you can develop ADF applications with Eclipse. For more information, refer to the official documentation at `http://www.oracle.com/technetwork/developer-tools/eclipse/overview/index.html`.

One of the main reasons behind ADF's fast growth is its Controller and View technology, which is famously known as **Oracle ADF Faces**.

ADF Faces is responsible for representing data to the end user and taking inputs back, passing data from and to the Data layer, respectively, to process.

If you are familiar with the **Model-View-Controller** (**MVC**) pattern, Oracle ADF Faces is the one that is responsible for all the Vs and Cs of the ADF application.

In this book, we will highlight our focus on the Oracle ADF Faces section of the ADF Framework, how to utilize it to our needs, and how to make the best data of it to create a beautiful user experience for the end user.

In this chapter, you will learn how to structure your development environment and how to organize and put everything in its right place. You will learn how to install your latest JDK and the options available for your database installation. You will practice how to install JDeveloper and how to tune it for your operational system, and how to change some general preferences inside JDeveloper. You will get an overview of Git and how to install the book's repository on your machine.

Preparing and structuring the OS for JDeveloper and ADF

It's important to understand the memory consumption of your software in order to work effectively without any trouble. If you would like to have a complete environment to work with ADF effectively, with your local machine, you might need to install JDeveloper and Oracle Database locally—if you like to work offline—which is a lot of memory consumption, not to mention when you debug and run your application against the application server, which would also have a medium to large memory footprint. So, make sure you have enough memory and processing power to start working with ADF effectively.

Getting ready

The following are considered minimum hardware requirements for your development machine:

- Minimum 4 GB Memory (RAM)
- Fast CPUs (for example, Intel Core i5)
- SSD Hard drive, HDD with minimum 7200 RPM, or Hybrid HDD

 For more information and guidance about performance and memory, check this great video by Chris Muir at `http://www.youtube.com/watch?v=GXABzw7qU9g`.

After making sure you have enough processing and memory power, you will still need to prepare your environment. You should always start by creating the directory structure to make sure everything goes into the right place, and to be in control especially after your project expands. It's always a good practice to organize how to reach your information effectively, after which you should start the installation process of your software.

How to do it...

In order to prepare and structure your operating system ADF, perform the following steps:

1. Create your directory structure properly. What I usually do is start from the root directory of my user, for example, `C:\Users\Amr` in Windows or `/Users/amr` in a Nix-based OS, and start adding the structure of my development environment. So, in Windows, for instance, my workspace under the user directory looks like the following screenshot:

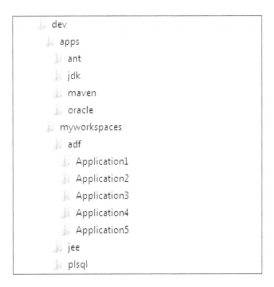

2. Create a `dev` directory where all the development will reside.

3. Create an `apps` directory, which will contain all the software starting from JDK to the middleware inside the Oracle directory.

4. Create a `myworkspaces` directory inside the `dev` directory, which will include different workspaces for each technology—you are free here to make it as per technology or per actual project—and then in each technology you have your different applications.

> I didn't introduce any whitespaces; this is important as whitespaces can cause too many troubles when dealing with JDeveloper and Java in general.

5. Create different environment variables for your development environment's `dev` directory, `apps` directory, and `myworkspaces` directory. This extra step will make it easy when you are installing different software to reach these directories easily using the command line. You should end up with the following environment variables:

   `$DEV_HOME=/Users/amr/dev`

   `$APPS_HOME=$DEV_HOME/apps`

   `$WORK_HOME=$DEV_HOME/myworkspaces`

6. You can do the same in Windows by simply navigating to **System Properties | Advanced | Environment variables** and create three variables with these names:

   `DEV_HOME=C:\Users\Amr\dev`

   `APPS_HOME=%DEV_HOME%\apps`

   `WORK_HOME=%DEV_HOME%\myworkspaces`

> Sometimes you might not have enough security privileges to access System Environment Variables. However, you can achieve the same results by opening the command prompt and using the `set` command as follows:
>
>   set DEV_HOME=C:\Users\Amr\dev
>   set APPS_HOME=%DEV_HOME%\apps
>   set WORK_HOME=%DEV_HOME%\myworkspaces

7. If you have Mac or other Nix-based systems, you can achieve the previous result by changing the `.bash_profile` file using a text editor or any text editing tools.

I always prefer to use **vi** or **vim** when it comes to Nix-based systems, but you can use any text editing tool of your choice. To know more about vi or vim, check these resources at `http://www.unix-manuals.com/tutorials/vi/vi-in-10-1.html` & `http://www.openvim.com/`.

8. You can create one if none exists by opening a terminal and entering the following command:

   ```
   vi ~/.bash_profile
   ```

9. Edit the file by pressing *I* to enter the edit mode, and add the following entries to the end of the file:

   ```
   export DEV_HOME=/Users/Amr/dev

   export APPS_HOME=$DEV_HOME/apps

   export WORK_HOME=$DEV_HOME/myworkspaces
   ```

   Save by pressing *Esc* and then *:wq*

How it works...

Creating environment variables will help you to map everything accordingly, and will give you a structured development environment for your IDEs and workspaces. This will also help you in your future applications, as you will be able to locate all the information you need in one place, and you will know where you should go fast and easy.

After you finish creating your environment variables and all the directory structures, you should be able to start installing the software, and we will start with the JDK.

Installing JDK

Java Development Kit (**JDK**) is the engine that runs everything from JDeveloper to the application server. The latest version of the JDK is JDK 7u25 at the time of writing, but if you find a newer version, don't hesitate to use it instead.

How to do it...

1. Download the latest JDK from `http://www.oracle.com/technetwork/java/javase/downloads/jdk7-downloads-1880260.html`.

   You should download the latest JDK and it should work just fine, but you have to select the JDK suitable for your Operating System and its architecture

You will need an oracle account. This is also important when installing the Oracle Database and JDeveloper, so you should get one now if you don't already have one, and it's free too!

Depending on the operating system, the installation should be straightforward, as for each operating system, there should be an installer with it, for example, for Windows an exe installer, for Mac you will have a dmg, and an rpm for Linux

2. Change the JDK installation directory to be inside `APPS_HOME`.

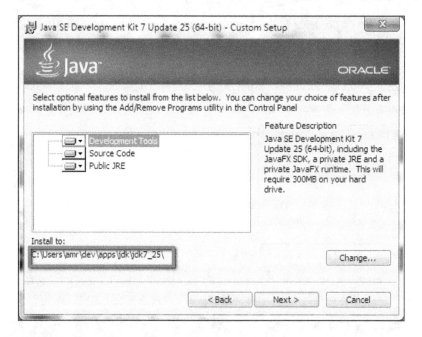

I chose the location to be `C:\Users\amr\dev\apps\jdk\jdk7_25` (jdk 7 update 25) in Windows or `/Users/amr/dev/apps/jdk/jdk7_25` in Nix-based systems

 You will be prompted to install the public JRE (Java Runtime Environment); you can create a directory for the JRE as well under `C:\Users\amr\dev\apps\jdk\jre7_25` or `/Users/amr/dev/apps/jdk/ jre7_25`.

3. Create a `JAVA_HOME` environment variable, and update the `PATH` environment variable to look at the `bin` folder inside our `jdk7_25` directory. This will help you greatly if you use the Java command line often.

4. If you are using Windows, you should add the following environment variable:

`JAVA_HOME=%APPS_HOME%\jdk\jdk7_25`

You should change the `PATH` environment variable to the following:

`PATH=%JAVA_HOME%\bin;`

 Alternatively, you can achieve the same result as previous by opening the command prompt without going to your environment variable settings and using the `set` command as `set PATH=%JAVA_HOME%\bin;%PATH%`.

Make sure you put `%JAVA_HOME%\bin` inside `PATH` and not `%JAVA_HOME%` as we want the path to reference all the Java executable files such as **java** and **javac**

 I put it in the front because some software, when installed, can edit this and put it in the end without inserting a semicolon at the start. So, it's safer to put it in the front of the `PATH` environment variable.

5. If you are using Mac or any other Nix-based system, you should edit the `.bash_profile` file to be the following:

`export JAVA_HOME=$APPS_HOME/jdk/jdk7_25`

`export PATH=$JAVA_HOME/bin:$PATH`

Notice that in Nix-based systems editing a `.bash_profile` is little bit different as the separator is a colon and not a semicolon

How it works...

Installing the JDK is the main part. JDeveloper runs on top of the **Java Virtual Machine** (**JVM**), which requires the JDK installed. The application server also uses the JDK to run.

Defining environment variables such as `JAVA_HOME` and putting them inside the `PATH` variable is crucial as we might need to start applications using the command line and these variables will become handy during such circumstances. Also, we will need this in order to start the installer of JDeveloper after installing the database.

Now that you have finished the installation of JDK, close any terminals (command prompts) opened and start installing the database.

Exploring different options to install the database

Almost all enterprise applications have a backend data layer that contains one or more **Database Management Systems** (**DBMS**), and since ADF is an enterprise-enabled framework, ADF is no exception to this rule.

ADF can work with any database as long as there is a **Java Data Base Connectivity** (**JDBC**) driver.

Users are encouraged to install a database if they want to follow all the recipes to the letter through all chapters of this book.

Getting ready

ADF works best with the Oracle Database, but as mentioned before it can work with any other DBMS, such as MySQL, PostgreSQL, or MSSQL. For the purpose of this book, you should install the Oracle Database, which comes in two flavors: Oracle Database Standard edition and Oracle Database **XE** (**Express Edition**).

 There is also an Oracle Database Enterprise edition, which has all the Standard Edition features plus management packs for highly critical performance such as for databases that are used in banks, which is outside the scope of this book.

Oracle XE is a version of Oracle Database that is easy to use and install; however, it only supports Windows 32-bit and Linux 64-bit versions. You can head over to `http://www.oracle.com/technetwork/products/express-edition/downloads/index.html` and install it if your operating system is one of the supported operating systems. If it isn't, you should install the Oracle Database Standard Edition from `http://www.oracle.com/technetwork/database/enterprise-edition/downloads/index.html`.

How to do it...

Depending on your operating system, you can know what kind of options you have:

> ▶ **Mac users**: You have only one option, and that is to have a virtual machine with Linux or Windows that hosts the database. Oracle provides multiple prebuilt Virtual Machines that you can install from `http://www.oracle.com/technetwork/community/developer-vm/index.html`.

- ▶ **Linux users**: Most of the Linux operating systems are 64-bit; if that is your case, then you are free to install either Oracle Database 12c or Oracle XE 11g. Other than that, you have to install Oracle Database 12c, or you can have a Virtual Machine with the database inside.

- ▶ **Windows users**: You can install Oracle XE 11g if your operating system is either 32-bit or 64-bit—you can use the database in its 32-bit mode; however, if you want to run the database on a 64-bit architecture, you can install Oracle Database 12c or you can have a Virtual Machine with the database inside.

How it works...

Installing the database will provide you with the data that your application will need to display, edit, add, and delete; one example database schema that is installed by default and that we will use in this book is the *HR* schema.

If you installed Oracle Database Standard edition, you should create at least one instance for you to work with.

There's more...

Make sure after installing your database that you can connect to it properly, and while the *HR* schema will be be installed with your database, it'll be locked by default.

In order to unlock the HR schema, log in with your system or sys user and execute the following command:

```
ALTER USER HR IDENTIFIED BY PASSWORD ACCOUNT UNLOCK;
```

This command will alter the *HR* schema and set the password to PASSWORD. You are free to change the password by changing the PASSWORD keyword in the previous command to whatever you like.

Installing JDeveloper

Now to the fun part that is installing your IDE. JDeveloper is a great IDE for Java, but it is the de facto IDE for ADF and Oracle Middleware products.

JDeveloper comes in two flavors: **Studio edition** and **Java edition**. If you are not planning to work with ADF in your JDeveloper, you can install Java edition; otherwise, Studio edition is the best when it comes to ADF development.

There are 5 installation options for JDeveloper:

- ▶ Windows 64 bit
- ▶ Windows 32 bit
- ▶ Linux 64 bit
- ▶ Linux 32 bit
- ▶ Generic

All installation options come with an embedded JDK except for the generic option, for which you need to preinstall JDK.

You can notice that there is no Mac version, but generic can work with any operating system.

In this recipe, we will download the generic installation option for the JDeveloper Studio edition and we will install it.

How to do it...

To install JDeveloper, perform the following steps:

1. Go to `http://www.oracle.com/technetwork/developer-tools/jdev/downloads/index.html` and download the latest JDeveloper (currently 12.1.2.0.0). Make sure you accept the agreement and pick the generic version from the drop-down menu.

2. After your download is complete, open your command prompt or terminal and change the directory—using the `cd` command—to the directory that contains the `.jar` file you just downloaded, and then execute the following command line:

```
java -jar jdev_suite_121200.jar
```

Note that you can execute the `java` command directly because you added the `%JAVA_HOME%` or `$JAVA_HOME\bin` directory inside the `PATH` environment variable, and this command basically says, start a Java application from the JAR file provided.

There are a couple of other arguments you can add to the previous command line such as `-Djava.io.tmpdir=/path/to/tmpdir`.

The previous argument uses another temp directory instead of the Java default one. If you don't have space in your system directory, you can also control the memory footprint of the Java program by adding the -xmX and -xmS arguments as well.

3. After executing this command, you should be able to see the JDeveloper installer screen as shown in the following screenshot:

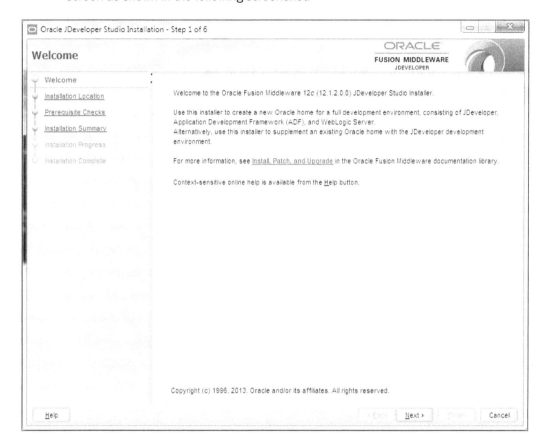

4. When you are prompted to enter your Oracle Home location you should choose C:\Users\<your_name>\dev\apps\oracle\Middleware\Oracle_Home.

If you have other middleware versions, you should install 12c on a different middleware directory, for example, `C:\Users\<your_name>\dev\apps\oracle\Middleware12c\Oracle_Home`

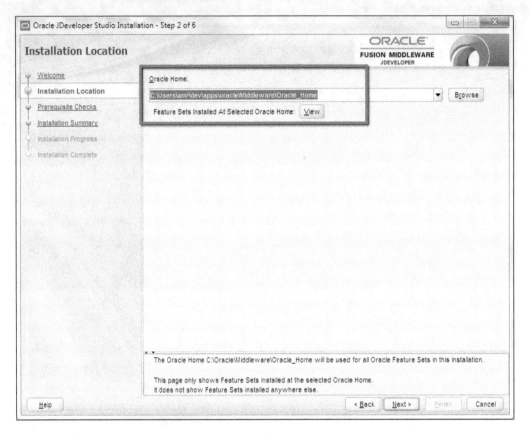

5. If you followed everything right and launched the JAR file with Java 7, the next step (prerequisites check) should pass without a problem. Click on **Next** and have a look at the summary of what will be installed by JDeveloper. Click on **Install** and let it install your favorite IDE that you will use during this book.

6. After a couple of minutes you should feel good as your JDeveloper is ready to go. Click on **Finish Installation** without opening JDeveloper and click on **Finish** to close your installer.

How it works...

When you executed the Java command, you started the JDeveloper installation process. Since we downloaded the Studio Edition, it'll ask you about your middleware home directory since it expects you to have multiple middleware products installed.

When you choose a middleware home directory, make sure not to pick up any existing middleware homes as different versions' installation on the same directory can cause lots of troubles.

There's more...

Don't be tempted to open JDeveloper just yet; we need to do a few things before starting JDeveloper.

First we need to create a new environment variable, which will point to the root directory of all our ADF applications; the environment variable needs to be named `JDEV_USER_HOME`.

You can set the environment variable in Windows to be under the `WORK_HOME` directory by executing the following command in the command prompt:

```
set JDEV_USER_HOME = %WORK_HOME%\adf
```

For the Nix-based version the environment variable can be set by using the following command:

```
export JDEV_USER_HOME = $WORK_HOME/adf
```

`JDEV_USER_HOME` is a reserved name that JDeveloper looks for before starting; if it's defined, JDeveloper will automatically create new applications in the directory.

> When setting `JDEV_USER_HOME`, all other JDeveloper versions you have in your operating system will be affected as well. If you want to still work with other older JDeveloper versions, make sure you don't create it as an environment variable and rather create a small Windows or Nix batch file to start JDeveloper which sets this variable for the session lifetime only. Check the Git repository, for example, of batch files at `https://github.com/agawish/ADF-Faces-Cookbook/tree/master/Chapter%201`.

After setting the variable, we need to tune some configuration of JDeveloper before starting it and we are going to use the next recipe for that.

Tuning JDeveloper

JDeveloper can work without tuning, but tuning is worth looking at for when you are looking at big enterprise applications that have many projects with source control and more than one team member.

How to do it...

In order to tune JDeveloper, perform the following steps:

1. Open your Oracle Home directory that we set up when installing JDeveloper, and navigate to `%MIDDLEWARE_HOME%` | `Oracle_Home` | `jdeveloper`. There are two files that you want to change: the first file is `ide.conf` located under `ide\bin\ide.conf`.

2. Open the file using your favorite text editor and locate the following lines:

   ```
   AddVMOption -Xms
   ```

   ```
   AddVMOption -Xmx
   ```

   You may want to increase these values if they are very low, for example, if you have more than 4 GB of RAM, you should set it to 1 GB each as shown in the following code:

   ```
   AddVMOption -Xms1024M
   ```

   ```
   AddVMOption -Xmx1024M
   ```

3. Save and close the file.

4. Open the `jdev\bin\jdev.conf` path under the `jdeveloper` directory.

5. Add the following entries at the end of the file:

   ```
   # optimize the JVM for strings / text editing
   AddVMOption -XX:+UseStringCache
   AddVMOption -XX:+OptimizeStringConcat
   AddVMOption -XX:+UseCompressedStrings

   # if on a 64-bit system, but using less than 32 GB RAM, this
   reduces object pointer memory size
   AddVMOption -XX:+UseCompressedOops

   # use an aggressive garbage collector (constant small collections)
   AddVMOption -XX:+AggressiveOpts

   # for multi-core machines, use multiple threads to create objects
   and reduce pause times
   AddVMOption -XX:+UseConcMarkSweepGC
   AddVMOption -XX:+UseGCOverheadLimit
   ```

These settings ensure that your JVM is optimized for your operating system. Also note that some of them are tailored depending on your Operating System architecture. So, don't just copy and paste them. Check what can apply and add accordingly.

 If you started JDeveloper and faced some troubles, try reducing the amount of memory assigned with Xms and Xmx and start it again.

6. Start JDeveloper now. You have tuned it for your operating system, and now it's time to change some general preferences of JDeveloper itself. So, let's start by starting your JDeveloper as shown in the following screenshot:

7. When you get a prompt that asks which mode you want to choose, leave the default value of the **Studio Developer (All Features)** option and click on **OK**.

 If this is not your first JDeveloper, you will also be prompted to migrate from the older JDeveloper versions. If you are planning to still use the old JDeveloper version and don't want to migrate your project, click on **No**; otherwise, click on **Yes**.

8. Go to the JDeveloper preferences by navigating to **Tools toolbar | Preferences**.

9. Change the following inside preferences:

    ❑ **Environment**: Change the **Encoding** to **UTF-8**

    ❑ Navigate to **Code Editor | Line Gutter** and enable **Show Line Numbers**

    ❑ Navigate to **Run | Weblogic** and click on **Load Extension** and enable **FastSwap**

10. Enable external tools by navigating to **Tools | External Tools** and making sure every item is selected and then clicking on **OK**.

How it works...

JDeveloper, like all IDEs, has configuration files that can be used to tune it to work without having memory problems. These configuration files are `ide.conf` and `jdev.conf`.

The first file controls the main JVM memory parameters that the JDeveloper thread will start using, and `jdev.conf` is used to add any additional configuration to the JDeveloper in order to enhance its performance with multicore processors or 64-bit architecture systems.

After that, we started JDeveloper for the first time and you were prompted to select a Role or Mode. Each role is tailored towards a specific behavior.

There are 5 roles you can choose from:

> ▸ **Studio Developer (All Features)**: This includes all the features of the IDE
> ▸ **Customization Developer**: This allows the developer to create customizable applications using the **Oracle Metadata Service** (**MDS**) framework
> ▸ **Database Edition**: This gives access to the core database development tools
> ▸ **Java EE Edition**: This includes features of core Java EE development only
> ▸ **Java Edition**: This includes only features of core Java development

After starting JDeveloper, we also need to tune the JDeveloper preferences themselves. This is different since you have control over them from the JDeveloper IDE. So, you may want to change them while you are working. Secondly, it doesn't relate to the JVM thread but it's totally an application-specific property.

Doing these changes to the JDeveloper preferences can increase your performance time by preventing you from facing some problems with encoding and other stuff when you are working with other team members or a multilanguage application.

See also

If you want to explore more properties that you can tweak with JDeveloper beyond the scope of this book, check the ADF EMG discussion at `https://groups.google.com/forum/#!topic/adf-methodology/g3q8TgHtsbk`.

Downloading the example code

You can download the example code files for all Packt books you have purchased from your account at `http://www.packtpub.com`. You can also download the files from GitHub at `https://github.com/agawish/ADF-Faces-Cookbook/archive/master.zip`. If you purchased this book elsewhere, you can visit `http://www.packtpub.com/support` and register to have the files e-mailed directly to you.

Downloading the book's Git repository

In order to keep your code organized, especially with bigger numbers of team members, you need to have a source control system. There are all sorts of version control systems starting from CVS passing by the famous SVN to the new distributed version control systems such as Git and Mercurial, which offer a different model, particularly for offline usage.

Git is a free and open source distributed version control system; you can learn about it very easily at `http://git-scm.com/documentation`.

Git also has a tiny footprint with lightning-fast performance. It outclasses SVN, CVS, Perforce, and ClearCase.

You don't have to follow the trend in here, just use what you and your team feel comfortable with.

I chose Git as a repository to have all the example applications used in this book.

You can check the book's repository content at `https://github.com/agawish/ADF-Faces-Cookbook` and start navigating through the code samples and files for each chapter. You can also download the whole thing and you can contribute if you find any bug or want to make some edits.

The great thing about JDeveloper, especially 12c, is that it comes with Git by default. So, you don't need to install anything. One thing you need to know is that terminology is quite different from SVN.

How to do it...

1. Clone the Git project by navigating to **Team** | **Git** and clicking on the **Clone** menu.

   The command is named Clone because of the distribution nature of Git, as you really clone the project locally on your machine

 Clone is the same as **Checkout** in SVN and CVS.

2. Leave the name as original, add `https://github.com/agawish/ADF-Faces-Cookbook.git` to the repository URL, enter your Github username and password, and click on **Next**.

   If you entered your information correctly, you should see the branch **master** in the **Include** list. This is another great feature. When you have a stable project, the main code base should be in the **master** branch, but if you decided to implement other features, you may want to create a new branch and migrate it to the **master** branch when you finish.

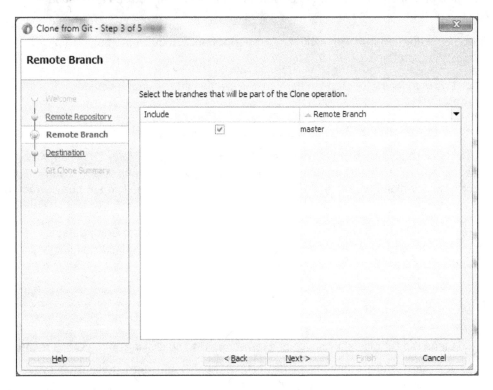

3. Click on **Next** to choose the cloned repository directory, a name of your repository, and to check which branch you want.

4. Click on **Finish** after you finish and you will have the entire book's Git repository locally.

5. Click on **No** when you are prompted to create a project out of the Git repository. However, you don't want to choose that option since the repository contains multiple applications.

6. Access specific applications from the filesystem.

How it works...

JDeveloper uses the concept of plugins or extensions. With each extension comes a set of features that can manipulate your project in a certain way.

With Git you get all the advantages of having a distributed version control system inside your IDE. You can commit your code within JDeveloper without the need to leave JDeveloper, which will increase your productivity and decrease the time you need to spend using third-party applications to manage your project.

See also...

To know more about Git, check the original website at `http://git-scm.com/`. Also, check these references at `http://stackoverflow.com/questions/315911/git-for-beginners-the-definitive-practical-guide` for a practical definitive guide to getting started with Git.

2
Getting Started with ADF Faces and JDeveloper

This chapter contains the following recipes:

- ▶ Creating an Application Workspace
- ▶ Connecting your application to a database
- ▶ Building Business Service
- ▶ Defining the page flow
- ▶ Creating a View page
- ▶ Adding ADF Faces components to JSF pages
- ▶ Running your first ADF Faces application

Introduction

In today's environment, enterprise applications have become more and more complex; they need the underlying technology to be scalable, distributed, component based, and mission critical.

Designing and developing such enterprise applications means going through hundreds of requirements; failure to meet any of these requirements can lead to the failure of the whole project. However, Oracle ADF comes to the rescue. Oracle ADF is a Java EE framework that inherits Java EE security, robustness, and scalability.

It also adheres to the rapid application development principles in today's agile world. These principles provide the developer with a rich out-of-the-box functionality to focus and give his/her 100 percent to the business logic.

Oracle ADF is an end-to-end framework that follows the **Model View Controller** (**MVC**) pattern as illustrated in the following diagram:

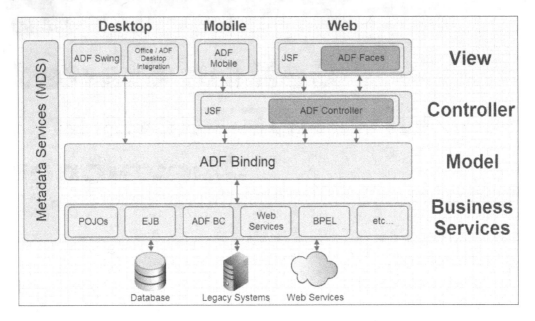

Oracle ADF offerings vary between mobile solutions with Oracle ADF Mobile and the Desktop Integration solution, which can be integrated with Microsoft Office Excel with Oracle ADF Desktop Integration. It also provides a free offering through which developers can download, develop, and deploy enterprise applications with Oracle ADF Essentials for free. Additionally, they are all evolved from the core Oracle ADF framework, which is the Java EE framework where they extend beyond MVC and integrate with other Oracle middleware solutions.

 To know more about what Oracle ADF has to offer, check its main page on Oracle, http://www.oracle.com/technetwork/ developer-tools/adf/overview/index.html.

In this book, we will only focus on ADF Faces and ADF Controller of the Oracle ADF framework. To make things easier, we will call them Oracle ADF Faces. Although Oracle ADF Faces exists in both the commercial Oracle ADF and Oracle ADF Essentials (the free version), we will only focus on the commercial part of it in this book since we are discussing the latest version of the Oracle ADF framework.

The latest version of Oracle ADF Essentials is 11.1.2.4, but this book focuses on Oracle ADF 12c. To know more about Oracle ADF Essentials, check the official page at `http://www.oracle.com/technetwork/developer-tools/adf/overview/adfessentials-1719844.html`.

Oracle ADF Faces is built on top of the **JavaServer Faces** (**JSF**) framework, which is the standard Java EE framework implementation. Being built on top of the JSF framework makes Oracle ADF a component-based framework just like JSF.

JSF uses XML files called View templates as its view layer and a **FacesServlet** that acts as a controller in which it processes requests, loads the appropriate View template, builds a component tree, processes events, and renders the response (typically in the HTML language) to the client. Check the following diagram for more information about the JSF lifecycle:

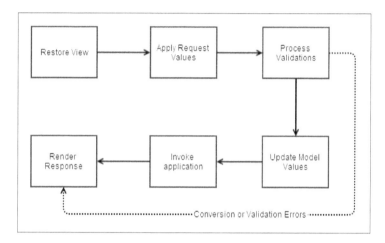

The state of UI components and other objects' of scope interest is saved at the end of each request in a process called state saving, which can be saved either on the client side or on the server side (more on this in *Chapter 10, Scaling Your Application*) and restored upon the next creation of that view.

Oracle ADF Faces extends all that we've discussed so far and adds the following to JSF:

▶ It adds more than 100 additional components that support Ajax

▶ It enhances the JSF lifecycle by adding ADF-specific phases that add support for task flows, more scope definitions, and the ADF Binding layer

In this chapter, we will take our first steps toward creating our first ADF application; in this application, we will start from scratch and even build the Business Service Layer quickly (this book doesn't focus on the Business Service Layer, but since it's the first step, it'll be included in this chapter).

In order to complete the recipes in this chapter, you need to have the HR schema in your database unlocked and up and running.

If you are a skilled ADF developer, you can skip this chapter.

Creating an Application Workspace

In this recipe, we will get to know a little bit about the JDeveloper IDE and how we can navigate around it; after this, we will start with the first steps of creating our ADF application by creating the ADF Application Workspace.

How to do it...

In order to create the ADF Application Workspace, perform the ensuing steps:

1. Start **JDeveloper**; you will find different panes highlighted in the following screenshot:

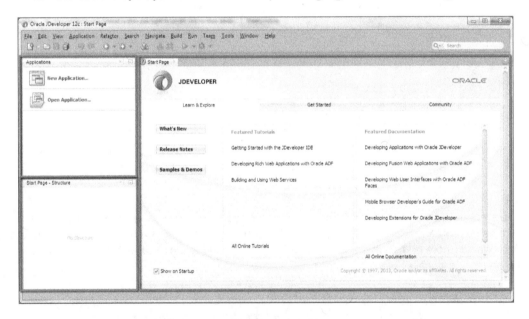

One of the main panes is the **Application** navigator pane (the top-left pane), which displays the application files. If there are no applications (such as the case when you open JDeveloper for the first time), you end up with two links: one for creating a new application and another for opening a pre-existing application.

The center pane is the main pane, which will be the **Start Page** when you start JDeveloper.

The bottom-left pane is the **Structure** pane, that gives you the structure of the center pane. If a Java class is in the main pane, the structure pane will contain all members and methods of this class. You can maximize or close any pane in JDeveloper, and if you want to open it again, you can do so from the **Window** menu.

Create a new ADF application by clicking on the **New Application...** link from the **Applications** pane or navigating to **File | New | Application**.

2. Choose **ADF Fusion Web Application** as your application type and click on **OK**.

   Now the **Create ADF Fusion Web Application** dialog pops up.

3. Choose a name for your application; I'll call it `HelloADFFaces`.

 You are free to have different names for your applications, pages, classes, and projects. It's actually better if you do this in order to keep your focus on the changes and map them to yours and not follow them blindly.

4. Choose an application package prefix for your application; for example, if your company is called ACME, and you are making this application commercial and the application name is HR, the prefix should be something like `com.acme.hr`. In this case, the application is `chapter2.helloadf` and it'll be commercial. So, the prefix will be `com` and the company `adffaces`; therefore, it'll be `com.adffaces.chapter2.helloadf`, as shown in following screenshot:

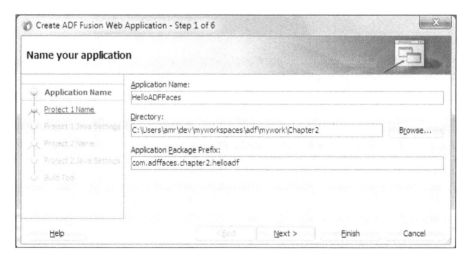

5. Click on **Finish** to end the wizard.

How it works...

When you finish the wizard, you will end up with a page in the center pane called **HelloADFFaces Overview**, which has a checklist of what you should do (the plan of your application). The **Applications** pane now has two projects: one called `Model` and the other `ViewController`. These projects have been created for you by the wizard. The `Model` project should hold your Business Service Layer and `ViewController` will hold your pages and all of your controller's logic.

 Notice that we clicked on **Finish** instead of **Next**, which is why you didn't witness the creation of the `Model` and `ViewController` projects. In the wizard, you can change their names and technology scopes. There is also another step at the end of the wizard in which you can specify your build tool, either the default JDeveloper build tools, Maven, or Ant.

The checklist is very helpful for planning your ADF application, especially if you are starting with ADF development; you should also check the plan to find good resources and references to start your ADF application.

We will put the ADF project together by embracing the JDeveloper ADF plan and following the checklist of steps to be done.

See also

For more information about the JDeveloper user experience, check the following excellent video: `http://download.oracle.com/otn_hosted_doc/jdeveloper/12cdemos/ JDevOverview12c/JDevOverview12c.html`.

Connecting your application to a database

In this application, we want to display employees' data from the HR schema on a web browser and be able to navigate between different records using buttons that help us go to the first, next, previous, and last records; employees' information should be displayed in a form-based view.

In order to retrieve employees' information, we need to establish a connection with the HR database.

In this recipe, we will use JDeveloper to establish a connection between our new ADF application and the HR schema, which comes by default with the Oracle database.

How to do it...

In order to establish a connection with the HR schema, follow the ensuing steps:

1. Expand the **Connect to a Database** checklist item from the checklist and click on the **Create a Database Connection** button that will open the **Create Database Connection** dialog.

 You can also create a connection by navigating to **File | New | From Gallery | General | Connections | Database Connection**.

2. Choose a connection name of your choice; I named it HRConnection for clarification.

3. Change the username and password of the HR user to match your database's HR schema; make sure you are pointing to the right host.

4. Click on the **Test Connection** button to make sure everything works fine, and if everything is fine, you should see a **Success!** message.

5. Click on **OK** to close the dialog box.

6. Mark this item as done in the checklist as well.

How it works...

When working with applications in ADF, you will need to have connections in order to establish a communication channel with different systems. One of the important connections that will be usually needed is a database connection, which establishes a connection between your application and database.

When you entered the information, you provided the connection with all the information needed in order to connect to a specific user in a specific database instance.

Your connection can be an application-based resource like the one we configured in this recipe; alternatively, it can be inside JDeveloper's resource catalog, which can be helpful if you have multiple applications that use the same database connection.

After creating a database connection, we need to create the Business Service Layer that will use the database connection.

Building Business Service

In this recipe, we are going to build our Business Service Layer, which consists of one entity object based on the EMPLOYEES table, one view object based on the entity object, and one application module to host the latest view object.

In a real application, it's always a good practice to establish a uniform naming convention for your business components, such as suffixes and package names, which can be found by navigating to **Tools | Preferences | ADF Business Components | Object Naming and Packages**.

This will be the only recipe that talks about Business Service in brief in this book. If you want to know more about building Business Service, check the official documentation at http://docs.oracle.com/middleware/1212/adf/ADFFD/partpage2.htm#ADFFD20093.

How to do it...

In order to build your Business Service, follow the ensuing steps:

1. Right-click on the **Model** project node from the **Applications** navigator pane and navigate to **New | Business Components from tables...**; by doing this, you are able to create all the three objects in one wizard instead of creating everything separately.

You can expand substeps in the Business Service checklist item and create each of them separately if you want; it'll be a good practice for you as well.

2. If this is the first time you're dealing with business components in this application, a dialog will pop up asking you to initialize the business components project. It also asks about database connection. If you only create one database connection, it should appear preselected; if not, you should select it from the drop-down list or create a new one using the green plus icon; once this is done, click on **OK** to proceed. The **Create Business Components from Tables** dialog should pop up.

3. Then, you define **Entity Objects**; click on the **Query** button to query all tables in the HR schema, select the EMPLOYEES table, and shuttle it into the selected panel.

4. Make sure that **Entity Objects** is created in the right Java package, which should exist in com.adffaces.chapter2.helloadf.model.entities based on the best practices of ADF BC. Also, it should not be mixed with application modules and view objects, so the result should be Employees.

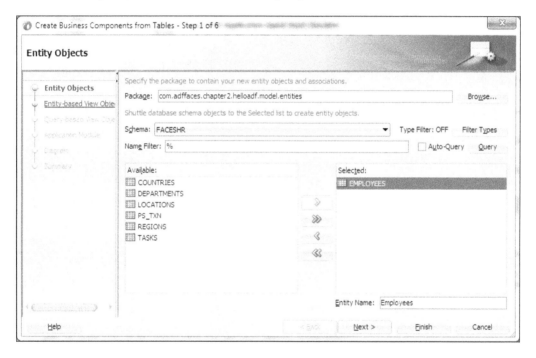

5. Click on **Next**.

To know more about ADF conventions and best practices, check the official PDF guide at http://www.oracle.com/technetwork/developer-tools/adf/learnmore/adf-naming-layout-guidelines-v1-00-1897849.pdf.

6. Create **Entity-based View Objects** that are traditionally known as updatable view objects; you should shuttle the `Employees` table from the left to the right panel.

7. Make sure that the package name follows the best practice by adding the `views` suffix; the package name will be `com.adffaces.chapter2.helloadf.model.views`. Also, make sure you follow the best practice by having a suffix for your view objects instances by adding the `View` suffix, which in this case should be `EmployeesView`.

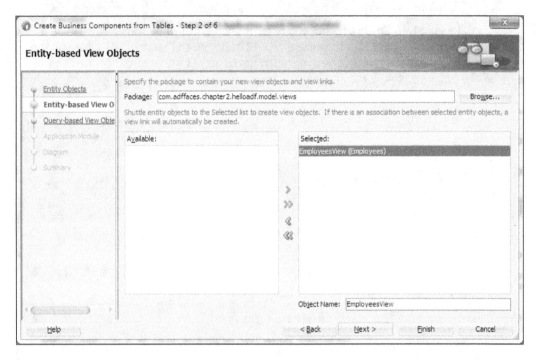

8. Click on **Next**.

9. Skip **Query-based View Objects** as we don't have any of these in this simple application; then click on **Next**.

10. Create an **Application Module** and naming it `HrAppModule`, which follows the best practice of adding the `AppModule` suffix at the end of the name and appending `services` to the package name. So, in this case, it should be `com.adffaces.chapter2.helloadf.model.services`.

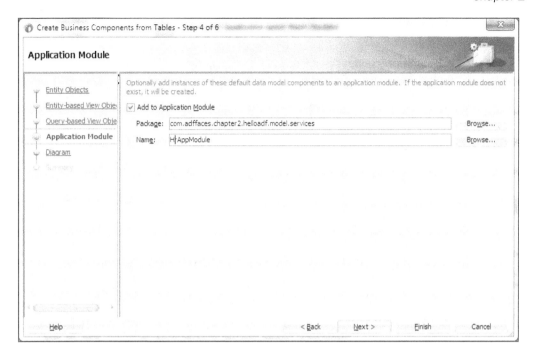

11. Click on **Finish** to close the dialog box. You should end up with the following structure in your **Applications** pane if you have followed the best practices in the ADF guide:

12. Place a tick on the third item of the checklist to indicate it is done.

How it works...

In order to build a proper Business Service, you need to create ADF business components from your database tables, which will require you to create the following:

> ► **Entity object(s)**: These are like one-to-one mappings with database tables so the structure of the entity bean should match the database table structure along with the added value of validations.

> ► **View object(s)**: These are like `select` statements. It's the data that users can see and is based on the Entity object that makes this view object support the Update, Add, and Delete row operations; alternatively, it can be based on a SQL statement, which means it'll be read-only.

> ► **Application module(s)**: The application module is the window of your Business Service to the user interface. You can expose view objects or other application modules inside of it, and it'll be available to the ADF Binding layer, where it can be dragged to the user interface inside JSF pages, using the drag-and-drop feature.

After you create your entity object, view object, and application module, your Business Service is in place, and with your `HrAppModule`, you automatically created your first Data Control.

 A Data Control can be created for Java objects, web services, and more; however, it is created automatically with every application module you create inside your Business Service Layer.

You can see the created Data Control by expanding **Data Control** from the **Applications** pane; you will find the `HrAppModuleDataControl`, and by expanding it, you will find `EmployeesView1` underneath it, which represents your view object.

 If you want to make sure that everything is correct with your Business Service, you can start the Oracle ADF Model Tester by right-clicking on the `HrModule` application module and then clicking on **Run**.

Now you are ready to define your application flow and Finish Step 4 in the Application Overview checklist.

Defining the page flow

When we talk about defining the page flow of our application, we talk about it in terms of how pages interact with each other, designing what is the right sequence of pages that the user has to navigate through; also, designing how work units are arranged in pages, and how they can be modularized and communicate with each other as well.

In this recipe, we move from the Business Service layer to the Controller layer. In order to work with page flows, we need to first understand what ADF Task Flow is.

ADF Task Flows provide a modularized approach to define the control flow in an ADF application. So, instead of representing an application as a single large page, you can break it up into a collection of reusable task flows.

Each task flow contains a portion of the application's navigational graph and can be considered as a logical business unit of work.

Each task flow contains one or more nodes that are called activities. An activity node can represent a simple logical operation such as displaying a page or a page fragment, executing an application's logic, or calling another task flow.

The transitions between the activities are called control flow cases and can represent navigations between different pages.

There are two types of task flows:

- **Unbounded task flows**: These are task flows without a specific start point that can contain one or more activities, control flow rules, and managed bean definitions. The application can interact with any activity inside of unbounded task flows without having to take a specific path. Usually, it represents the application's main navigational page model such as the `adfc-config` Task Flow.

- **Bounded task flows**: Unlike the unbounded task flow, a bounded task flow has a single entry point (activity) and zero or more exit points. It has its own private activities, control flows, and Managed Bean definitions. Bounded task flow allows the reuse of parameters, transaction management, re-entry, and routing; it also allows us to save a state and more. Unlike unbounded task flows, it can be rendered within the ADF region inside a JSF Page.

 You can have an overview of task flow and task flow-oriented architecture by watching this great video: `http://www.youtube.com/watch?v=TajCHL7Hw5M`

In this recipe, we will create one bounded task flow. We won't create any unbounded task flows, but we will be using the `adfc-config` task flow later.

How to do it...

In order to create the bounded task flow, follow the ensuing steps:

1. Expand the **Design Application Flow** checklist item and click on the **Create a Task Flow** button. A pop-up window will pop up asking which project you wish to create this task flow for; choose `ViewController` and click on **OK**. Another dialog window will pop up asking you to create your task flow.

2. Name the task flow file `retrieve-employees-information`. The name should be meaningful. It'll be better if you arrange your task flows into different physical directories under the `WEB-INF` directory based on their functionalities; however, for my simple application, I'll retain the default setup.

3. Make sure that the **Create as Bounded Task Flow** checkbox is checked.

4. Uncheck the **Create with Page Fragments** option and then click on **OK**.

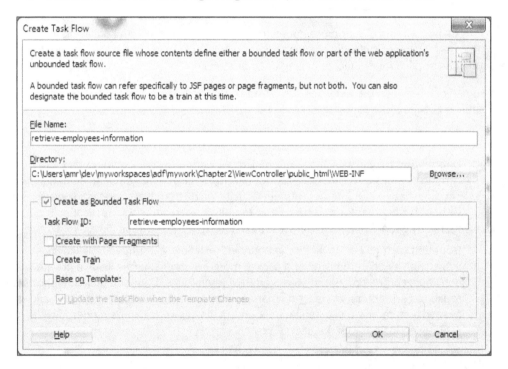

 You can create your task flow with page fragments but then this task flow can't be executed on its own and needs to be part of a JSF page inside the ADF region.

Once you create your task flow, you should be directed to it; if this doesn't happen, you can easily locate it by navigating to **Applications Navigation pane | ViewController | Web Content | Page Flows**.

When you open the task flow, you will be directed to the Diagram view asking you to place components from the Components pallet on the right-hand side.

1. Expand the **Components** category under **Components** palette if not expanded; locate the View activity and drag-and-drop it inside the task flow diagram view.

2. Name the newly added View activity `employees`. You can see that there is a green circle around it, which indicates default activity; you will also see a purple triangle over it, which means that this page has not been created yet.

3. Save everything using _Ctrl + S_ or clicking on the double disk icon on the toolbar.

4. Open the **HelloADFFaces Overview** tab and check the **Design Application Flow** checklist item as done.

 If you close the Overview window, you can re-open it again by navigating to **Application menu | Show overview**.

How it works...

In this recipe, we created a simple bounded task flow that has one activity, which represents a View; a View means a page in our case, which will be physically created in the next recipe.

Creating a View page

In this simple recipe, we will create the actual JSF page behind the `Employees` View activity inside the `retrieve-employees-information` task flow that was created in the previous recipe.

How to do it...

In order to create the JSF page behind the View activity, follow the ensuing steps:

1. Open the `retrieve-employees-information` task flow and then double-click on the `employees` View activity. A dialog should pop up asking for the filename and the page template for this page and/or Managed Beans for it. For this simple application, we won't create page templates as we will use **Oracle Three Column Layout**.

2. Leave the default filename as is.

3. Choose the **Oracle Three-Column** layout under **Page Layout tab | Reference ADF Page Template**. In *Chapter 5, Beautifying Application Layout for Great User Experience*, we will learn how to create our own rich page template.

4. Close the pop-up window by clicking on the **OK** button.

5. Open the **HelloADFFaces Overview** tab and check the **Design Pages** checklist item as done.

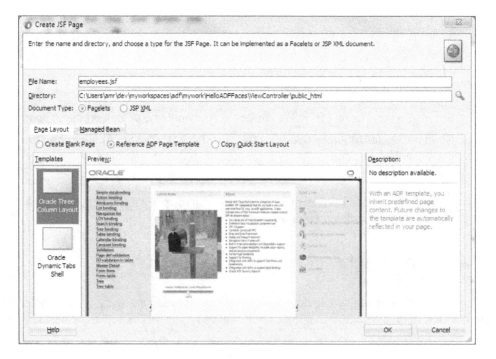

The page should be opened automatically, but if it isn't, you can open `employees.jsf` by navigating to **Applications Pane | ViewController | Web Content**. You can see that the Oracle three-column template is loaded, and you are able to see the main structure of the page.

How it works...

When you create a page, you have two options:

► Creating a `.jsf` page (recommended since 11g Release 2) that uses Facelets

► Creating a `.jspx` page, which is given for backward compatibility with JDeveloper release 1 so that you can have a seamless migration from 11gR1 to 12c

You are also asked to choose a page template, which is a great way to have a page structure that can be applied to your pages, without having to worry about maintaining it for each page separately. You can also have a single point of change that can be applied to all the pages that use this template. JDeveloper and ADF come with the Oracle three column template that can be used.

While creating this page, we reached a status where we can run and display what we've done; however, the page is currently empty and we want to have the employees' data, so first let's place some components on the page before running it.

Adding ADF Faces components to JSF pages

Now, for the magic to happen from the Business Service Layer to the view layer, in order to place the data, you can select the data that you want to insert from the Data Control and drag-and-drop it onto our page and choose the format that this page should have. So let's do that.

What we want is to have a form that has all employees' information inside our page.

How to do it...

Let's see how to add ADF Faces components to JSF pages:

1. Expand **HrAppModuleDataControl** under **Data Controls** and drag `Employees1` into the white square inside of the `employees.jsf` page. Remember this is the view object that contains all employees' information, and it's based on the `Employees` Entity object.

2. Choose **ADF Form...** when the drag-and-drop dialog appears as shown in the following screenshot:

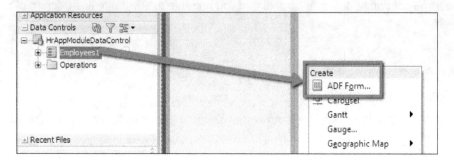

Now, a new dialog pops up asking you what you want to display in your form.

3. Check the **Row Navigation** checkbox.

   This will place all navigation buttons such as **First**, **Next**, **Previous**, and **Last** under the form.

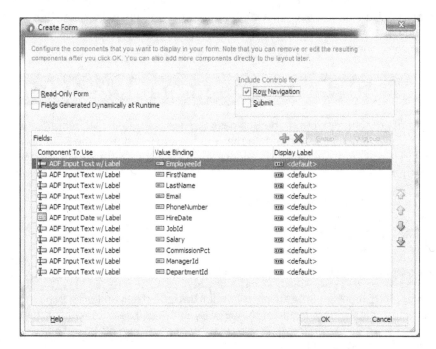

4. Click on **OK** to close the dialog.

5. Open the **HelloADFFaces Overview** tab and check the **Add Common Components** checklist item as done.

How it works...

You can notice that, inside the form's input, you have something like #{bindings. FirstName.inputValue}. This **Expression Language** (**EL**) expression represents the binding that gets created automatically once you have dragged-and-dropped the view object onto the page, which is a proof of the ADF Binding layer in action.

You can see these bindings by navigating to the **Bindings and Executables** tab, which will open the **Page Data Binding Definition** of the employees.jsf page, which looks like the following screenshot:

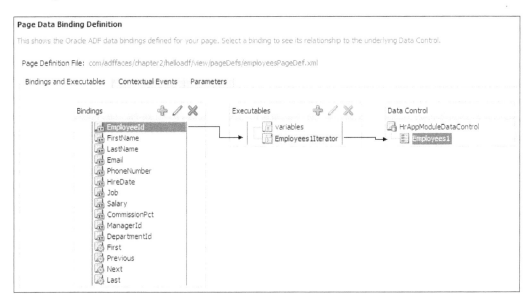

You can see that FirstName is under the **Bindings** section, and FirstName is pointing to something called Employees1Iterator under the **Executables** section. The **Executables** section is pointing to Employees1, which is the child of HrAppModuleDataControl under the **Data Control** section.

The **Bindings and Executables** sections are very important to understand since the whole ADF Binding mechanism is based on them. The **Executables** section represents activities that get executed when the page is ready to be viewed. So, Employees1Iterator is getting executed to get all the data from the Employees1 view object, and the data will be available inside the Employees1Iterator object. Thats why, when you click on it, you will get to edit some properties like how often this iterator should get refreshed, should the result get cached, and more features such as these.

As for the **Bindings** section, they are bound to those results data, and to items that can be referenced by components in your JSF page such as input Texts and Buttons. Also if you check the last four bindings, you will find them corresponding to four buttons in the page. These are actual actions that manipulate the data inside the iterator, which by definition manipulates the data in the view object as well. You can also see all these actions from the Data Controls pallet directly by expanding the view object, and you will find a folder called `Operations`; expanding it will reveal all the operations you can have for this view object, which covers the main **CRUD** (**Create Retrieve Update Delete**) operations plus a few other operations. You also have two operations that are not related to a specific view object but related to the whole Data Control, and these are Commit and Rollback (To commit to database or roll-back changes).

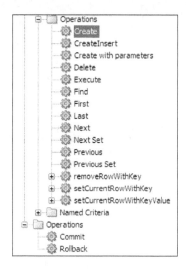

The Page Definition is an XML file that is linked to the `employees.jsf` page. This link is the one that makes **Bindings** available to the `employees.jsf` page's EL as part of the ADF Faces lifecycle. The link between the page and Page Definition happens in a specific file called `DataBindings.cpx`, which is also an XML file that has all pages and their corresponding Page Definitions.

 To learn more about ADF Model and ADF Binding layer, check the official documentation at `http://docs.oracle.com/middleware/1212/adf/ADFFD/bcdcpal.htm#BABHJJHA`.

Now that you have finished creating the form inside the page, it is time to see everything in action and run your application.

Running your first ADF Faces application

In this recipe, we will run our application in multiple scenarios by trying the worst scenario first and enhancing it till we reach the best scenario.

How to do it...

To run your first ADF Faces application, perform the following steps:

1. Locate your task flow `retrieve-employees-information` and right-click on it.

2. Click on **Run** or select it and click on **Run** (the green arrow icon) on the toolbar, and the page will start appearing.

 If this is the first time you run an application in JDeveloper, a pop-up window will ask you to instantiate your first Weblogic instance and will ask you about the password for your weblogic user and port numbers.

If you did everything correctly, you should see a form that you can navigate through with **Next**, **Previous**, **First**, and **Last**.

However, if you check the URL, it's quite ugly. It's not quite what you have in mind, so how can it be enhanced?

 This method is not recommended and is only used for debugging and testing Page-based task flows, but it's worth mentioning.

The second scenario is where you run the page directly. So let's try that and see if there are any changes.

1. Right-click on the `employees.jsf` page and run it. You will probably get a warning message from JDeveloper telling you that running the page itself is not recommended, which is true, but ignore it for the moment and click on **Yes**; let's examine the end result.

   The URL is much better now; it doesn't show all the `adf.task-flow` parameters in the URL that expose a bit of sensitive information about our task flow.

   But still, the warning from JDeveloper means that this way is also not recommended, so what is the best way to run your application?

   Well, if you remember, we said that the `adfc-config` task flow and usually any unbounded task flows are generally responsible for the application's navigation model, so why don't we use it? In order to do so, all we have to do is expose the `employees.jsf` page as a View activity in that task flow.

2. Open the `adfc-config` task flow.

3. Drag-and-drop the `employees.jsf` page from the Application Pane into the body of the task flow to have it look like the following screenshot:

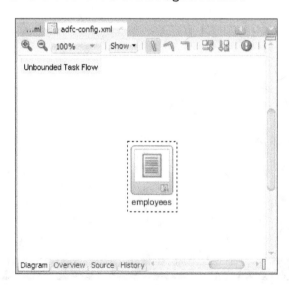

4. As you can see, the activity's name is `employees` without the `.jsf` part, and this is what is going to be shown in the URL.

    By doing this, we added the `employees.jsf` page as a View activity inside the `adfc-config` task flow, which as you know can act as an entry point since unbounded task flow has unlimited entry points.

5. Right-click on `adfc-config` and run it; you will now see an even more enhanced version of the URL. You will see something like the following:

    `http://127.0.0.1:7101/ViewController/faces/employees`

    This is good, but `ViewController` isn't really the name of our application. So, in order to make the name reflect your application, let's rename it to what JDeveloper thinks is the name of our application.

6. Right-click on the `ViewController` project and click on **Project Properties...** at the end of the list; select **Java EE Application**.

7. Change **Java EE Web Application Name** and **Java EE Web Context Root** to something like `helloadf` and then run again; now, you can see your application with a nicely formatted URL like the following: `http://127.0.0.1:7101/helloadf/faces/employees`

 You can also run the page directly from the `ViewController` project. It'll ask you for a target to run; choose the `adfc-config`. It'll also ask you for the target inside `adfc-config`; choose `employees`.

How it works...

In this recipe, we tried three different methods to run our ADF application; however, it is preferable to always use the third method; `adfc-config` is the heart of your ADF application and contains all of the project's navigation information. From the task flow, you can notice that there are no green circles behind the page, which means that if you have any other activity, then the new activity can also be called directly and it doesn't have to follow any order.

If you run your application using any one of the scenarios and this is the first time you run an application in JDeveloper's lifetime, it'll create the weblogic domain first with no managed servers and only one admin server. It'll be created under the JDEV_USER_HOME environment variable that we created. After the domain is created successfully, the Admin Server starts, and after it does, JDeveloper starts packaging the application into a **WAR (Web Archive)** file. You can see this deployment profile by right-clicking and navigating to **ViewController** | **Properties** | **Deployment**; you will find an entry that represents the WAR packaging of this project. This project is also dependent on the Model project, which means that packaging will include all the stuff created in the Model Project. After the WAR file is created successfully, JDeveloper starts deploying the WAR file into the Admin Server. If the operation is successful, it will start to access the URL of the application inside the embedded Weblogic Server to show the target.

When you view the page, you can see that each input that has bindings represents a data field from the Employees table. When you start clicking on the buttons, you can see that the row of focus is changing to the next, previous, first, or last row, and you can validate this data against the database.

3
Presenting Data Using ADF Faces

The chapter will cover the following topics:

- ▶ Presenting single records on your page
- ▶ Presenting multiple records using ADF Table
- ▶ Presenting multiple records using ADF List View
- ▶ Presenting multiple records using ADF Iterator
- ▶ Presenting master-details records using ADF Tables and Forms
- ▶ Presenting master-details records using ADF Tree and tree table components
- ▶ Presenting master-details records using ADF List with a group header
- ▶ Internationalizing and localizing your representation

Introduction

In the previous chapter, we went through creating our first ADF application that gave us an idea of how the ADF application works. In this chapter, we will look at different ways of presenting data to give the best user experience possible and how to internationalize and localize pages to target multiple languages and locales.

In this chapter, you will learn how to present a single record, multiple records, and master-details records on your page using different components and methodologies.

You will also learn how to enable the internationalizing and localizing processes in your application by using a resource bundle and the different options of bundle you can have.

Starting from this chapter onward, we will not use the HR schema. We will rather use the FacerHR schema in the Git repository under the BookDatabaseSchema folder and read the README.txt file for information on how to create the database schema. This schema will be used for the whole book, so you need to do this only once.

You can find all the recipes of this chapter inside the Chapter 3 folder of the book's Git repository. Make sure you validate your database connection information for your recipes to work without problem.

Presenting single records on your page

In this recipe, we will address the need for presenting a single record in a page, which is useful specifically when you want to focus on a specific record in the table of your database; for example, a user's profile can be represented by a single record in an employee's table.

The application and its model have been created for you; you can see it by cloning the PresentingSingleRecord application from the Git repository.

How to do it...

In order to present a single record in pages, follow the ensuing steps:

1. Open the PresentingSingleRecord application.

2. Create a bounded task flow by right-clicking on **ViewController** and navigating to **New | ADF Task Flow**. Name the task flow single-employee-info and uncheck the **Create with Page Fragments** option.

> You can create a task flow with a page fragment, but you will need a page to host it at the end; alternatively, you can create a whole page if the task flow holds only one activity and is not reusable. However, in this case, I prefer to create a page-based task flow for fast deployment cycles and train you to always start from task flow.

3. Add a **View** activity inside of the task flow and name it singleEmployee.

4. Double-click on the newly created activity to create the page; this page will be based on the Oracle Three Column layout. Close the dialog by pressing the **OK** button.

5. Navigate to **Data Controls pane | HrAppModuleDataControl**, drag-and-drop EmployeesView1 into the white area of the page template, and select **ADF Form** from the drop-down list that appears as you drop the view object.

6. Check the **Row Navigation** option so that it has the first, previous, next, and last buttons for navigating through the task.

7. Group attributes based on their category, so the `Personal Information` group should include the `EmployeeId`, `FirstName`, `LastName`, `Email`, and `Phone Number` attributes; the `Job Information` group should include `HireDate`, `Job`, `Salary`, and `CommissionPct`; and the last group will be `Department Information` that includes both `ManagerId` and `DepartmentId` attributes.

8. Select multiple components by holding the *Ctrl* key and click on the **Group** button at the top-right corner, as shown in the following screenshot:

9. Change the **Display Label** values of the three groups to `eInfo`, `jInfo`, and `dInfo` respectively.

The **Display Label** option is a little misleading when it comes to groups in a form as groups don't have titles. Due to this, **Display Label** will be assigned to the **Id** attribute of the `af:group` component that will wrap the components, which can't have space and should be reasonably small; however, **Input Text w/Label or Output Text w/Label** will end up in the **Label** attribute in the **panelLabelAndMessage** component.

10. Change the **Component to Use** option of all attributes from **ADF Input Text w/ Label** to **ADF Output Text w/Label**. You might think that if you check the **Read-Only Form** option, it will have the same effect, but it won't. What will happen is that the `readOnly` attribute of the input text will change to `true`, which will make the input text non-updateable; however, it won't change the component type.

11. Change the **Display Label** option for the attributes to have more human-readable labels to the end user; you should end up with the following screen:

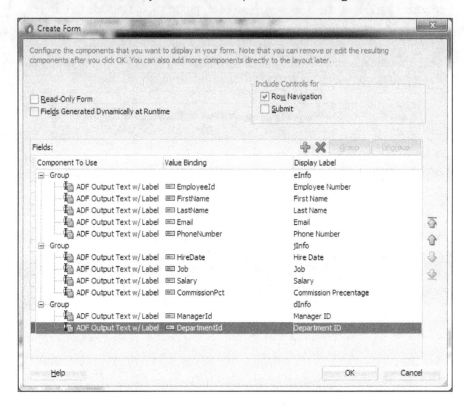

12. Finish by pressing the **OK** button.

You can save yourself the trouble of editing the **Display Label** option every time you create a component that is based on a view object by changing the `Label` attribute in UI Hints from the entity object or view object. More information can be found in the documentation at `http://docs.oracle.com/middleware/1212/adf/ADFFD/bcentities.htm#sm0140`.

13. Examine the page structure from the **Structure** pane in the bottom-left corner as shown in the following screenshot. A panel form layout can be found inside the center facet of the page template. This panel form layout represents an ADF form, and inside of it, there are three group components; each group has a panel label and message for each field of the view object.

At the bottom of the panel form layout, you can locate a **footer** facet; expand it to see a panel group layout that has all the navigation buttons. The **footer** facet identifies the locations of the buttons, which will be at the bottom of this panel form layout even if some components appear inside the page markup after this facet.

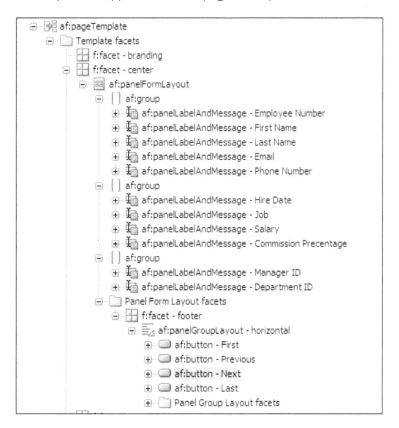

14. Examine the panel form layout properties by clicking on the **Properties** pane, which is usually located in the bottom-right corner. It allows you to change attributes such as **Max Columns**, **Rows**, **Field Width**, or **Label Width**. Change these attributes to change the form and to have more than one column.

If you can't see the **Structure** or **Properties** pane, you can see them again by navigating to **Window menu | Structure** or **Window menu | Properties**.

15. Save everything and run the page, placing it inside the `adf-config` task flow like we did in *Chapter 2, Getting Started with ADF Faces and JDeveloper*; to see this in action, refer to the following screenshot:

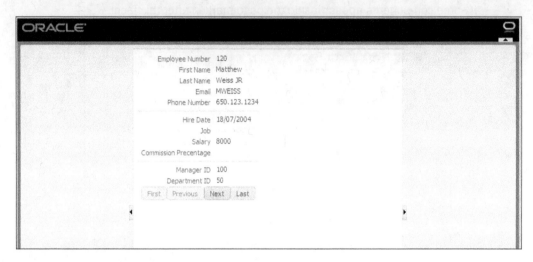

How it works...

The best component to represent a single record is a panel form layout, which presents the user with an organized form layout for different input/output components.

If you examine the page source code, you can see an expression like `#{bindings.FirstName.inputValue}`, which is related to the `FirstName` binding inside the `Bindings` section of the page definition where it points to `EmployeesView1Iterator`. However, iterator means multiple records, then why `FirstName` is only presenting a single record? It's because the iterator is aware of the current row that represents the row in focus, and this row will always point to the first row of the view object's `select` statement when you render the page. By pressing different buttons on the form, the `Current Row` value changes and thus the point of focus changes to reflect a different row based on the button you pressed.

When you are dealing with a single record, you can show it as the input text or any of the user input's components as we did in the previous chapter; alternatively, you can change it as the output text if you are just viewing it.

In this recipe, you can see that the **Group** component is represented as a line in the user interface when you run the page.

If you were to change the panel form layout's attributes, such as **Max Columns** or **Rows**, you would see a different view. **Max Columns** represents the maximum number of columns to show in a form, which defaults to **3** in case of desktops and **2** in case of PDAs; however, if this panel form layout is inside another panel form layout, the **Max Columns** value will always be **1**. The **Rows** attribute represents the numbers of rows after which we should start a new column; it has a default value of 2^{31}-1.

 You can know more about each attribute by clicking on the gear icon that appears when you hover over an attribute and reading the information on the property's **Help** page.

The benefit of having a panel form layout is that all labels are aligned properly; this organizes everything for you similar to the HTML `table` component.

See also

Check the following reference for more information about arranging content in forms:

`http://docs.oracle.com/middleware/1212/adf/ADFUI/af_orgpage.`
`htm#CDEHDJEA`

Presenting multiple records using ADF Table

In this recipe and the next two recipes, we will get to know how to present multiple records at once using three different components so that you can have control over what can be displayed and how you want to display it. In this recipe, you will learn how to do this using ADF Tables.

ADF Tables is one of the main components in the ADF Faces family, and it's commonly used, that is, you hardly find an enterprise application without one. ADF Tables provides great functionalities such as pagination, sorting, and filtering without compromising the ease of use for the application's user.

You can continue from the previous recipe, or you can grab this project's recipe by cloning the `PresentingMultipleWithTable` application from the Git repository.

How to do it...

In order to present multiple records using ADF Table, follow the ensuing steps:

1. Create a task flow with a view like the previous recipe, but change the attributes as shown in the following steps:

   1. **Task Flow name**: Enter the value `multiple-employees-info-table` in this field.

   2. **Create with Page Fragments**: Check this option.

      This will create a task flow with page fragments instead of pages; it's good time to understand how this works. Create a view and double-click on it to create it and make sure it has the following properties:

   3. **View name**: Enter the value `employeesTable` in this field.

   4. **Page Fragment Directory**: Enter the value `public_html\fragments` in this field.

   5. **Page Fragment Layout**: Set this option as **Create Blank Page**.

2. Navigate to **Data Control pane | HrAppModuleDataControl**, drag-and-drop `EmployeesView1` inside the page fragment, select **Table/List View** from the list, and select **ADF Table**, as shown in the following screenshot:

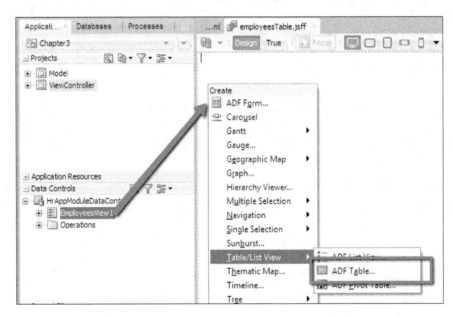

A dialog will open providing multiple options for row selection, sorting, filtering, and making the table read only.

3.   Check the **Single Row** option.

4.   Check the **Enable Sorting**, **Enable Filtering**, and **Read-Only Table** options.

 Notice how the **Component to Use** column changes when you check the **Read-Only Table** option.

5.   Create three groups exactly the same way as the previous recipe, but change the **Display Labels** option for **Groups** to **Personal Information**, **Job Information**, and **Department Information** respectively.

6.   Change the **Display Label** values for all attributes to have more human-readable column names as we did in the previous recipe; you should end up with the following screen:

7.   Click on **OK** to close the dialog window and return back to your screen, which should render the table successfully. You can see how the grouping looks like in the table, which looks like an Excel sheet.

8. Surround the table with a panel collection by right-clicking on the table from the **Structure** pane, clicking on the **Surround with...** option (as shown in the following screenshot), selecting **Panel Collection** from the list, and then clicking on **OK**.

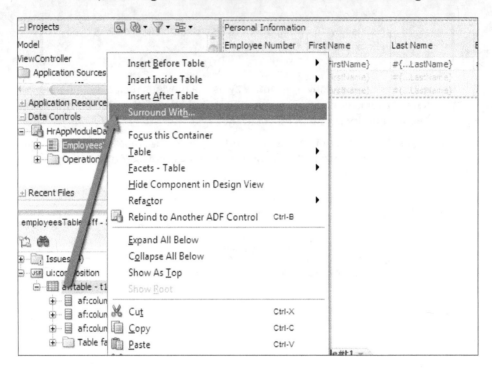

Notice the new **View** menu and a **Detach** button above the table.

9. Enable page pagination by changing the ADF Table's **Scroll Policy** property to **Page** from the **Properties** pane under **Appearance**.

The **Scroll Policy** option is newly introduced in Oracle ADF since 11.1.1.7, 11.1.2.3, and 12c; changing this property will not affect how the table looks in the **Design** view of the page fragment.

10. Surround the panel collection with the panel group layout as we did before, and now you are ready to run your page.

11. Open the `faces-config` task flow from the `WEB-INF` folder.

12. Drag-and-drop a view activity inside `faces-config`.

13. Change the name to `employeesTable`.

14. Double-click on the newly created activity to create the page and select **Oracle Three Column Layout** as the page template.

15. Drag-and-drop the `multiple-employees-info-table` task flow from the application navigation inside the `employeesTable.jsf` page to the blank area of the page template (center facet); select **Region** from the dialog list as shown in the following screenshot:

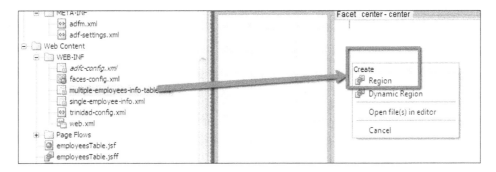

16. Run the page by clicking on the **Run** button (the green arrow) and run the `employeesTable.jsf` page, which looks like the following screenshot:

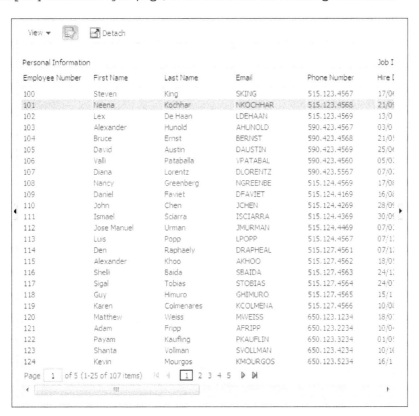

You can see from the layout that you have multiple options, such as filtering and sorting, which are used to hide columns from the **View** menu or detach the table to view it in a pop up that consumes the whole screen; you can try changing different properties in the **Appearance** section of the ADF Table to see how they effect its display.

How it works...

To understand how ADF Table works, let's view the source code of the `employeesTable.jsff` page fragment; you will find the structure is different from what the form is about. You can see the `value` attribute of the ADF Table referencing to the expression `#{bindings.EmployeesView1.collectionModel}`. The `var` attribute equals to `row`. These two attributes provide important information, but they also make you wonder: where are these rows? How are they resembled by the `value` attribute? How to represent multiple rows inside the table?

 There are also other values such as **Row Selection**, **Empty Text**, **Selection Listener**, **Selected Rows**, **Fetch Size**, **Filter Model**, **Query Listener**, and **Scroll Policy**, which are optional properties.

To answer these questions, let's look at the structure of the table. The ADF Table component has multiple `Column` components inside of it, and you can see nested columns that represent the **Groups** feature of the table. So, you can find a column inside a column. The uppermost will be the group column, and the one inside will be the subgroup until you end up with innermost column that represents an actual column. Inside the innermost column, you will find the output text with a value, something like `#{row.EmployeeId}` or `#{row.FirstName}`. By opening the page definition, you can see that there are no row bindings inside the `Bindings` section, which means there is something else happening.

First, let's take a step back to understand the `value` attribute of the table, and to do that, let's go to the `bindings` view of the page and see what `#{bindings.EmployeesView1.collectionModel}` means. As you can see, there is something called `EmployeesView1` in the `Bindings` section, and if you double-click on it, you can see that this binding is called a **tree binding**, which represents a table, tree, or basically any collection of rows inside a page.

You can also see that **Tree Level Rules** is pointing to the `EmployeesView` view object, and there is **Display Attributes**, which has all the attributes of the view object inside of ADF Table. Also, this tree binding is referencing `EmployeesView1Iterator`. If you have selected this, you can see on the **Properties** pane that it has range size of **25**, which represents the number of records that you saw on a single page of the table. Also, the iterator points to the `EmployeesView1` view object under the application module, which gives you the indication that this tree binding has a property called `CollectionModel` that corresponds to the attributes under the **Display Attributes** section of the tree binding.

Go back to the page source; now we can understand what the table's `value` attribute means; however, how can we target a specific column inside this `CollectionModel`? This is the role of the `var` attribute. It represents a single variable (`row`) inside the table, which means whatever the value of the `var` attribute is, you can use it to represent a single row value; if you want to display a specific column inside this row, you can just use `#{varValue.columnName}`, which is what the output text component is displaying.

The following are the attributes that the table uses:

- `emptyText` – This attribute tells the table what to display in case there are no records.

- `rowSelection` – This attribute represents the type of selection this table should have; you have three options: `None`, `Single`, or `Multiple`.

- `selectedRowKeys` – This attribute indicates selected rows inside the collection model that indicates the selected row(s) if `rowSelection` is either `Single` or `Multiple`.

- `selectionListener` – This attribute indicates an event that gets triggered every time you select a new record from the table and the selection listener, which by default executes a method called `makeCurrent`. This method changes the current row of the `collectionModel` inside the iterator, which means if you have a form and a table that point to the same iterator and select a record inside the table, the form should display the same record.

- `fetchSize` – This attribute represents the number of rows in the data fetch block.

- `filterModel` – This attribute is responsible for the inline filtering feature that you see when you enable the filter. This is the query that gets executed when you enter some text in the filter's textbox and hit *Enter*. This points to `#{bindings. EmployeesView1Query.queryDescriptor}` in the `Executables` section in the `Bindings` view.

- `queryListener` – This attribute indicates an event such as `selectionListener`, but the filter executes every time you hit *Enter* on your filter textboxes.

- `scrollPolicy` – This attribute indicates how the pagination in the table should work; there are two policies, either `Scroll` or `Page`, and you have to have a non-stretchable parent in order for page's `scrollPolicy` to work effectively.

- `varStatus` – This attribute indicates the status of the `var` attribute which focuses on getting the status of the current row and not the row data, that is, information such as index number, count, and step.

 Instead of having the inline filter of ADF Table, you could replace it to have another component called **search form**. You can learn all about it from `http://docs.oracle.com/middleware/1212/adf/ ADFFD/web_search_bc.htm`.

You might wonder where sorting is occurring in the table attributes, but sorting is something up to the column itself not for the table as a whole. So inside the column, you will find properties such as `sortable` and `sortProperty` that tell the column what is the name of this column field in order to sort it; also, inside the column, you can change the `headerText` attribute or change other properties such as the `alignment` attribute of the column.

Surrounding the table with the **Panel Collection** component—which can surround any collection of components such as tables, trees, and tree tables—will provide a container for these components. It can also provide more functionalities to interact with the table, such as detaching the table to view it fullscreen, removing the filter, hiding columns, or reordering columns inside the table. You have the option to add more to the toolbar or the menu by using the **Panel Collection** facets.

See also

To know more about ADF Tables, check the reference documentation at `http://docs.oracle.com/middleware/1212/adf/ADFFD/web_tables_forms.htm`.

Presenting multiple records using ADF List View

In this recipe, we will get to know how to present multiple records at once using the ADF List View component, which is pretty similar to ADF Table with some minor differences.

If you don't care about sorting or filtering and you want to have more control of how the rows look, ADF List View is the component to use.

 ADF List View is a newly introduced component starting from release 11.1.1.7 in the 11gR1 release stack and 12c.

You can continue from the previous recipe or you can grab this project's recipe by cloning the `PresentingMultipleWithListView` application from the Git repository.

How to do it...

To present multiple records using ADF List View, follow the ensuing steps:

1. Create a task flow and a view page fragment like the previous recipe, but this time, change the following attributes:

    1. **Task Flow name**: `multiple-employees-info-list`.
    2. **Create with Page Fragments**: Checked.
    3. **View name**: `employeesList`.
    4. **Page Fragment Directory**: `public_html\fragments`.
    5. **Page Fragment Layout**: **Create Blank Page**.

2. Navigate to **Data Control pane | HrAppModuleDataControl**, drag-and-drop `EmployeesView1` inside the page fragment, select **Table/List View** from the list, and select **ADF List View...** as shown in the following screenshot:

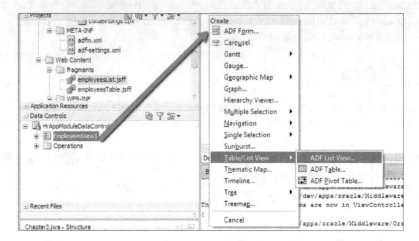

3. A dialog will open up asking about the list view layout; this is really important as it depends on how you want to present your data. If the attributes of the row are stacked vertically, you should choose **Panel Group Layout** (as shown in the following screenshot); if they are taking the whole width of the page, choose **Panel Grid Layout**; if you have a master-details view object, you may want to choose the last option—we will talk about it later in this chapter.

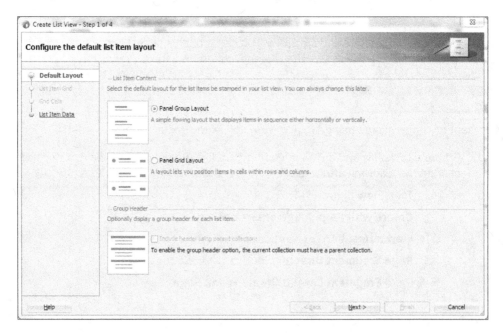

4. Select the **Panel Grid Layout** option for this recipe, as it'll give you a good introduction to the panel grid layout component that is newly added to Oracle ADF Faces and is great to work with.

5. Click on **Next** to specify how the panel grid will look and how many columns and rows you want; arrange it in three columns: `Personal Information`, `Job Information`, and `Department Information`. Choose four rows to display up to four attributes inside the same column. Leave the margin between columns as is.

6. Click on **Next** to identify how much space each column should have. Change the value of the first column to **50%** and **25%** for the other two. Specify the span which can be useful; because the last column only has two attributes, so create a span from **gc2,3** (grid cell (2,3)) to **gc4,3** so that you end up with only two rows inside the last column as shown in the following screenshot:

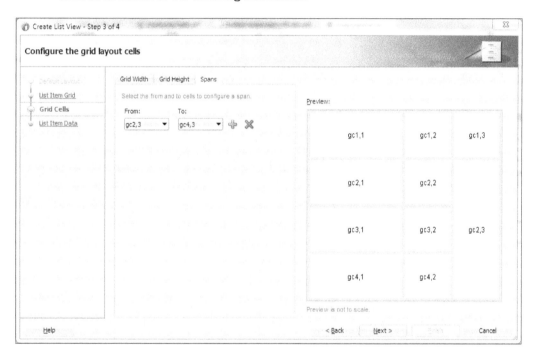

7. Click on **Next** to bind your cells to your attributes by changing the **Value Binding** attribute. In the first column, select `First Name`, `Last Name`, `Email`, and `Phone Number` in `gc1,1`, `gc2,1`, `gc3,1`, and `gc4,1` respectively, which have the `gcn,1` form.

    In the second column, select `Job`, `Hire Date`, and `Salary & Commission Pct` in `gc1,2`, `gc2,2`, `gc3,2`, and `gc4,2` respectively, which have the `gcn,2` form.

In the last column, select `Manager Id` and `Department Id` in gc1,3 and gc2,3 respectively, which have the gcn,3 form. You should end up with the following screen:

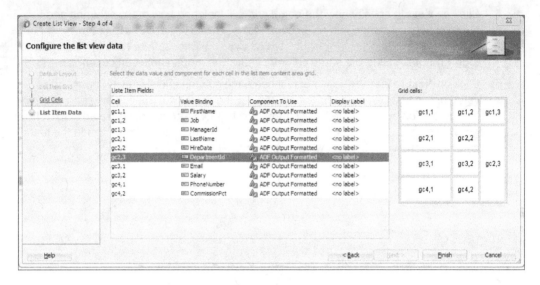

8. Click on **Finish** to close the dialog.

9. Examine the **Structure** pane; you can notice that the list view consists of a list item that represents a single row inside the panel grid layout; you can easily spot the similarity between list views and tables, as is evident from the following screenshot:

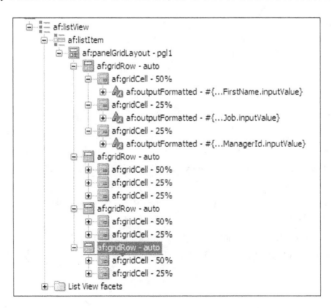

10. Surround the ADF List View with the panel accordion by right-clicking on the list view from the **Structure** pane; then, click on the **Surround with...** option, select **Panel Accordion** from the list, and click on **OK**.

11. Drag-and-drop `af:ListView` inside `af:showDetailItem` from the **Structure** pane.

12. Select `af:showDetailItem` from the **Structure** pane and change the `text` attribute value to **ADF List View**.

13. Surround the ADF List View again, but this time with the panel group layout, by right-clicking on the list view from the **Structure** pane, clicking on the **Surround with...** option, selecting **Panel Group Layout** from the list, and then clicking on **OK**.

14. Select `af:panelGroupLayout` from the **Structure** pane and change the `layout` attribute value to `scroll`; this will enable the ADF List View to have `scroll` inside the panel accordion.

    Now we have finished creating the list view; let's go and put the task flow under a JSF page to run and test it.

15. Open the `faces-config` task flow under the `WEB-INF` folder.

16. Drag-and-drop a view activity inside `faces-config`.

17. Change the name to `employeesList`.

18. Double-click on the newly created activity to create the page and select **Oracle Three Column Layout** as the page template.

19. Drag-and-drop the `multiple-employees-info-list` task flow from the application navigation inside the `employeesList.jsf` page, which is inside the white area of the page template (center facet), and select **Region** from the dialog list.

20. Run the page by clicking on the **Run** button (the green arrow) and run the `employeesList.jsf` page, which looks like the following screenshot.

21. When you run the page, you will notice a link at the end that displays **Load more items**; this is the pagination option. When you click on it, you can display the next 25 records or the number of records mentioned in the fetchSize attribute.

How it works...

Under the hood, the ADF List View behaves exactly like ADF Table, except that it looks different. So, if you opened the source view, you would see that the same attributes are in ADF List View. Attributes such as value, var, emptyText, and fetchSize look and act similar to ADF Table; however, this time, instead of having a column, we have a list, so you get the data from an item instead of a row.

 As you know, rows and items are irrelevant. You can use any keyword to represent a single record; however, in ADF List View, item suits the context more, while in a table, row suits the context more.

Also, having panel grid layout is totally irrelevant; you can add any ADF Faces component and organize it the way you see best fit, but panel grid layout can make sure that everything looks nice inside the list view component.

We surrounded the ADF List View with panel accordion and panel group layout. The panel group layout is necessary to provide scrolling capabilities of rows inside the panel accordion.

You haven't seen the panel accordion in action yet. In the next recipe, we will see how panel accordion works in more detail.

Presenting multiple records using ADF Iterator

Iterator is not a component in nature, as it doesn't have generated HTML specific to it, which makes it perfect if you want to create something completely different from what ADF Table or List View offer; however, at the same time, using iterator will make it a little bit harder for you, as you will have to add everything manually.

In this recipe, you're not going to create a new task flow; instead, we will use the `employeesList.jsff` page fragment created in the previous recipe to display a list of the employees' full names in another accordion panel under the list view.

You can continue from the previous recipe, or you can grab this project's recipe by cloning the `PresentingMultipleWithIterator` application from the Git repository.

How to do it...

To present multiple records using ADF Iterator, follow the ensuing steps:

1. Open the `employeesList.jsff` page fragment if it's not already opened, and select the **Panel Accordion** component from the **Structure** pane.

2. Right-click on it and navigate to **Insert Inside | Show Detail Item**.

3. Change the text of the new `showDetailItem` attribute to **ADF Iterator**.

4. Right-click on `showDetailItem` and navigate to **Insert Inside | Panel Group Layout**.

5. Change the layout of the new `panelGroupLayout` attribute to **scroll**.

6. Drag-and-drop the **Panel List** component from the **Layout** option in **Components** palette inside the `panelGroupLayout` attribute we created in the previous step.

7. Select the **Panel List** option inside the **Structure** pane, right-click on it, navigate to **Insert inside Panel List | ADF Faces | Iterator**, and click on **OK**.

8. Select the **Iterator** component from the **Structure** pane, hover over the `value` attribute in the **Properties** pane on the bottom-right side, click on the gear icon that appears to the right, and select the **Expression Builder** option.

9. Navigate to **ADF Bindings | bindings | EmployeesView1**, select **collectionModel**, and then click on **OK**, as shown in the following screenshot:

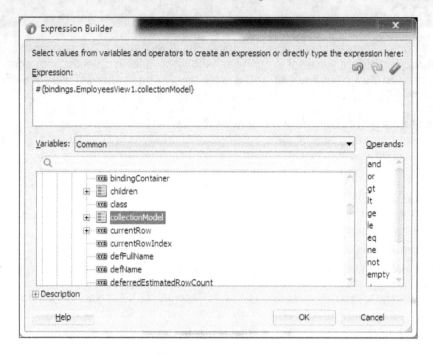

10. Now you should see the **Value** property filled; change the `var` property to **emp**.

11. Change the `rows` attribute to **50** to show the first 50 employees.

    Now it is time to show the full name.

12. Right-click on the iterator from the **Structure** window, navigate to **Insert inside Iterator | ADF faces**, and select **Output Text** from the list in the dialog.

You can right-click and use **Insert Inside**, drag-and-drop the component from the **Components** pallet into the design view directly, or drag-and-drop the component from the **Components** pallet inside the **Structure** window; however, if you choose the drag-and-drop option, drop it inside the **Structure** window as it provides more control over where your component will get dropped.

13. Change the `value` attribute of the output text to the following:

```
#{emp.FirstName} #{emp.LastName}
```

You should end up having the following inside your **Structure** pane:

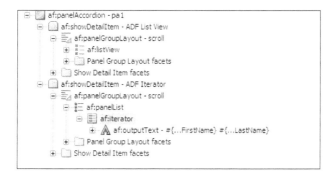

14. Run the application by running the `employeesList.jsf` page. Click on **ADF Iterator**, which will collapse the first item of the accordion to show a list with the first 50 employees' full names as shown in the following screenshot:

How it works...

What we did here is that we replicated what the table does but on a small scale; after we added the panel list, we added the iterator component inside of it so that the panel list items can be generated dynamically. We pointed to the same `value` binding as the ADF List View and ADF Table, and this `value` binding was retrieved from the `Bindings` section of the page definition using the expression builder.

We also chose a different name for the var attribute. This time it was called emp as each record represents an employee; however, you are free to choose whatever name you would like. Inside the iterator, we added the output text that has the value #{emp.firstName} #{emp.lastName}, which is the full name of the employee.

Notice that this time we didn't create a new page, and we reused the same binding model that I used with list view. JDeveloper doesn't provide the drag-and-drop functionality to the iterator, so we have to do things manually; you can create the tree binding from the binding view manually, or you can create a dummy table and remove it from the source—don't remove it from the **Structure** pane or else it'll remove the bindings with it—and use the same collection model.

Presenting master-details records using ADF Tables and Forms

To have multiple records in a page is one thing, but to have a master-details relationship, whether this relationship is originally based on a one-to-many or many-to-many database relationship, is essential to many applications.

In this recipe and the following two recipes, we will get to know three different approaches to display master-details records in pages. One of the most basic yet effective approaches is the use of a combination of forms and tables to view master-details information, and this gives us four options:

- ▶ Master form, details table
- ▶ Master form, details form
- ▶ Master table, details form
- ▶ Master table, details table

These four options cover how you can use master-details scenarios with tables and forms.

In this recipe, you will walk through the first option, and by finishing it, you will grasp the rest on your own.

In order to use the master-details approach, you need to have a master-details model. In pure Java language, a master-details model means that one object has a collection of another object. From Oracle ADF Business Component's perspective, this means you should have a view link between two view objects.

You can learn more about defining master-details-related view objects and how to create view links from http://docs.oracle.com/middleware/1212/adf/ADFFD/bcquerymasterdetail.htm#ADFFD23702.

Lucky for us that our `Employees` table has a one-to-many relationship with itself to accomplish the manager-employees relationship, which we will utilize to display master-details records in this recipe and the next two recipes.

You can continue from the previous recipe, or you can grab this project's recipe by cloning the `presentingMasterDetailTables` application from the Git repository.

How to do it...

To know how to present master-details relationship using tables and forms, follow the ensuing steps:

1. Create a task flow and a view JSF page fragment with the following properties:

    1. **Task Flow name**: `master-details-employees-table`.

    2. **Create with Page Fragments**: Checked.

    3. **View name**: `mdEmployeesTable`.

    4. **Page Fragment Directory**: `public_html\fragments`.

    5. **Page Fragment Layout**: **Create Blank Page**.

2. Navigate to **Data Control pane** | **HrAppModuleDataControl** | **EmployeesView1**, drag-and-drop `EmployeesView2` inside the page fragment, select **Master-Detail** from the list, and select **ADF Master Form, Detail Table**, as shown in the following screenshot:

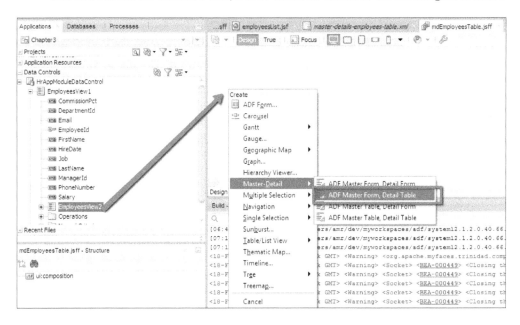

As you can see, there are no wizards for this; if you check the **Structure** pane, you will find that you have a panel group layout with two panel headers. In the first panel header, you will find a panel form layout, and in the second one, you can see an ADF Table. You can change the panel header `text` attribute of the first one to `Manager` and to `Department employees` for the second panel header.

3. Open the `faces-config` task flow under the `WEB-INF` folder.

4. Drag-and-drop a view activity inside `faces-config`.

5. Change the name to `mdEmployeesTable`.

6. Double-click on the newly created activity to create the page and select **Oracle Three Column Layout** as the page template.

7. Drag-and-drop the `master-details-employees-table` task flow from the application navigation inside the `mdEmployeesTable.jsf` page, which is inside the white area of the page template (center facet), and select **Region** from the dialog list.

8. Run the page by clicking on the **Run** button (the green arrow) and run the `mdEmployeesTable.jsf` page, which looks like following screenshot:

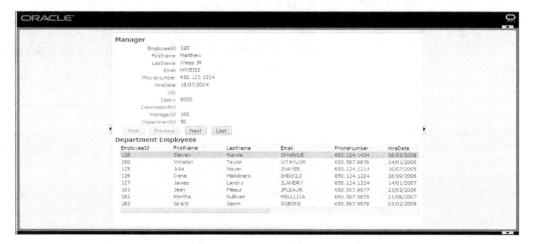

As you navigate through the manager form, you will see that the table gets updated with the data of different departments' employees, which represents tabular-form information about the hierarchy of the company.

How it works...

JDeveloper provides an easy way to implement a master-details relationship; as you can see, here we chose to drag-and-drop `EmployeesView2` instead of `EmployeesView1`. It is important for JDeveloper to know that there are parent view objects and they are linked through a view link.

When you do this, a couple more options appear when you drag-and-drop it into your page, and you can see the four scenarios of master-details reports that we talked about.

What we did is exactly equal to the following four steps:

1. Drag-and-drop `EmployeesView1` as a read-only form with navigation buttons.

2. Drag-and-drop `EmployeesView2` as a read-only table with a single selection without sorting and filtering.

3. Set the **Partial Submit** attributes of the buttons inside the form (first, previous, next, and last) to **true**. (More on this in *Chapter 7, Handling Events and Partial Page Rendering*.)

4. Put the table and the form inside **Panel Headers**.

If you open the `Bindings` view, you will find all the bindings that were mentioned earlier in the form and table; however, this time the table binding will reference to `EmployeesView2`, which will reference `EmployeesView2Iterator`.

Presenting master-details records using ADF Tree and tree table components

As you can see from the previous recipe, we presented a hierarchy that can be mapped to a tree instead of tables and forms, and ADF provides a great way to deal with hierarchical data by having two components; a tree component and a tree table component.

In this recipe, you will represent the same relationship between manager and employees as tree and tree table respectively.

You can continue from the previous recipe, or you can grab this project's recipe by cloning the `presentingMasterDetailTrees` application from the Git repository.

How to do it...

To present master-details relationship using trees and tree tables, follow the ensuing steps:

1. Create a task flow and a view JSF page fragment with the following properties:

    1. **Task Flow name**: `master-details-employees-tree`.

    2. **Create with Page Fragments**: Checked.

    3. **View name**: `mdEmployeesTree`.

    4. **Page Fragment Directory**: `public_html\fragments`.

    5. **Page Fragment Layout**: **Create Blank Page**.

2. Drag-and-drop a panel splitter from the **Components** palette into the root of the page fragment.

3. Navigate to **Data Control pane | HrAppModuleDataControl**, drag-and-drop `EmployeesView1` into the *first* facet of the panel splitter, select **Tree** from the list, and select **ADF Tree...** as shown in the following screenshot:

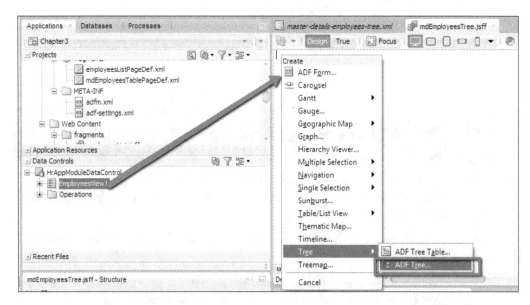

A dialog will show asking you to edit tree binding; we want to show a tree of employee names.

Shuttle `First Name` and `Last Name` from **Available Attributes** to **Display Attributes** and remove `EmployeesId` from the **Display Attributes** section.

4. Click on the plus icon inside the **Tree Level Rules** section.

5. Select `Employees1` from the list in which we will add another employee level under the main level, as shown in the following screenshot:

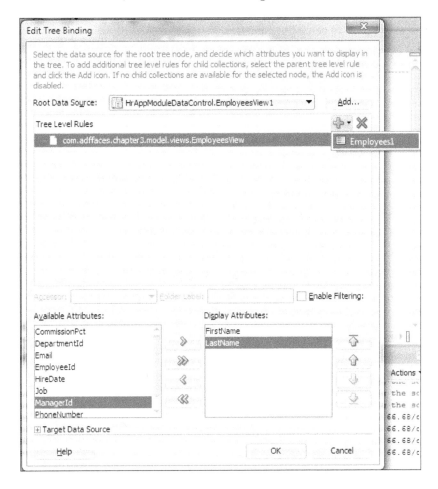

In the **Tree Level Rules** section, you should see something like `com.adffaces.chapter3.model.views.EmployeesView(<Employees1>)`.

The last bracket means that it has details of the same view object.

6. Finish by clicking on **OK** to close the dialog.

7. Examine the **Structure** window to see what was generated. You will see a tree component, and you can see a facet inside of it called `nodeStamp`. It has the output text with the value `#{node}` that represents the displayed attributes we just defined.

Now let's add the tree table component, which will go just below the tree component.

8. Drag-and-drop `EmployeesView1` inside the *second* facet of the panel splitter component and navigate to **Tree | ADF Tree Table**.

9. Shuttle `First Name`, `Last Name`, and `Salary` into **Display Attributes**.

10. Click on the plus button at the **Tree Level Rules** section, add **EmployeesView**, and click on **OK** to close the dialog.

    Now we will edit the tree table component a little bit to show the `First Name` and `Last Name` attributes in one column and `Salary` in another column.

11. Expand the tree table from the **Structure** pane and expand the `nodeStamp` facet.

12. Select the column and change the `headerText` value to `Employee`.

13. Select the output text and change the value from just `#{node}` to `#{node.FirstName}` `#{node.LastName}`.

14. Repeat the previous step for the `pathStamp` facet to have `#{node.FirstName}` `#{node.LastName}` as well.

15. Select the tree table component as a whole from the **Structure** pane, right-click on it, and navigate to **Insert inside Tree Table | Column**.

16. Change the `headerText` attribute of the newly created column to `Salary`.

17. Right-click on the column from the **Structure** pane and navigate to **Insert inside Column | Output Text**.

18. Change the `value` attribute of the newly created output text to `#{node.Salary}`; you should end up with something like the following screenshot:

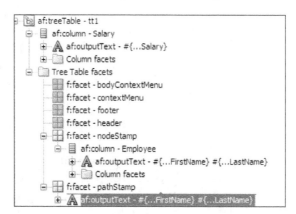

19. Open the `faces-config` task flow under the `WEB-INF` folder.

20. Drag-and-drop a view activity inside `faces-config`.

21. Change its name to `mdEmployeesTree`.

22. Double-click on the newly created activity to create the page and select **Oracle Three Column Layout** as the page template.

23. Drag-and-drop the `master-details-employees-tree` task flow from the application navigation inside the `mdEmployeesTree.jsf` page, which is inside the white area of the page template (center facet), and select **Region** from the dialog list.

24. Run the page by clicking on the **Run** button (the green arrow) and run the `mdEmployeesTree.jsf` page, which looks like following screenshot:

You can see the names of all the employees, and if you expand the first one, `Matthew Weiss JR`, you can see who he manages, and you can drill down indefinitely.

You can also use the mouse's right-click on any tree element. A menu will pop up with different options such as **Collapse**, **Expand**, and **Set as top**.

How it works...

The tree works in a top-down approach unlike JDeveloper's master-details feature, so you start with the top branch and then you add subbranches to the tree using the plus icon.

In our example, both branches belong to the same view object; that's why you saw the same attribute twice. If you were to have different view objects, you would see different attributes in different branches, and you could also have a master-details-details format if you like; however, if you want the tree to have unlimited number of levels, you have to have the same view object twice or else you will end up with the number of levels you specified inside your tree binding.

If you examine the structure, you will find the tree has a similar structure to the table; however, what's new in here is that first you work with a facet called `nodeStamp` instead of a column in a table or `listItem` in list view, and secondly, the `var` attribute has a *node* instead of a *row*. You just put #{node} in the `var` attribute without specifying a particular attribute, which by default will concatenate all **Displayed Attributes** values together in one string separated by a space. The bindings are exactly the same as in the table and list view, which point to tree bindings. This means that you can still specify the attribute you want to use inside your `nodeStamp` facet explicitly, which was illustrated using the tree table component.

If I had left the tree table component as is, it'd have generated something like `Matthew Weiss JR 8000`, which is not what I wanted. This is why I had to explicitly specify `First Name` and `Last Name` in the `nodeStamp` facet and create a new column for the `Salary` attribute.

The problem with specifying values directly is that if you have different view objects for your levels with different attributes, you will have to have some condition to view and hide different output texts using the `rendered` attribute or the `switcher` component.

> The `switcher` component dynamically decides which facet component should be rendered. The `switcher` component is a purely logical server-side component. It does not generate any content itself and has no client-side representation.
>
> To know more about the `switcher` component, check the official documentation at `http://jdevadf.oracle.com/adf-richclient-demo/docs/tagdoc/af_switcher.html`.

Trees and tree tables also contain a `pathStamp` facet. This facet determines how the content of the hierarchical selector dialog is rendered, just like the `nodeStamp` facet determines how the content of the tree is rendered. The component inside the `pathStamp` facet can be a combination of simple output text, an image, and the `outputFormatted` tags; it cannot be any input component. If this facet is not provided, then the hierarchical selector icon is not rendered. Refer to the following screenshot showing what the `pathStamp` looks like at runtime:

Using pathStamp

In this recipe, we also saw panel splitter in action; panel splitter is one of the stretching components that lets you create two panes separated by a splitter, which can be resized at runtime. More about panel splitter in *Chapter 6, Enriching User Experience with Visualization Components*.

Presenting master-details records using ADF List with a group header

The previous master-details recipe that has a great UI look and feel is the list view component with group header enabled; this will allow you to have a master-details relationship inside the list view component.

In this recipe, you will represent the same relationship between the manager and his/her employees as a list view with group header.

You can continue from the previous recipe, or you can grab this project's recipe by cloning the `presentingMasterDetailList` application from the Git repository.

How to do it...

The steps for presenting master-details records using the ADF list with a group header are as follows:

1. Create a task flow and a view JSF page fragment with the following properties:
    1. **Task Flow name**: `master-details-employees-list`.
    2. **Create with Page Fragments**: Checked.
    3. **View name**: `mdEmployeesList`.
    4. **Page Fragment Directory**: `public_html\fragments`.
    5. **Page Fragment Layout**: **Create Blank Page**.

2. Navigate to **Data Control | HrAppModuleDataControl | EmployeesView1** and drag-and-drop `EmployeesView2` inside the page fragment root, select **Table / List View** from the list, and select **ADF List View**.

3. Leave the **Panel Group Layout** checkbox checked as the **Create List View** dialog opens up.

4. Check the **Include header using parent collection: EmployeesView1** checkbox; this will enable the master-details feature of list view.

5. Click on **Next**; you will find two tabs: **Content Data** and **Group Header Data**. The group header data is the data for the manager and the content data is for the employees of that manager.

6. Add two fields, `FirstName` and `LastName`, by clicking on the plus icon, and change the value binding to `FirstName` and `LastName` respectively under **Value Binding** as shown in the following screenshot:

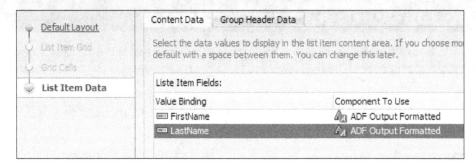

7. Do the same for **Group Header Data** to add `FirstName` and `LastName` as well, then click on **Finish**.

8. Navigate to **af:listView | af:listItem** and select **af:panelGroupLayout** from the **Structure** pane.

9. Right-click on `af:panelGroupLayout` and navigate to **Insert Inside | Spacer**.

10. Put `Spacer` between the two `af:outputFormatted` tags.

11. Repeat the previous two steps for **af:listView, af:facet – groupHeaderStamp, af:listItem**, and **af:panelGroupLayout**. You should end up with the structure shown in the following screenshot:

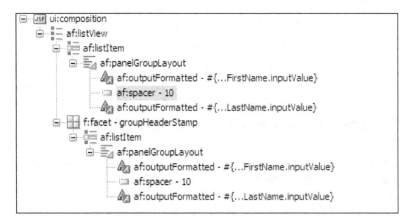

12. Examine what got inserted in the page by using the **Structure** pane. You can find that there is a new facet added inside the list view called `groupHeaderStamp`, and it has a list item as well, which has the `FirstName` and `LastName` value bindings that we added.

13. Open the `faces-config` task flow under the `WEB-INF` folder.

14. Drag-and-drop a view activity inside `faces-config`.

15. Change the name to `mdEmployeesList`.

16. Double-click on the newly created activity to create the page and select **Oracle Three Column Layout** as the page template.

17. Drag-and-drop the `master-details-employees-list` task flow from the application navigation inside the `mdEmployeesList.jsf` page, which is inside the white area of the page template (center facet), and select **Region** from the dialog list.

18. Run the page by clicking on the **Run** button (the green arrow) and run the `mdEmployeesList.jsf` page, which looks like the following screenshot:

How it works...

Behind the scene, the list component tree binding is exactly the same as for the tree and tree table components. If you check the `Bindings` section, you will actually see that it references `EmployeesView1` even if we dragged-and-dropped `EmployeesView2`. This is because list view is also a top-down approach, so if you double-click on this binding, you will see it has two levels, just like the bindings in table and tree table.

The only difference is the new facet that you saw in the **Structure** pane when you examined what was inserted in the page. This facet will render at the topmost level, and the content of the list view will be rendered as **Content Data**. The only limitation in list view is that it only has two levels and can't have infinite levels like trees.

There is more...

Just like list view has some capabilities to view master-details relationship, tables also have the same capabilities, but they don't have a wizard to make it easy like the list view. In order to do this, you will first need to add the new level from the `Bindings` section inside the bindings view of your page (try it on `employeesTable.jsff`).

After you add the sub-level, go back to the design view, select the table from the **Structure** pane, right-click on the **Table**, and navigate to **Insert inside the table | JSF | Facet - detail Stamp**.

This facet will create an expander just like the one in the list view and help you expand the record to see more details. You can use it in other ways to show more information about a single employee for instance, but you can also utilize the ADF Iterator component to show details of the master table and iterate over a subview. For instance, in the `EmployeesView` example, you will have to create an iterator with a different `var` attribute, say `subEmp`, and the value of the iterator will be `#{row.EmployeesView}`. By iterating over this view, you will iterate over subrows, and you can get all the data you want using `#{subEmp.FirstName}`.

An example is given inside the Git repository, and for this chapter, inside `employeesTable.jsf`.

Internationalizing and localizing your representation

Internationalization is the process of designing and developing products for easy adaptation to specific local languages and cultures. **Localization** is the process of adapting a product for a specific local language or culture by translating text and adding locale-specific components. A successfully localized application will appear to have been developed within the local culture.

In this recipe, we will get to know how to localize the application representation to enable content to be viewable in multiple languages and regions and how to enable the application to change the locale at runtime.

ADF Faces not only provides an easy way to use localization as part of JSF's capabilities, but also extends it to include it in the ADF BC. It also adds additional ways of formatting your text by using well known methods of localization.

In order to localize your application, you first have to have a bundle that can hold your string texts for a specific locale—a locale is a combination of a language and an optional country that can give you a specific variation of the language in that country.

...

There are three types of bundle that can be created in ADF as follows:

- **List resource bundle**: This is a Java file that holds all your string text
- **The properties file**: This is a text file that holds all your string text
- **XML Localization Interchange File Format (XLIFF) resource bundle**: This file is a standardization of localization interchange files (if you are using big enterprise applications, you will appreciate it)

You can continue from the previous recipe, or you can grab this project's recipe by cloning the `i18nADFFaces` application from the Git repository.

How to do it...

In order to internationalize and localize your representation, follow the ensuing steps:

1. Right-click on the `ViewController` project node in the application's navigator pane and select **Project Properties**.

2. Select **Resource Bundle** from the menu on the left-hand side to see the options you have, as shown in the following screenshot:

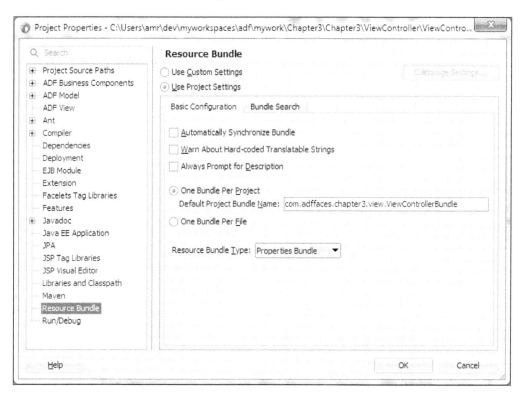

You have two main options: you either have one bundle for the whole project or have one bundle per file (page or page fragment). You have another list to choose which resource bundle type you want, and the properties bundle is selected by default. You can also have multiple options that warn you about hardcoded strings, which can be helpful if you start with hardcoded text and then start to localize everything afterwards.

Using the default properties file is the easiest and most common option.

3. Check the **Warn about Hard-coded Translatable Strings** option to show where you can find the hardcoded text.

    We want to change the `singleEmployees.jsf` page we created in the beginning of this chapter in a way that it is localized, and you can practice this and apply it to all other pages as an exercise.

4. Open the `singleEmployees.jsf` page after clicking on **OK** to save the changes of the **Project Properties** page. You will find some yellow squares that identify warnings in the page.

5. Click on the first small yellow rectangle, which will be the `af:document` tag and the `title` attribute.

6. Click on the gear icon in the property inspector and select **Select Text Resource**; a pop up will appear.

7. Enter the value `Single Employee form`, which will create a default key for this text string in the resource bundle. A good convention is to prefix your key with your page name, or if you have something that is common to all the pages, name it after the project name.

8. Change the key from `SINGLE_EMPLOYEE_FORM` to `EMPLOYEE.PAGE_TITLE` to be more meaningful.

9. Click on **Save and Select**.

    You will see that you have one less yellow square.

10. Examine your application navigator; you can see the resource bundle file, that is, the `ViewControllerBundle.properties` file created.

11. By double-clicking on it, you can see the key-value pair that you just created.

12. Repeat the same steps to remove all yellow rectangles from all the buttons. Notice that the input text and input dates don't provide you with a warning as they are pointing to control hints inside the model, which can also reference to a resource bundle.

You should end up with the following list inside the resource bundle file, `ViewControllerBundle.properties`:

```
EMPLOYEE.PAGE_TITLE=Employees form
EMPLOYEE.FIRST=First
EMPLOYEE.NEXT=Next
EMPLOYEE.PREVIOUS=Previous
EMPLOYEE.LAST=Last
```

13. Drag-and-drop another button beside the `Last` button.

14. Use the **Select Text Resource** option to add another key-value pair inside the resource bundle like the following:

```
EMPLOYEE.CHANGE_LANG=Change Language
```

15. Change the `partialSubmit` attribute to `false`.

    This will disable the automatic partial submit of the button and will force a full submit to the server, which is needed in this case to alert all the components that the locale has been changed.

16. Select the `view` node by navigating to **Applications Navigator | View Controller | Application Sources | com.adffaces.chapter3 | view**.

17. Right-click on `view` and navigate to **New | From Gallery**.

18. Go to **General Category | File**.

19. Name the file `ViewControllerBundle_fr.properties`, which will create the French version of our resource bundle.

20. Add the following entries inside the file, which are the French equivalents to the English values:

```
EMPLOYEE.PAGE_TITLE=Employés forme
EMPLOYEE.FIRST=Première
EMPLOYEE.NEXT=Prochain
EMPLOYEE.PREVIOUS=Précédent
EMPLOYEE.LAST=Dernier
EMPLOYEE.CHANGE_LANG=Change Language
```

21. Open the `singleEmployees.jsf` page.

22. Select `f:view` from the **Structure** pane.

23. In the `Locale` attribute, enter the expression `#{sessionScope.`
    `locale==null?'en': sessionScope.locale}`, which basically instructs the
    page to change based on the `sessionScope` variable called `locale`. If `locale`
    is not found inside `sessionScope` (first time), fall back to `English`. (More about
    scopes in *Chapter 7, Handling Events and Partial Page Rendering.*)

24. Select the button that we created in step 13 from the **Structure** pane.

25. Right-click on it, go to **Insert Inside... | ADF Faces**, and select **Set Property
    Listener** from the list.

26. In the `From` field, add the following expression:

    ```
    #{(sessionScope.locale == null or sessionScope.locale ==
    'en')?'fr':'en'}
    ```

27. In the `To` field, add the following expression:

    ```
    #{sessionScope.locale}
    ```

28. In the `Type` field, select **action** from the combobox.

29. Click on **OK** to close the dialog.

    This dialog will set the `locale` variable inside the session scope, and when a user
    clicks on it—the action trigger type—the locale value will be changed to French if
    `locale` is `null` or `English`.

> You can learn more about providing locale runtime changes from the
> following documentation:
> `http://docs.oracle.com/middleware/1212/adf/ADFUI/af_`
> `global.htm#CIHIJJDG`

Another thing which is great is that you can use it to have parameterized messages;
follow the next steps to know how to do this.

30. Change the `NEXT` and `PREVIOUS` keys inside the resource bundle
    `ViewControllerBundle.properties` to be like the following:

    ```
    EMPLOYEE.NEXT=Next {0} record(s)
    EMPLOYEE.PREVIOUS=Previous {0} record(s)
    ```

31. Open `singleEmployees.jsf` and change the `Text` attribute of the `Next` button
    from `#{viewcontrollerBundle['EMPLOYEES.NEXT']}` to `#{af:formatStrin`
    `g(viewcontrollerBundle['EMPLOYEES.NEXT'], '1')}`.

32. Repeat the previous step with the `Previous` button. You can see when you run the page, `0` is replaced by `1` at runtime, which can be very helpful for getting customized error message, counting messages, and so on.

33. Run the page to see your `singleEmployees.jsf` page in action. The following screenshot shows the change:

How it works...

Under the hood, the JSF view root has a default locale that comes from the user's browser by default, and you can specify multiple supported languages inside the `faces-config` file itself; however, ADF makes it an optional requirement, as it can assign a resource bundle dynamically inside each JSF page.

With a powerful IDE like JDeveloper, it becomes a pretty easy task to create multilingual applications by creating multiple variations of this `properties` file. For instance, you can create a file with the name `ViewControllerBundle_fr.properties`, or you can specify a language for a specific country like `ViewControllerBundle_fr-fr.properties` or `ViewControllerBundle_fr-ca.properties` to specify French in France or French in Canada and edit these values. When a Canadian French or a French user uses the French locale in his browser, he will see the French language automatically; alternatively, you can enable changing the locale at runtime like we did in the recipe.

Also, by having parameterized strings, you don't have to worry about concatenation and having hideous-looking labels or text, as they can be formatted nicely using `af:formatString`. You can also use another variation of formatting text like `af:formatNamed2`, which can be used as shown in the following example:

```
<af:outputText value="#{af:formatNamed2(
   'The disk named {disk}, contains {fileNumber} files', 'disk', bean.
disk, 'fileNumber', bean.fileNumber)}" />
```

This can be useful if you don't remember the order of your parameters; also, locations can be different in different languages.

Also, the resource bundle is not only about text; you can also have the date format, number format, currency format, messages, and much more.

4
Using Common ADF Faces Components

The chapter will cover the following topics:

- ▶ Using the inputText component
- ▶ Using the inputNumber components
- ▶ Using the inputDate component
- ▶ Using the inputColor component
- ▶ Using the selection components
- ▶ Using the richTextEditor component
- ▶ Using the inputFile component
- ▶ Using the codeEditor component
- ▶ Using the ListOfValues components
- ▶ Using the pop-up dialogs, menus, and windows
- ▶ Using menus, toolbars, and toolboxes
- ▶ Using different output components
- ▶ Using buttons and links for navigation
- ▶ Using buttons and links to invoke functionalities
- ▶ Utilizing the XML Menu Model with NavigationPane, Breadcrumbs, and MenuBar
- ▶ Using the train components
- ▶ Working with dynamicComponent

Introduction

In this chapter, we will get to know more about common ADF Faces components. This includes input components; output components; pop ups, menus, and toolbars; navigation components; and dynamic components.

You can find all the recipes of this chapter inside the `Chapter 4` folder of the book's Git repository. As in the previous chapter, make sure you have the `faceshr` schema already created in order for your recipes to work without problem. Also, don't forget to change the database connection with the right information pointing to your local database settings.

Using the inputText component

In this recipe and the next seven recipes, we will describe how to create different input components that allow end users to enter data (such as `inputText`), select values and components (such as `inputNumber`, `inputRange`, `inputColor`, and `inputDate`), edit text (such as `richTextEditor`), and load files (such as `inputFile`).

In these eight recipes, a model has been created for you; you can see it by cloning the `ADFFacesInputComponents` project from the Git repository.

In this recipe, we will talk about the `inputText` component, which is one of the basic input components for entering values; in spite of this, it's so powerful that it can display multiple forms of look and feel based on its attributes. Also, in this simple recipe, we will create a page; inside the page, we will have an ADF form with three `inputText` components.

How to do it...

To add the `inputText` components, follow the ensuing steps:

1. First, we need to create a page to host the components as shown in the following steps:

    1. Open the `ADFFacesInputComponents` application.

    2. Double-click on `adfc-config.xml` to open it.

    3. Drag-and-drop a view activity from the **Components** palette and name it `inputComponents`.

    4. Double-click on the newly created view to create the page and select **Oracle Three Column Layout**.

2. Now we will start adding components inside an ADF Form using the following steps:

    1. Drag `EmployeesView1` in `Chapter4AppModuleDataControl` from the **Data Control** pane and drop it inside the page, which is inside the `center` facet of the **Oracle Three Column Layout** page template, by choosing the option **ADF Form**.

    2. Remove all of the attributes except for the first three attributes: `EmployeeId`, `FirstName`, and `LastName`.

    3. Check the **Row Navigation** option.

    4. Click on **OK** to close the ADF Form creation dialog.

    5. Select `inputText` - `EmployeeId` from the **Structure** pane.

    6. Change the `Secret` attribute to `true`.

    7. Select `inputText` - `LastName` from the **Structure** pane.

    8. Change the `Rows` attribute to `3`.

    9. Save everything.

    10. Run the `inputComponents.jsf` page. You should see the output window as shown in the following screenshot:

How it works...

In this recipe, we used `inputText` to show three different attributes `EmployeeId`, `FirstName`, and `LastName`. First, we showed `EmployeeId` as the password by changing the `Secret` attribute, then we showed `FirstName` normally without any modifications, and finally we showed `LastName` as the text area by changing the `Rows` attribute.

You can control the width of the `inputText` component by changing the `Columns` attribute by providing a smaller number.

You can also show `inputText` without a label by setting the `Simple` attribute to `true`; this is especially useful if it is placed inside a table.

To know more about `inputText`, check the official documentation at `http://jdevadf.oracle.com/adf-richclient-demo/docs/tagdoc/af_inputText.html`.

Using the inputNumber components

The `inputNumber` components are created to give a user an easy way to select a number instead of writing the number in an `inputText`, thereby reducing human errors and giving rich controls to the end user.

There are three `inputNumber` components as shown in the following list:

> ▶ `inputNumberSlider` – This component displays a single marker to choose from and returns a single number between the specified minimum and maximum values. This can be displayed horizontally or vertically.

> ▶ `inputRangeSlider` – This component displays two markers to set the minimum and maximum values of a range. This can be displayed horizontally or vertically.

> ▶ `inputNumberSpinbox` – This component displays an input field with up and down keys to increase and decrease the number in the field by a defined step.

Both `inputNumberSlider` and `inputNumberSpinbox` components return a single number while `inputRangeSlider` returns two numbers (minimum and maximum).

In this recipe, we will add the `inputNumberSlider` component to the `Employees` form we created in the previous recipe to show the `Salary` attribute.

How to do it...

In order to add the `InputNumberSlider` component, follow the ensuing steps:

1. Open the `inputComponents.jsf` page.
2. Drag the `Salary` attribute under `EmployeesView1` in `Chapter4AppModuleDataControl` from the **Data Control** pane and drop it inside the panel form layout.
3. Select **Text** from the drop-down menu and click on **ADF Input Text w/Label**.
4. Right-click on the `Salary` input text and go to **Convert to... | Slider (Number)**.
5. Change the `Minimum` attribute to `2000`.

6. Change the `Maximum` attribute to `30000`.

7. Change the `MajorIncrement` attribute to `500`.

8. Save everything.

9. Run the `inputComponets.jsf` page. You should see the output page as shown in the following screenshot:

How it works...

The `inputNumberSlider`, `inputRangeSlider`, and `inputNumberSpinbox` components are all acting in the same way, and all are presented to the end user to make the operation of picking a number easy.

So, the question might be what to choose, and you can choose easily based on your use case:

- If you have definite minimum and maximum numbers to choose between, `inputNumberSlider` is the best choice.
- If you want to know the minimum and maximum values from the end user, `inputRangeSlider` is designed exactly for that.
- If you don't have a definite minimum or maximum value, `inputNumberSpinbox` is best suited for the task at hand.

In this recipe, we showed how to use the `inputNumberSlider` component to represent the `Salary` attribute, with a `Salary` value that is not less than `2000` and not more than `30000`, along with `increment` that is equal to `500`.

This will make it easier for the end user to choose the right value quickly and also to make sure that he/she doesn't exceed the maximum limit.

Using the inputDate component

The `inputDate` component presents a text input field for entering dates and a button for picking dates from a pop-up calendar.

In this recipe, we will add an `inputDate` component to the `Employees` form created in the first recipe to show the `Hire Date` attribute.

How to do it...

In order to add the `inputDate` component, follow the ensuing steps:

1. Open the `inputComponents.jsf` page.

2. Drag the `HireDate` attribute under `EmployeesView1` in `Chapter4AppModuleDataControl` from the **Data Control** pane and drop it inside the panel form layout.

3. Select **Date** from the drop-down menu and select **Date Input w/Label.**

4. Save everything.

5. Run the `inputComponets.jsf` page. You should now see the output as shown in the following screenshot:

How it works...

The `inputDate` component is used to make it easier for the user to enter a date at runtime. There is also a complementary component called the `chooseDate` component that can be used along with `inputDate` to allow the user to quickly select a date value without having to navigate to a secondary dialog to choose the date.

In order to indicate that a particular `inputDate` component should be updated in response to the changes made to the `chooseDate` selection, the `inputDate` component's `chooseId` attribute must be set to the ID of the associated `chooseDate` components.

The `inputDate` component accepts any date object of the type `java.util.Date`, `java.sql.Date`, or `oracle.jbo.domain.Date`; you can also specify the date pattern using `af:convertDateTime`.

 More details about converters and validators will be discussed in *Chapter 8, Validating and Converting inputs.*

Using the inputColor component

The `inputColor` component allows users to pick a color from a color palette. It presents a text input field for entering a color's hexadecimal code, usually in the format #RRGGBB. The component also displays a button for picking colors from a palette in a pop up.

In this recipe, we will add an `inputColor` component to the `Employees` form created in the first recipe to show the `Favorite Color` attribute.

How to do it...

In order to add `inputColor`, follow the ensuing steps:

1. Open the `inputComponents.jsf` page.

2. Drag the `FavColor` attribute under `EmployeesView1` in `Chapter4AppModuleDataControl` from the **Data Control** pane and drop it inside the panel form layout.

3. Select **Text** from the drop-down menu and select **ADF Input Text w/Label**.

4. Right-click on the `inputText` component and go to **Convert to...** | **Input Color**.

5. Change the `Compact` attribute to `true`.

6. Save everything.

7. Run the `inputComponets.jsf` page. You should see the page as shown in the following screenshot:

How it works...

The `inputColor` components are used to make it easier for the user to enter a color at runtime; just like `chooseDate`, there is also a `chooseColor` component that reacts in the same fashion.

The `inputColor` value attribute should be a `java.awt.Color` object. So, in order to work with it effectively, the `Employee` entity in the `Model` project has a transient attribute named `FavColor` of the type `java.awt.Color`; also in the the `entityObject` class, the getter and setter of this attribute is set to convert the hexadecimal string of attribute `Color` to `java.awt.Color` and vice versa. The getters and setters are defined by the following Java code:

```java
public Color getFavColor() {
    if(getColor()!=null){
        return new Color(
                    Integer.valueOf( getColor().substring( 1, 3 ), 16
),
                    Integer.valueOf( getColor().substring( 3, 5 ), 16
),
                    Integer.valueOf( getColor().substring( 5, 7 ), 16
) );
    }
    return null;
}
```

```
public void setFavColor(Color value) {
    String rgb = Integer.toHexString(value.getRGB());
    setColor("#"+rgb);
    setAttributeInternal(FAVCOLOR, value);
}
```

Setting the `compact` attribute of the component to `true` hides the `inputText` part of the component and only shows the color panel. You can also specify the color pattern using the `af:convertColor` component inside `inputColor`.

 More details about converters and validators will be discussed in *Chapter 8, Validating and Converting Inputs*.

Using the selection components

The selection components allow end users to select single or multiple values from a list or group of items. ADF Faces provides a number of different selection components that range from simple Boolean checkboxes and radio buttons to order shuttle boxes that allow the user to select multiple items and order them.

Almost all of the selection components present items as either multiple tags of `af:selectItem` or `f:selectItem` or one tag of `f:selectItems`. This rule applies to all `select` components except for the `selectBooleanCheckbox` and `selectBooleanRadio` components. The following list explains different `select` components:

> * `selectBooleanCheckbox` – This is a component that is used to create an HTML checkbox as shown in the following screenshot; its value must always be a `boolean` or `java.lang.Boolean` and not an object as with other `select` components. It toggles between selected (`true`) or unselected (`false`) states.

> * `selectBooleanRadio` – This component is exactly like the `selectBooleanCheckbox` component but in a radio button format (as shown in the following screenshot). It also allows grouping multiple `selectBooleanRadio` components together using the same `group` attribute.

- `selectOneRadio` – This is a component that is used to create a list of radio buttons through which the user can select a single value from a list. It returns a single object. The following screenshot shows the list of radio buttons created using `selectOneRadio`:

- `selectManyCheckbox` – This is a component that is used to create a list of checkboxes from which the user can select one or more values. It returns a list of objects. The following screenshot shows one such list of checkboxes:

- `selectOneListbox` – This is a component that allows the user to select a single value from a list of items displayed in a listbox, as shown in the following screenshot. It returns a single object.

- `selectManyListbox` – Like `selectOneListbox`, this component shows a list that allows the user to select one or more items from the list; it also provides the **All** option that selects all items of the list and returns a list of objects. The following screenshot shows an example of such a list:

- selectOneChoice – This is a component that allows the end user to select items from a drop-down list (also known as combobox) and returns a single object. The following screenshot shows an example of this list:

 The selectOneChoice component is best used for a relatively small number of items in a drop-down list.

- selectManyChoice – This is a component that allows the user to select multiple values from a list of items displayed in a combobox and returns a list of objects, as shown in the following screenshot. This component can be configured to include the **All** option, just like selectManyListbox.

▶ `selectManyShuttle` – This is a component that presents end users with two different list boxes, namely, **Available Values** and **Selected Values**, as shown in the following screenshot. The end users can shuttle from one list to the other using different arrows provided between the lists. This component returns a list of objects (the items of the **Selected Values** list).

▶ `selectOrderShuttle` – This is similar to the `selectManyShuttle` component, but additionally, it includes the up and down arrow buttons that the users can use to reorder values in the **Selected Values** list box as shown in the following screenshot:

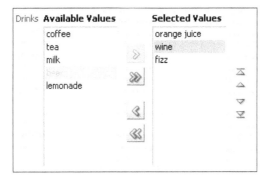

In this recipe, we will add the `DepartmentId` attribute as `selectOneChoice` inside the `Employees` form we created in the first recipe.

How to do it...

In order to add the `selectOneChoice` component, follow the ensuing steps:

1. Open the `inputComponets.jsf` page.

2. Drag the `DepartmentId` attribute under `EmployeesView1` in `Chapter4AppModuleDataControl` from the **Data Control** pane and drop it inside the panel form layout.

3. Select **Single Selection** and choose **ADF Select One Choice**.

4. Save everything.

5. Run the `inputComponents.jsf` page. You should now see the following output page:

How it works...

The `select` components are categorized into three types as shown in the following list:

▶ **Boolean selection** – Components of this type provide a user with two states: either `true` or `false`. Two components are included in this category: `selectBooleanCheckbox` and `selectBooleanRadio`.

▶ **Single selection** – Components of this type present multiple values and expect a single value to be selected. In order to present multiple options, these components have to nest `f:selectItems`, `f:selectItem`, or `af:selectItem`. You can also create items programmatically by creating a list of `javax.faces.model.SelectItem`. The components that are included in this category are `selectOneRadio`, `selectOneListbox`, and `selectOneChoice`.

▶ **Multiple selections** – Like single selection components, these components present multiple values and expect multiple values to be selected. The components that are included in this category are `selectManyCheckbox`, `selectManyListbox`, `selectManyChoice`, `selectManyShuttle`, and `selectOrderShuttle`.

In this recipe, we have a very common example of `selectOneChoice` to present the user with a more friendly input. Instead of seeing a bunch of numbers that represent department IDs, the user can now see what these IDs are presenting; this is done by creating a list of values of the `DepartmentId` attribute in the `EmployeesView` view object.

When a value is selected and the form is submitted, the `DepartmentId` value will be submitted and not `DepartmentName`, even though the `DepartmentName` value is the one that is displayed.

See also

You can learn more about creating ADF BC **List of Values** (**LOV**) from the official documentation at `http://docs.oracle.com/middleware/1212/adf/ADFFD/bcquerying.htm#CHDHBDDE`.

Using the richTextEditor component

The `richTextEditor` component provides an input field that can accept text with formatting. You can copy the formatted text from a place and paste it inside the `richTextEditor` component, use the `richTextEditor` controls to format the text inline by using the formatting toolbar that comes with the component, or edit the HTML source file directly using the toolbar button that toggles between the HTML mode and normal mode.

In this recipe, we will add the employee's `biography` attribute as `richTextEditor` to the `Employees` form we have.

How to do it...

In order to add the `richTextEditor` component, follow the ensuing steps:

1. Open the `inputComponets.jsf` page.

2. Drag the `Biography` attribute under `EmployeesView1` in `Chapter4AppModuleDataControl` from the **Data Control** pane and drop it inside the panel form layout.

3. Navigate to **Text | ADF Input Text w/ Label**.

4. Right-click on the `inputText` component and navigate to **Convert to... | Rich Text Editor**.

5. While selecting the `inputText` component from the **Structure** pane, change the `converter` attribute to `ClobConverter` in order to convert the biography from Oracle Clob to `java.lang.String` and vice versa.

6. Save everything.

7. Run the `inputComponents.jsf` page. You should see the output page as shown in the following screenshot:

How it works...

The `richTextEditor` component is one of the powerful components to display formatted text, yet it can be very risky because it accepts HTML code that can make it vulnerable to cross-site scripting attacks; however, it is for this exact reason that `richTextEditor` was carefully created so it does not accept any `script`, `noscript`, `frame`, `frameset`, `noframes`, or any form- or document-related elements. It also doesn't accept any unknown tags. The `richTextEditor` component accepts all other tags including the `iframe` and `img` tags.

You can customize the `richTextEditor` toolbar by adding multiple facets inside the component and changing the `toolboxLayout` attribute to customize what the toolbar looks like; you can use the defaults and add more icons, or you can replace the entire toolbar with your icons.

In this recipe, we used a `richTextEditor` component to show the employees' biography. Since the biography can have more than 4,000 characters, which is the limit of the database field for the `VarChar` type, a `Clob` type was used instead; also, just for your information, in order to seamlessly convert the biography from clob to string and vice versa, a custom `ClobConverter` converter is used.

 You will learn more about converters in *Chapter 8, Validating and Converting Inputs*.

See also

You can learn more about customizing toolbars of the `richTextEditor` component from the official documentation at `http://docs.oracle.com/middleware/1212/adf/ADFUI/af_input.htm#BABECJJF`.

Using the inputFile component

The `inputFile` component provides end users with file uploading and updating capabilities. It allows selecting a local file and uploading the `inputStream` component to a selectable location on the server.

In this recipe, we will add an `inputFile` component to mimic saving the user's uploaded image and saving the image filename in the `Image` attribute of the `Employees` table.

How to do it...

In order to add the `inputFile` component, follow the ensuing steps:

1. Open the `inputComponets.jsf` page.

2. Drag the `Image` attribute under `EmployeesView1` in `Chapter4AppModuleDataControl` from the **Data Control** pane and drop it inside the panel form layout.

3. Navigate to **Text | ADF Input Text w/ Label**.

4. Right-click on the `inputText` component and go to **Convert to... | Input File**.

5. While selecting the `inputText` component, change the `AutoSubmit` attribute to `true`.

6. Change the `Converter` attribute to `FileConverter`.

7. Save everything.

8. Open the `inputComponents.jsf` page.

9. Select `af:form` from the **Structure** pane.

10. Change the `useUpload` attribute to `true`. This is mandatory for the form to set the `enctype` attribute to `multipart/form-data` to support the file upload.

11. Run the `inputComponets.jsf` page and see the console for more information. You should see the output page as shown in the following screenshot:

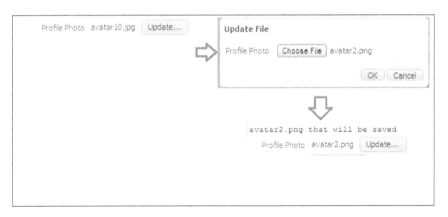

How it works...

The value property of an inputFile component is set to an instance of the org.apache.myfaces.trinidad.model.UploadedFile class when the file is uploaded.

In order for the inputFile component to work properly, we must configure the page's form to allow uploads by changing the useUpload attribute to true just like what we did in step 10.

In this recipe, we created an inputFile component that represents the Employee table's Image attribute and used the autoSubmit attribute in order to submit the value as soon as the end user enters it. Also, we used a converter to save the filename instead of the UploadedFile object. This converter sends a message to the console as you can see in the previous screenshot.

By default, the inputFile component allows the upload of only one file, but it can be configured to upload multiple files by setting the maximumFiles attribute to more than 1 or -1 if you want to upload an unlimited number of files. You can also use the uploadType attribute to specify whether the files should be uploaded automatically or they require the user to click on the **Upload** button to upload all of the files.

See also

To know more about the capabilities of uploading multiple files, see the official documentation at http://docs.oracle.com/middleware/1212/adf/ADFUI/af_input.htm#sthref124.

Using the codeEditor component

A new component added to the ADF Faces family from the 12c version is the codeEditor component which provides an in-browser code editing capabilities.

The codeEditor component is used by end users to enter code-like text with editing functionalities like what a typical IDE would provide, such as syntactical color coding of keywords, indention, validation, search, error highlighting, and logs pane.

In this recipe, we will present the CodeSample attribute in a codeEditor component inside the inputComponets.jsf page.

How to do it...

In order to add the `codeEditor` component, follow the ensuing steps:

1. Open the `inputComponets.jsf` page.

2. Drag the `CodeSample` attribute under `EmployeesView1` in `Chapter4AppModuleDataControl` from the **Data Control** pane and drop it inside the panel form layout.

3. Navigate to **Text** | **ADF Input Text w/ Label**.

4. Open the source mode of the `inputComponets.jsf` page.

5. Manually change `af:inputText` to `af:codeEditor` and don't forget the closing tag as well.

6. Remove the `maximumLength` attribute.

7. Change the `Converter` attribute to `ClobConverter`.

8. Change the `Language` attribute to `xml`.

9. Change the `Rows` attribute to `20`.

10. Save everything.

11. Run the `inputComponets.jsf` page and try to add XML tags inside the code editor. You should see the output as shown in the following screenshot:

How it works...

The `codeEditor` component is one of the great new additions to the ADF Faces components family; it supports JavaScript, XML, and Groovy languages. The `codeEditor` component provides multiple functionalities such as line numbering, using jump to move to a specific line, find and replace, auto-indent, and more.

You can use tabs inside the `codeEditor` component by going into the **Edit** mode by pressing *F2*. This way you can use the **Tab and Shift** tab, which converts the component into a small IDE.

In this recipe, we added the `CodeSample` attribute of the `Employees` table to showcase an XML representation of the `Employee` table; we also used the same `ClobConverter` component we used in `richTextEditor` to convert `CodeSample` from clob to string and vice versa.

Using the ListOfValues components

ADF Faces provides the following two LOV input components:

> ▸ `inputListOfValues` – This component displays an `inputText` component with a magnifier glass icon. Upon clicking on this icon, a search pop up will appear to provide the user with the **Search and Select** functionality as shown in the following screenshot:

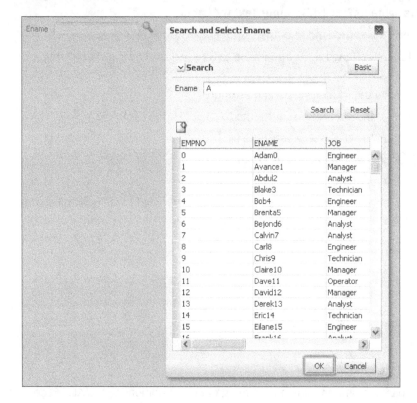

> ▸ `inputComboboxListOfValues` – This component displays a list instead of `inputText` and the user can open the **Search and Select** pop up by clicking on the **Search** link at the end of the list.

These LOV components are useful when you have a huge result list; trying to add them into normal **Select** components can make it harder for the user to select them properly.

In this recipe, we will continue from the previous recipes by adding the `ManagerID` attribute as an `inputComboboxListOfValues` component inside the `inputComponets.jsf` page. You can continue from the previous recipe, or you can grab the `ADFFacesListOfValues` application from the Git repository.

How to do it...

In order to add `inputComboboxListOfValues`, follow the ensuing steps:

1. Open the `inputComponets.jsf` page.

2. Drag the `ManagerId` attribute under `EmployeesView1` in `Chapter4AppModuleDataControl` from the **Data Control** pane and drop it inside the panel form layout.

3. Navigate to **List of Value | ADF LOV Choice List**.

4. Save everything.

5. Run the `inputComponets.jsf` page. You should see the page as shown in the following screenshot:

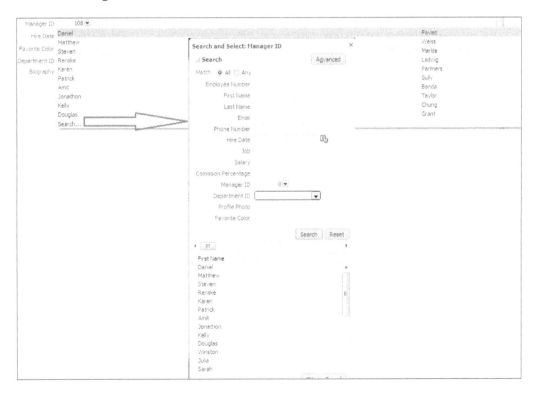

How it works...

In this recipe, we were able to drag-and-drop the component directly without providing any information about the relationship. This is because the `Model` project was made to support LOV just as in the *Using the Selection Components* recipe, but this time the component is displayed as a `inputComboboxListOfValues` component instead of `selectOneChoice`.

Also, in this recipe, the model was created with an LOV by referencing the `ManagerId` attribute with a foreign key to `EmployeesView.EmployeeId`.

If a developer doesn't use ADF BC or any business service layer, he/she can also generate the model behind it programmatically.

See also

To know more about creating the LOV data model programmatically, check the official documentation at `http://docs.oracle.com/middleware/1212/adf/ADFUI/af_lov.htm#CACBHJBF`.

Using the pop-up dialogs, menus, and windows

The pop-up components are used with a number of other ADF Faces components to create dialogs, menus, notes, and windows that provide information or request input from end users. They can be configured to show a secondary window to request information or to edit inline without enforcing the user to leave the current page.

In this recipe, we will create a page, which will have pop-up dialogs, context menu pop ups, note windows, and pop-up windows. You can continue from the previous recipe, or you can grab the `ADFFacesPopups` application from Git repository.

How to do it...

To add different pop ups, follow the ensuing steps:

1. Open the `adfc-config.xml` file.
2. Drag-and-drop a view activity inside the diagram and name it `employeesPopup`.
3. Double-click on the view activity to create the JSF page and choose the **Oracle Three Column Layout** as a template.
4. Drag `EmployeesView1` under `Chapter4AppModuleDataControl` from the **Data Control** pane, drop it into the `center` facet, and save it as an **ADF Table**.

5. Change the **Row Selection** option to **Single Row** when the dialog opens.

6. Check on the **Read-Only Table** option.

7. Remove all attributes except for `EmployeeId`, `FirstName`, `LastName`, and `Biography`. You should end up with the following screenshot:

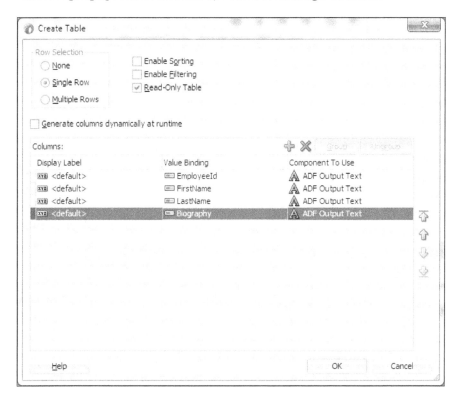

8. Click on **OK** to close the table-creation dialog.

9. Drag a pop-up component from the **Components** palette and drop it below the table we just inserted (you can find the pop-up component under **Layout | Secondary Windows**).

10. Change the `ContentDelivery` attribute to `lazyUncached`.

11. Right-click on the pop up, select **Insert inside...**, and navigate to **popup | Dialog**.

12. Change the `Type` attribute to `ok`.

13. Change the `Title` attribute to `Employee Details`.

14. Drag `EmployeesView1` under `Chapter4AppModuleDataControl` and drop it inside the dialog by choosing the option **ADF Form**.

15. Check on the **Read-Only form** option.

16. Remove the `Image`, `Color`, `FavColor`, `Biography`, and `CodeSample` attributes. You should end up with the following screenshot:

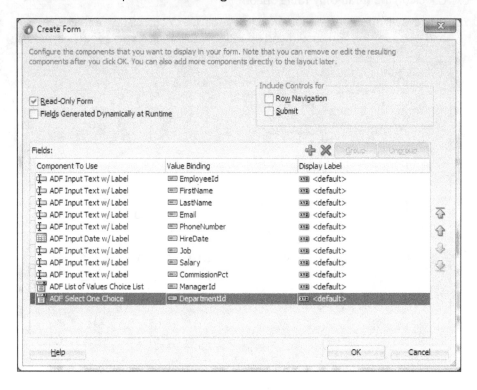

17. Click on **OK** to close the form creation dialog.

    We have created the dialog, but there is no trigger to open it yet. We will create a trigger based on the context menu of the table.

18. Select the table we created in step 4 from the **Structure** pane.

19. Change the `ColumnStretching` attribute to `last`.

20. Right-click on the table and navigate to **Insert Inside | JSF | Facet - contextMenu**.

21. Right-click on the newly created facet and navigate to **Insert Inside | Popup**.

22. Right-click on the newly created pop up and go to **Insert Inside | Menu**.

23. Right-click on the newly created menu and go to **Insert inside | Menu Item**.

24. Change the `Text` attribute of the menu item to `View Details`.

25. Right-click on the menu item and navigate to **Insert Inside | ADF Faces | Show Popup Behavior**.

26. Change the `PopupId` value to reference to the pop up we created in step 9 using the gear icon.

27. Change the `TriggerType` attribute to `action`.

     We created the trigger for the dialog pop up; we will now create two more pop ups.

28. Select the first column on the table (the one that holds the `EmployeeId` value) from the **Structure** pane.

29. Drag-and-drop another pop up inside the column.

30. Right-click on the pop up and navigate to **Insert Inside | Note Window**.

31. Drag-and-drop an `outputText` component inside the note window.

32. Change the `Value` attribute of the `outputText` component to `This employees was hired on #{bindings.HireDate.inputValue}`.

33. Select the first column again (the one that holds the `EmployeeId`).

34. Right-click on it and go to **Insert Inside | JSF**.

35. Select the facet from the list and select **context** from the list of facet names.

36. Right-click on the **context** facet and navigate to **Insert Inside | Context Info**.

37. Right-click on the newly created `contextInfo` attribute and navigate to **Insert Inside | ADF Faces | Show Popup Behavior**.

38. Change the `PopupId` value to the last pop up we created using the gear icon.

     We have finished creating the second pop up which is a note window.
     We will now add a third pop up associated with the `Biography` attribute.

39. Select the last column on the table (the one that holds the `Biography` attribute) from the **Structure** pane.

40. Drag-and-drop another pop-up component inside the column.

41. Right-click on the pop up and navigate to **Insert Inside | Panel Window**.

42. Change the `Title` attribute to `Edit Biography`.

43. Drag the `Biography` attribute from under `EmployeesView1` in `Chapter4AppModuleDataControl` from the **Data Control** pane, drop it inside the panel window, and save it by navigating to **Text | ADF Input Text w/Label**.

44. Right-click on the `InputText` component and go to **Convert to... | Rich Text Editor**.

45. Select the last column on the table again (the one that holds the `Biography` attribute).

46. Select the `OutputText` component under the column from the **Structure** pane.

47. Change the `TruncateAt` attribute to `5`.

48. Drag a link component from **Components** palette into the column.

49. Change the `Text` attribute to `(edit)`.

50. Right-click on the link and navigate to **Insert Inside | ADF Faces | Show Popup Behavior**.

51. Change the `PopuId` attribute to point to the last pop up we created.

52. Change the `TriggerType` attribute to `action`.

53. Change the `Align` attribute to `overlap`. This will overlap the window on top of the link.

54. Save everything.

55. Run the `employeesPopup.jsf` page. You should now see the page as shown in the following screenshot:

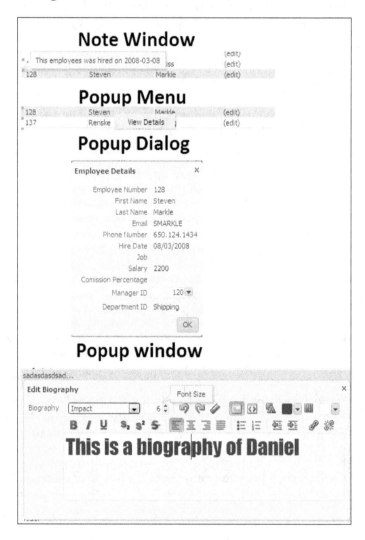

How it works...

The pop-up component is invisible by default. However, it can be used with other components (like the ones you saw in this recipe) to display other inline information in dialogs, windows, and menus.

ADF Faces provides a dialog framework to help present pages and task flows inside pop ups. This framework can be used to create more advanced dialogs to provide a nice, rich user experience for the end user. The best thing is that it's inside the page, so the end user won't face any problem with browser's pop-up blockers.

In this recipe, we showcased all of these types and used the showPopupBehavior ADF tag to declaratively open different pop ups. In the showPopupBehavior tag, you specified the popupId value you want to open, the triggerType attribute to listen to specific trigger-like button action (press) or mouse over, and the alignment attribute to control where the pop up will appear.

See also

 ▶ To know more about pop ups, check the official documentation at http://docs. oracle.com/middleware/1212/adf/ADFUI/af_dialog.htm#CHDFFFJD.

 ▶ To know more about how to run task flows as a pop-up dialog, check the documentation at http://docs.oracle.com/middleware/1212/adf/ADFFD/ taskflows_dialogs.htm#CHDCBFHB.

Using menus, toolbars, and toolboxes

Menu bars and toolbars allow you to organize menus, buttons, and other simple components in a horizontal bar. Menus can be nested to show multiple levels and hierarchical data. At the leaf of the hierarchy, each menu item can trigger an action or redirect completely.

In this recipe, we will create a single page to showcase the menu of a system similar to the file explorer, where the buttons will not be perform any actions; this page will just be an example. You can resume from the previous recipe, or you can grab the ADFFacesMenus application from the Git repository.

How to do it...

To add menus, toolbars, and toolboxes, follow the ensuing steps:

1. Open the adfc-config.xml file.
2. Drag-and-drop a view activity inside the diagram and name it fileExplorerMenu.

3. Double-click on the view activity to create the JSF page, and then choose **Oracle Three Column Layout** as a template.

4. Drag-and-drop the `Toolbox` component from the **Components** palette (you will find it under **Menus and Toolbars**) to the `center` facet of the page.

5. Drag a menu bar from the **Components** palette and put it inside the `Toolbox` component.

6. Drag a menu from the **Components** palette and put it inside the menu bar.

7. Change the `Text` attribute to `File`.

8. Drag-and-drop another menu under the **File** menu.

9. Change the `Text` attribute to `New`.

10. Change the `Icon` attribute to point to the `new_ena.png` image under the `src/META-INF/resources/images` folder by using the gear icon.

11. Drag-and-drop a menu item under the new menu created in step 8 and change the `Text` attribute to `New File`.

12. Change the `Accelerator` attribute to `control F`. This will trigger the menu when the user presses *Ctrl + F* on keyboard.

13. Repeat step 11 to change the `Text` attribute to `New Folder`, and change the `Accelerator` attribute to `control D`.

14. Put another menu item inside the `File` menu created in step 6.

15. Change the `Text` attribute to `Find`.

16. Change the `Icon` attribute to point to `find_ena.png` under the `src/META-INF/resources/images` folder.

17. Put another menu item inside the `File` menu created in step 6.

18. Change the `Text` attribute to `Word Wrap`.

19. Change the `Type` attribute to `Check`.

20. Add another menu inside the menu bar from step 5 and change the `Text` attribute to `View`.

21. Drag a menu item (`Go`) and drop it inside the `View` menu.

22. Change the `Text` attribute to `Search in Oracle`.

23. Change the `Destination` to `http://www.oracle.com`.

24. Change the `TargetFrame` attribute to `_blank`.

25. Add another menu inside the menu bar from step 5 and change the `Text` attribute to `Edit`.

26. Drag the menu item (Go) and drop it inside the Edit menu.

27. Change the Text attribute to Undo.

28. Change the Icon attribute to point to undo.png under the src/META-INF/resources/images folder.

    Now that we have created the menu, let's create the toolbar.

29. Drag-and-drop a toolbar from the **Components** palette inside the toolbox.

30. Right-click on the toolbar and go to **Insert inside | Group**.

31. Drag a button and drop it inside the group. Change the Text attribute to Undo and change the Icon attribute to the undo.png image under the src/META-INF/resources/images folder.

32. Drag another button and drop it inside the group, change the Text attribute to Redo, and change the Icon attribute to the redo.png image under the src/META-INF/resources/images folder.

33. Create another group by right-clicking on the toolbar and navigate to **Insert inside | Group**.

34. Drag-and-drop an inputText component from the **Components** palette into the new group.

35. Change the Simple attribute to true.

36. Change the Placeholder attribute to Find inside files.

37. Drag a button from the **Components** palette and drop it inside the group as well.

38. Remove any text inside the Text attribute.

39. Change the Icon attribute to point to find_ena.png under the src/META-INF/resources/images folder.

40. Drag a choice component (selectOneChoice) from the **Components** palette and drop it inside the toolbar directly.

41. Click on **Create List** and this will create a static list.

42. Add the following three items:

Item Label	Item Value
Blue Skin	blue
Red Skin	red
Green Skin	green

43. Click on **Next**.

44. Change the `Label` attribute to `Choose Skin`.

45. Click on **Finish**. If you have done everything successfully, you should end up with the following screenshot of the **Structure** pane:

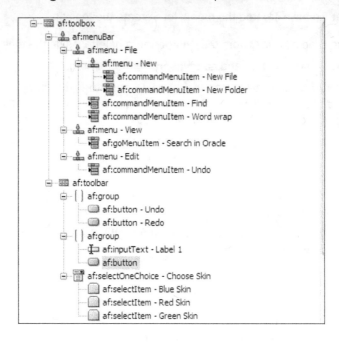

46. Save everything.

47. Run the `fileExplorerMenu.jsf` page. You should see the output page as shown in the following screenshot:

How it works...

By organizing toolbars and menu bars inside a toolbox, you will be able to define relative sizes for the toolbars on the same line and define several layers of toolbars and menu bars vertically.

In this recipe, we created a toolbox to host a menu bar and a toolbar that are aligned vertically.

The menu bar had three menus. The first menu has a nested menu with two menu items with the `accelerator` attribute, which can be used to trigger the action using a keyboard. Also, we used the `Go` menu item to redirect the users to different pages, which in this case, is `oracle.com`.

We then added the toolbar that can have multiple components, such as `inputText`, `selectOneChoice`, or `buttons`. We grouped multiple components together in order to distinguish between them inside the toolbar. We used the `Group` component inside the menu bar to group menu items together.

Using different output components

This recipe describes how to use the `outputText`, `outputFormatted`, `image`, `icon`, `statusIndicator`, and `media` components of ADF Faces.

In this recipe, we will create a page to showcase a different output component. You can continue from the previous recipe, or you can grab the `ADFFacesOutputComponents` application from Git repository.

How to do it...

In order to add different output components, follow the ensuing steps:

1. Open the `adfc-config.xml` file.

2. Drag-and-drop a view activity inside the diagram and name it `outputComponents`.

3. Double-click on the view activity to create the JSF page and choose **Oracle Three Column Layout** as a template.

4. Drag a panel group layout and drop it inside the `center` facet.

5. Change the `Layout` attribute to `scroll`.

6. Drag an `outputText` component inside the panel group layout.

7. Change the `Value` attribute to `Sample Date`.

8. Drag another `outputText` component.

9. Change the `Value` attribute to `#{viewScope.output.sampleDate}`. This is an existing managed bean that has a date and two strings.

10. Right-click on the last `OutputText` component and go to **Insert inside | ADF Faces | Convert Date Time**.

11. Change the `DateStyle` attribute to `long`. This will show the long version of the current date.

12. Drag a `Separator` component from the **Components** palette and drop inside the panel group layout. You can find the `Separator` component under the **Layout** category.

13. Drag another `outputText` component inside the panel group layout and change the `Value` attribute to `Unformatted Text Truncated`.

14. Add another `outputText` component and change the `Value` attribute to `#{viewScope.output.textWithoutFormat}`.

15. Change the `TruncateAt` attribute to `5`.

16. Drag another `Separator` component inside the panel group layout.

17. Drag another `outputText` component and drop it inside the panel group layout and change the `Value` attribute to `Formatted Text`.

18. Add another `outputText` component and change the `Value` attribute to `#{viewScope.output.bigTextWithFormat}`.

19. Drag a `Separator` component inside the panel group layout.

20. Drag `outputText` component inside the panel group layout and change the `Value` attribute to `Formatted Text Escaped`.

21. Add another `outputText` component and change the `Value` attribute to `#{viewScope.output.bigTextWithFormat}`.

22. Change the `Escape` attribute to `false`. This will escape any HTML tags but will create a web application vulnerable to cross-site scripting attacks, so the `outputText` component is not really fit for showing HTML tags.

   In the next steps, we will see how to avoid that vulnerability by using the `outputFormatted` component instead of `outputText`.

23. Drag a `Separator` component inside the panel group layout.

24. Drag `outputText` inside the panel group layout and change the `Value` attribute to `Formatted Text using Output Formatted`.

25. Drag `outputFormatted` from the **Components** palette and change the `Value` attribute to `#{viewScope.output.bigTextWithFormat}`.

   This will show some of the HTML tags used in the Rich Text Editor without making the application vulnerable to cross-site scripting attacks. We will now see how to use the `Icon` component.

26. Drag a `Separator` component inside the panel group layout.

27. Drag `outputText` and drop it inside the panel group layout, and change the `Value` attribute to `Icon example`.

28. Drag the `Icon` component from the **Components** palette under **General Controls** and drop it inside the panel group layout.

29. Change the `Name` attribute to `logo`. These icons can be changed in your skin. This is explained in *Chapter 5, Beautifying Application Layout for Great User Experience*.

    We will showcase the `Image` component and how to use it.

30. Drag a `Separator` component inside the panel group layout.

31. Drag `outputText` inside the panel group layout and change the `Value` attribute to `Image example`.

32. Drag the `Image` component from the **Components** palette under **General Controls** and drop it inside the panel group layout.

33. Change the `Source` attribute to point at the `36H.jpg` image located under the `src/META-INF/resources/images` folder.

34. Change the `ShortDesc` attribute to `Two Trees`.

35. Change the `inlineStyle` attribute to `width:700px;height:549px`. This will decrease the size of the image to 700 x 549 pixels. (It's not really recommended that you add `inlineStyle` and should be replaced by `styleClass`. However, we will learn how to use it in *Chapter 5, Beautifying Application Layout for Great User Experience*).

36. Drag another `Separator` component inside the panel group layout.

37. Drag `outputText` inside the panel group layout and change the `Value` attribute to `Image Link example`.

38. Drag a `Link` component from the **Components** palette under **General Controls** and drop it inside the panel group layout.

39. Change the `Destination` attribute to `http://www.oracle.com`.

40. Change the `TargetFrame` attribute to `_blank`.

41. Drag the `Image` component and drop it just under the `Link` component.

42. Change the `Source` attribute to point at the `37H.jpg` image located under the `src/META-INF/resources/images` folder.

43. Change the `ShortDesc` attribute to `One Tree`.

44. Change the `inlineStyle` attribute to `width:700px;height:549px`. This will decrease the size of the image to 700 x 549 pixels.

45. Switch to the **Source** mode and put the `af:image` tag inside the `af:link` tag and manually close the `af:link` tag by adding `</af:link>` at the end.

 You might see an error in JDeveloper, but you can ignore it.

In the next steps, we will see another interesting component that indicates if the page is busy or not. This is especially helpful for long-running processes.

46. Drag a `Separator` component inside the panel group layout.

47. Drag `outputText` inside the panel group layout and change the `Value` attribute to `Status Indicator example`.

48. Drag a button and drop it under the `outputText` component and change the `Text` attribute to `Make Status busy`.

49. Drag a `Status Indicator` component from the **Components** palette under **General Controls** and drop it inside the panel group layout.

    The last thing to showcase is the `Media` component, so let's see how to add it.

50. Drag a `Separator` component inside the panel group layout.

51. Drag `outputText` inside the panel group layout and change the `Value` attribute to `Media example`.

52. Drag a `Media` component from the **Components** palette under **General Controls** and drop it inside the panel group layout.

53. Change the `Source` attribute to point the `sample_video.wmv` file under the `public_html/media` folder.

54. Change the `StandbyText` attribute to `Loading...`; this will be displayed when the media is loading.

55. Change the `AutoStart` attribute to `true`. This will make sure the media is started automatically when displayed.

56. Save everything. You should have the following structure in your **Structure** Pane by now:

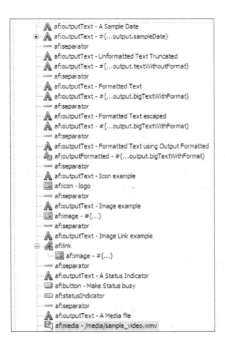

57. Run the `outputComponents.jsf` page. You should now see the page as shown in the following screenshot:

How it works...

In this recipe, we worked with multiple output components to showcase some of their common functionalities.

The `outputText` component is best used to show unformatted text. It can be used for formatted text as well by using the `escape` attribute, but it's not recommended.

We saw how to truncate text which generates . . . at the end of the text. When we hover over it, we can see all of the text.

Setting the `escape` attribute to `false` can be dangerous, and if you are displaying an input from the user, it can be even vulnerable to a cross-scripting attack; that's why you should present formatted text with `outputFormatted` instead of `outputText`, which can work great to show the output of a `richTextEditor` component.

We also saw how to add the `icon`, `image`, `image link`, `statusIndicator`, and `Media` components inside the page. Note that if the `Media` component is not running in the browser, another link will be provided to download the media instead.

Using buttons and links for navigation

Navigation components allow users to submit data, show more information, and navigate between different pages. Typical ways of navigation are buttons and links. There are different types of buttons and links in ADF; most of them can work on their own and a few of them need to be used in conjunction with other components.

ADF Faces provides more than just buttons and links. Some components render tabs, breadcrumbs, and trains to navigate through hierarchical pages, keeping track of the user's current location in the page hierarchy. Also, they render links and buttons that can be used to guide users through a multistep task.

In this recipe and the next three small recipes, we will get to know more about navigation components: how to use them and how to make the best out of them. You can continue from the previous recipe, or you can grab the `ADFFacesNavigationComponents` application from Git repository.

Also, in this recipe, we will showcase the use of the `Button` and `Link` components, both of which can be used in navigation. Depending on your use case, you can configure these components to navigate directly to another location, to submit requests, or to fire the `ActionEvent` events.

We will create a page with couple of links and buttons that can be used in different ways: either to navigate to a page based on the control flow or to redirect to an external page.

How to do it...

In order to use buttons and links for navigation, follow the ensuing steps:

1. Open the `adfc-config.xml` file.

2. Drag a `Wildcard` component from the **Components** palette and drop it inside the **Diagram** mode.

3. Drag-and-drop a control flow from the `Wildcard` component to `inputComponents` and name the control flow `inputs`.

4. Repeat the previous step with the `employeesPopup`, `fileExplorerMenu`, and `outputComponents` views with the control flow names `popups`, `menus`, and `outputs` respectively.

5. Drag-and-drop another view activity inside the diagram and name it `navigationComponents`.

6. Drag a control flow from the `Wildcard` component to `navigationComponents` and name the control flow `navigations`. You should end up with something similar to the following screenshot:

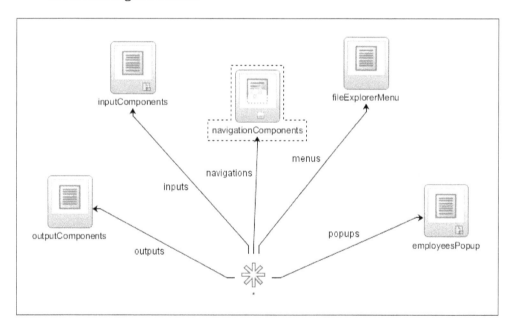

7. Double-click on `navigationComponents` to create the page and choose the **Oracle Three Column** template.

8. Drag a panel group layout and put it inside the `center` facet.

9. Change the `Layout` attribute to `vertical`.

10. Drag a button inside the panel group.

11. Change the `Text` attribute to `Go to Inputs page`.

12. Change the `Action` attribute and select `inputs` from the combobox.

13. Drag another button inside the panel group.

14. Change the `Text` attribute to `Go to oracle.com`.

15. Change the `Destination` attribute to `http://www.oracle.com`.

16. Change the `TargetFrame` attribute to `_blank`.

17. Drag a link inside the panel group.

18. Change the `Text` attribute to `Go to Outputs page`.

19. Change the `Action` attribute and select `outputs` from the combobox.

20. Drag another link inside the panel group.

21. Change the `Text` attribute to `Go to packtpub.com`.

22. Change the `Destination` attribute to `http://www.packtpub.com`.

23. Change the `TargetFrame` attribute to `_blank`.

24. Save everything.

25. Run the `navigationComponents.jsf` page (as shown in the following screenshot) and see the different behaviors of the buttons and links.

How it works...

In 11g, there used to be two ADF components for buttons, namely, `af:commandButton` and `af:goButton` and two ADF components for links, namely, `af:commandLink` and `af:goLink`. In 12c, this has changed to have only one button component and one link component that can have both behaviors depending on the attributes specified.

In this recipe, we will showcase two buttons and two links; the first button shows how you can use the button to move forward to another page in the system, that is, it acts like an `af:commandButton` tag in 11g, which delivers an `ActionEvent` component (more on that in *Chapter 7, Handling Events and Partial Page Rendering*) or use it without delivering `ActionEvent` to redirect to `oracle.com`, that is, acts like a `af:goButton` tag, like the case with the second button and we will create two links the same way we created the two buttons

If both the `destination` and `action` attributes are specified, `destination` will take precedence.

Using buttons and links to invoke functionalities

In addition to using the `action` components for navigation, ADF Faces also includes `listener` tags that can be used in conjunction with the `action` components to have specific functionalities executed when the `action` event fires. The `listener` tags include the following tags:

- ▶ `exportCollectionActionListener` – This tag is used to export data from the table, tree, and tree table components to an Excel spreadsheet.

- ▶ `fileDownloadActionListener` – This tag is used to initiate a file download from the server to the local hard drive.

- ▶ `resetListener` – This tag is used to reset submitted values.

In this recipe, we will create a button that will download a file using `fileDownloadActionListener` instead of navigating.

How to do it...

In order to use buttons and links to invoke functionalities, follow the ensuing steps:

1. Open the `navigationComponents.jsf` page.
2. Drag-and-drop a button inside the panel group layout.
3. Change the `Text` attribute to `Download readme file`.
4. Right-click on the button and navigate to **Insert Inside | ADF Faces**.
5. Choose the `File Download Action` listener from the list.
6. Change the `ContentType` attribute to `text/plain`.
7. Change the `FileName` attribute to `readme.txt`.
8. Click on the gear icon beside the `Method` attribute and click on **Edit**.
9. Click on **New**.
10. Change the `Bean Name` attribute to `navigationBean`.
11. Change the `Class Name` attribute to `NavigationBean`.
12. Change the `Package Name` attribute to `com.adffacescookbook.chapter4. view.beans`.
13. Click on **OK**.
14. In the `Method` attribute, click on the **New** button to create the method.
15. Name the method `downloadReadmeFile` and click on **OK**.

16. Open the `NavigationBean` class from the application explorer.

17. Add the following lines inside the `downloadReadmeFile` function:

```
OutputStreamWriter w = null;
try {
    w = new OutputStreamWriter(outputStream, "UTF-8");
    w.write("This is the Readme File.");
    w.write("Start Reading me!");
    w.close();
} catch (Exception e) {
    e.printStackTrace();
}
```

18. Save everything.

19. Run the `navigationComponents.jsf` page and click on the **Download readme file** button to download the file, as shown in the following screenshot;

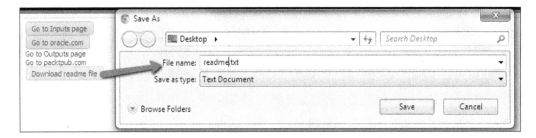

How it works...

In this simple recipe, we used `fileDownloadActionListener` to download a file. This file is created on the fly in the managed bean that was created in the recipe itself by getting the `outputStream` writer and writing a couple of words.

Utilizing XML Menu Model with NavigationPane, Breadcrumbs, and MenuBar

An application may consist of pages that are related and organized in a tree-like hierarchy, where users gain access to specific information on a page by drilling down a path of links.

In this recipe, we will create an XML Menu Model and show how we can display it using different components.

How to do it...

In order to create the XML Menu Model and use it with different components, follow the ensuing steps:

1. Open the `adfc-config.xml` file.

2. Right-click on the white area in the **Diagram** mode and select the **Create or Update ADF Menu** option.

3. Leave the defaults in the pop up and click on **OK**.

4. Examine the `root_menu` attribute from the **Structure** pane; you can see that every page is represented by `itemNode`.

5. Click on the `inputComponents` node and change the `Label` attribute to `Input Components`.

6. Repeat step 5 for the `employeesPopup`, `fileExplorerMenu`, `navigationComponents`, and `outputComponents` nodes and change the `Label` attributes to `Popup component`, `Menu component`, `Navigation components`, and `Output Components` respectively.

7. Drag the `navigationComponents` component of `itemNode` inside the `fileExplorerMenu` component of `itemNode`.

8. Right-click on the menu (the root), select **Insert Inside**, and choose **groupNode**.

9. Change the `id` attribute to `groupNode_inputOutput`.

10. Change the `idref` attribute to `itemNode_inputComponents`.

11. Drag the newly created group node to be the first on the list.

12. Change the `Label` attribute to `Inputs and Outputs`.

13. Drag the `inputComponents` component of `itemNode` inside the group node.

14. Also, do the same for the `outputComponents` component of `itemNode`. You should end up with the following screenshot of the **Structure** pane of the `root_menu` attribute:

15. Open the `navigationComponents.jsf` page.

16. Drag a `Separator` component inside the panel group layout.

17. Drag a `menuBar` component inside the panel group layout.

18. Change the `Value` attribute to `#{root_menu}` (you can also select it by using the gear icon menu and navigating to **Expression Builder | ADF Managed Beans | root_menu**).

19. Change the `Var` attribute to `menuItem`.

20. Right-click on the `MenuBar` component and navigate to **Insert Inside | JSF | Facet NodeStamp**.

21. Right-click on the `nodeStamp` facet and navigate to **Insert Inside | Navigation Item**.

22. Change the `Text` attribute to `#{menuItem.label}`.

23. Change the `Action` attribute to `#{menuItem.doAction}`.

    Now that we have created the menu bar that represents the menu model, let's create a breadcrumb to show the current page location relative to the hierarchy.

24. Drag a `Breadcrumb` component from the **Components** palette under **General Controls**, and then drop it inside the panel group layout.

25. Change the `Value` attribute to `#{root_menu}`.

26. Change the `Var` attribute to `crumbItem`.

27. Right-click on the breadcrumb and navigate to **Insert Inside | JSF | Facet | NodeStamp**.

28. Right-click on the `nodeStamp` facet and navigate to **Insert Inside | ADF Faces | Navigation Item**.

29. Change the `Text` attribute to `#{crumbItem.label}`.

30. Change the `Action` attribute to `#{crumbItem.doAction}`.

    Now let's add two navigation panes (one for each level) to present the menu model differently.

31. Drag a navigation pane from the **Components** palette (from the **Layout** section) and drop it inside the panel group layout.

32. Change the `Hint` attribute to `bar`.

33. Change the `Value` attribute to `#{root_menu}`.

34. Change the `Var` attribute to `item`.

35. Right-click on `NavigationPane` and go to **Insert Inside | Facet NodeStamp**.

36. Right-click on the `nodeStamp` facet and navigate to **Insert Inside | ADF Faces | Navigation Item**.

37. Change the `Text` attribute to `#{item.label}`.

38. Change the `Action` attribute to `#{item.doAction}`.

39. Drag another navigation pane inside the panel group layout.

40. Change the `Hint` attribute to `tabs`.

41. Change the `Level` attribute to `1`.

42. Change the `Value` attribute to `#{root_menu}`.

43. Change the `Var` attribute to `item`.

44. Right-click on `NavigationPane` and navigate to **Insert Inside | Facet NodeStamp**.

45. Right-click on the `nodeStamp` facet and navigate to **Insert Inside | ADF Faces | Navigation Item**.

46. Change the `Text` attribute to `#{item.label}`.

47. Change the `Action` attribute to `#{item.doAction}`.

48. Save everything.

49. Run the `navigationComponents.jsf` page and see the different navigation components as shown in the following screenshot:

How it works...

When we created a menu model in step 2, we created an XMLMenuModel metadata file. Each XMLMenuModel file represents a navigation menu for a page hierarchy in XML (think site maps). You are free to have only one or multiple XMLMenuModel files to present the page hierarchy.

The `XMLMenuModel` file is an XML file with `menu` tag as its root element. Inside the `menu` tag, you can see multiple tags for the following nodes:

- **Item node** – This represents a single page in the page menu hierarchy which is typically represented by a JSF or JSPX page.

- **Group node** – This represents a group of pages (but not a page itself) which can be useful to create main menus in the hierarchy without needing to create physical pages, as it simply aggregates their children nodes.

- **Shared node** – This is used to maximize reusability by creating a separate menu for a subtree and use it as a shared menu in other menus.

All of the previous nodes can be nested to create the hierarchy.

In this recipe, we created an `XMLMenuModel` file based on the few pages we had and we restructured them in a way to showcase the group node and nested item nodes.

To represent this menu model, we used the `MenuBar` and `NavigationPane` components. (Typically, these components should be inside a page template since it should be there for all pages. More on that in *Chapter 5, Beautifying Application Layout for Great User Experience.*) We also used the `Breadcrumb` component which is great to show the derivative hierarchy of the current page related to the entire menu model. The `NavigationPane` component can only represent one level unlike `MenuBar` that represents the entire menu model, and each level can have different hints such as tabs, bar, buttons, choice, and list.

As you can see in all these components, the common thing is the `nodeStamp` facet which represents a single menu item inside the menu model, which reacts in a similar fashion to an ADF Table.

Using the train components

When you have a set of pages which users should visit in a particular order, you should consider using the `train` component on each page to display a series of navigation items that guide users through the multistep process. In this recipe, we will create a train-enabled task flow to showcase the train controls.

How to do it...

In order to use `train`, follow the ensuing steps:

1. Create a new task flow with the name `train-flow`.

2. Check the **Create Train** checkbox and click on **OK**.

3. Drag a view inside the task flow and name it `trainStep1`.

4. Drag another view inside the task flow and name it `trainStep2`.

5. Drag a third view inside the task flow and name it `trainStep3`.

6. From the **Structure** pane, expand `view - TrainStep1` and select the `train-stop` node.

7. Right-click on `train-stop` and navigate to **Insert Inside | Display Name**.

8. Change the `Display Name` to `Step 1`.

9. Repeat the last three steps and change the `Display Name` to `Step 2` and `Step 3` for `trainStep2` and `trainStep3` respectively.

10. Double-click on `trainStep1` to create the page fragment and put it inside the `fragments` folder (you can create the folder or you can enter it in the path to be created automatically).

11. Drag a panel group layout inside the page fragment and set the `Layout` attribute to `vertical`.

12. Drag a `train` component from **General Controls** inside the panel group layout. When prompted, click on **OK** of the **Bind Train** dialog.

13. Drag `outputText` inside the panel group layout and change the `Value` attribute to `This is Step 1 of the Train`.

14. Drag a `Train Button Bar` component from **General Controls** of the **Components** palette and drop it inside the panel group layout. When prompted, click on **OK** of the **Bind trainButtonBar** dialog.

15. Repeat the steps 10 to 14 for the other two page fragments and change the `value` attribute of `outputText` for `trainStep2` and `trainStep3` to `This is Step 2 of the Train` and `This is Step 3 of the Train` respectively.

16. Open the `navigationComponents.jsf` page.

17. Drag `train-flow` from the application navigator and drop it inside the panel group layout. Save it as **Region**.

18. Save everything.

19. Run `navigationComponents.jsf` and click on the train buttons to navigate between the three fragments, as shown in the following screenshot:

How it works...

The train component renders each configured step represented as a train stop and with all the stops connected by lines. Each train stop has an image (for example, a square block) with a label (display name) underneath the image.

In this recipe, we created a train-enabled task flow with three stops. Also, we changed the label of the three stops to Step1, Step2, and Step3 respectively. In each of the three stops, we added both the train and trainButtonBar components that were bound automatically.

Both the train components work by binding the value attribute to a train model of the type org.apache.myfaces.trinidad.model.MenuModel which you can configure programmatically or which can be bound automatically when you check the **Create train** checkbox in the task flow that contains this page.

See also

You can know how you can create the train model programmatically from the official documentation at http://docs.oracle.com/middleware/1212/adf/ADFUI/af_navigate.htm#CACCJEHI.

Working with dynamicComponent

There are certain cases when you want to render different components on page dynamically based on a changing model (think programmatic view object), and this cannot be determined before runtime. This can generate a huge code to generate components which can be very tedious for the developer.

Oracle ADF Faces provides a solution for the use cases with the af:dynamicComponent tag. The af:dynamicComponent tag can determine the component type to display and its value at runtime.

In this recipe, we will create a new page to see how can we display different input components based on of the EmployeeView attributes using af:dynamicComponent.

How to do it...

In order to use the dynamicComponent, follow the ensuing steps:

1. Open the adfc-config.xml file.
2. Drag a view and name it dynamicComponent.

3. Double-click on the newly created view and choose the **Oracle Three Column Layout** template.

4. Drag `EmployeesView1` under `Chapter4AppModuleDataControl` from the **Data Controls** pane and drop it inside the `center` facet.

5. Check the **Fields Generated Dynamically at Runtime** checkbox.

6. Check the **Row Navigation** checkbox.

7. Examine the **Source and Structure** pane of the page. You can see that a dynamic component has been generated inside an `af:iterator` tag to dynamically generate the input fields for `EmployeesView1`.

8. Save everything.

9. Run the `dynamicComponent.jsf` page and see how different inputs have been generated from the `dynamicComponents` based on their model type, as shown in the following screenshot:

How it works...

Dynamic components can be used greatly when you are uncertain about what will be generated at runtime. Here's what happens when you insert an `af:dynamicComponent` tag: at runtime it determines the data type associated with this attribute and then represents it with the right input field.

If the attribute data type is date, then `af:inputDate` is going to represent this attribute and so on for the rest of types.

The following are the supported components that get rendered at runtime:

- ▶ af:inputText
- ▶ af:inputDate
- ▶ af:inputListOfValue
- ▶ af:selectOneChoice
- ▶ af:selectManyChoice
- ▶ af:selectOneListbox
- ▶ af:selectManyListbox
- ▶ af:selectOneRadio
- ▶ af:selectBooleanRadio
- ▶ af:selectBooleanCheckbox
- ▶ af:selectManyCheckbox

As you can see, it almost covers all of the ADF Faces input and select components.

In this example, we used the dynamic converter to dynamically generate the inputs based on the EmployeesView view object.

You can also create the model of the dynamicComponent programmatically, and you can develop it to support the grouping of inputs together and provide an even greater user experience.

See also

You can see how you can create a dynamic component model programmatically from the official documentation at http://docs.oracle.com/middleware/1212/adf/ADFUI/af_dynamic.htm#BHCDHCCA.

5
Beautifying the Application Layout for Great User Experience

This chapter contains the following recipes:

- ▶ Creating a page template for your application
- ▶ Adding layouts to the header and footer of the page template
- ▶ Creating an ADF skin for your application
- ▶ Changing skins at runtime
- ▶ Using skins like a pro by using Sass and compass
- ▶ Using media queries for a responsive web design
- ▶ Using flat design techniques

Introduction

In the last chapter, we saw different components of ADF Faces and how to work with them, but components alone don't provide a user experience, and without a great user experience developed applications can go underappreciated. In this chapter, we will discuss how to improve the user experience by creating an application template, enhance your page layout, and skin your application.

We will also learn how to create a page template to uniform your design across different pages, how to use ADF Layout components to structure your page, how to create and use ADF skins, and how to change skins at runtime.

We will even get exposed to more advanced approaches of using ADF skin by converting the skin into Syntactically Awesome Style Sheets (SASS), a CSS language, how to use media queries to create responsive web design, and finally, how to add variations to the style sheet and use a flat design in your application.

You can find all the recipes of this chapter inside the `Chapter 5` folder of the book's Git repository. As in the previous chapter, make sure you have the `faceshr` schema already created in order for your recipes to work without problems. Also, don't forget to change the database connection with the right information pointing to your local database settings when you open JDeveloper.

Creating a page template for your application

Page templates are the first step towards creating a beautiful, consistent looking application. A page template represents the layout structure of your pages, which if created carefully can provide a great user experience for your application's audience.

Page templates let you define entire page layouts, including values for certain attributes of the page. When pages are created based on a template, the page inherits the defined layout, and when a modification is required for the page template, you can change it once in the page template and all of the pages that are based on this template will automatically have the new changes.

In this recipe, the application and its model have been created for you. You can see it by cloning the `ADFFacesPageTemplate` project from the Git repository.

We will start by creating a page template, which looks like the next screenshot, based on the `minimaxing` template from `http://html5up.net/minimaxing/`.

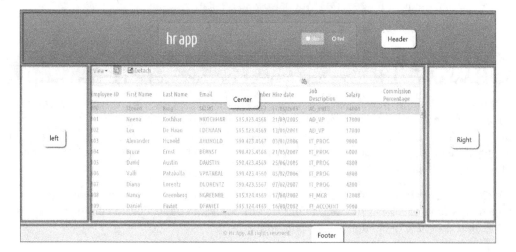

How to do it...

To create a page template, perform the following steps:

1. Open the `ADFFacesPageTemplate` application in JDeveloper.

2. Expand the **ViewController** node from Applications Navigator Pane.

3. Right-click on **ViewController** and select **ADF Page Template** under **New**.

4. Change the name of the template to `defaultHrTemplate`.

5. Change the directory of the template to `public_html\template`, as shown in the following screenshot:

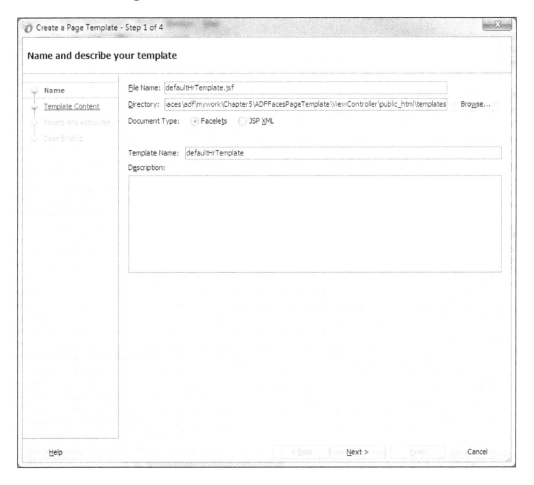

6. Click on **Next**.

7. Click on the **Blank Template** option since we want to start from scratch and then click on **Next**.

8. Define three facets inside the **Facets Definition** section since we have a three-column structure with names:

   ❑ Left

   ❑ Center

   ❑ Right

9. Define two attributes inside the **Attributes** section with the following details:

   ❑ **leftColumnWidth**: (Type: `java.lang.String`, Default Value: `100px`, Required: `false`)

   ❑ **rightColumnWidth**: (Type: `java.lang.String`, Default Value: `100px`, Required: `false`)

10. Click on **Next**.

11. Check the **Create Page Definition File** option.

12. Click on **Finish** to close the dialog.

13. Open **defaultHrTemplate.jsf** if it's not already opened.

14. Examine the page from the **Structure** pane. If you select the **af:pageTemplateDef** tag from the **Structure** pane, you can see all your facet definitions and attributes. Also, notice the `Var` attribute which equals to `attrs`. This is important because we will use it to reference the attributes we defined in step 9.

15. Drag the panel stretch layout component from the **Components** palette in the **Layout** section and drop it into the page template.

16. Select the component in the **Structure** pane.

17. Change the `DimensionsFrom` attribute to `Parent`.

18. Change the `StartWidth` attribute to `#{attrs.leftColumnWidth}`.

19. Change the `EndWidth` attribute to `#{attrs.rightColumnWidth}`.

 You don't need to memorize these expressions since you can select them by navigating to **Expression Builder | Scoped Variables | attrs**

20. Change the `TopHeight` attribute to `150px`.

21. Right-click on the center facet under panel stretch layout from the **Structure** window and navigate to **Insert Inside | ADF Faces | Facet Definition (facetRef)**.

22. Choose `Center` as a facet name when the dialog appears.

23. Repeat the last two steps to add the left facet definition inside the panel stretch layout's start facet, and the right facet definition inside the panel stretch layout's end facet. You should end up with the following screenshot:

```
af:pageTemplateDef
    c:set - viewcontrollerBundle
    af:xmlContent
    af:panelStretchLayout
        f:facet - bottom
        f:facet - center
            af:facetRef - Center
        f:facet - start
            af:facetRef - Left
        f:facet - end
            af:facetRef - Right
        f:facet - top
```

24. Save everything.

How it works...

In this recipe, we laid down the main structure of the page template that will be used in the next recipes. In this page template, we defined three facets, which represent three content place holders which all of the pages that are based on this template can use for their components. You can see that we didn't specify facets for footers or headers as they will be the same in all of the pages and won't need to change.

Also, you specified two attributes, which control the width of the left and right facets. This feature is very useful as it can create different looking pages from the same page template, which provides great flexibility over the page design. For instance, if you don't want a three-column layout and you only want two columns, you can make `rightColumnWidth` equal to `0px` and that way you will end up with only two columns. Also, if you want to have only one-column structure, you can make `leftColumnWidth` and `rightColumnWidth` both equal to `0px` and that way you'll end up with one column. This flexibility was provided by using just two attributes.

We also checked the **Create Page Definition File** option in the last step of the page template creation wizard, which will create a page binding for the page template exactly like a page definition for your JSF pages. This is extremely useful when you need to put task flows or other generic bindings from your data control that are common across all pages. When you create a page based on a page template, the template page definition will be included along with the page definition itself, so that anything inside the page template bindings will be available inside the page bindings as well.

Your application can have multiple page templates. You don't have to be stuck with one page template for your entire application.

You can also add a page template dynamically inside a page by using EL. Refer to the following link for more information: `http://docs.oracle.com/middleware/1212/adf/ADFFD/web_getstarted.htm#ADFFD22211`

See also

▶ You can know more about page templates from the official site at `http://docs.oracle.com/middleware/1212/adf/ADFUI/af_reuse.htm#CACCFCJC`

Adding layouts to the header and footer of the page template

ADF Faces provides a high number of layout components that can be used to arrange ADF components on a page. Usually, you begin building your page with one of the layout components as your root, and then you add components that provide other functionalities (for example, rendering data or rendering buttons) either inside facets or as child components to these layout components.

Layout components can be overwhelming. With so many of them, you might get lost considering which is the best one to choose from. During this recipe, you will get to know some of these layout components, and during the course of the book you will grow your understanding of the difference between most of the layout components, which can help you easily decide what you want.

In this recipe, we will continue working on the page template we created in the previous recipe and lay the main structure of the header and footer area using different layout components.

How to do it...

To know how to lay down the structure of the page template, perform the following steps:

1. Open the `defaultHrTemplate.jsf` page template.

   First we need to finish the layout of the header, so let's do that.

2. Drag a panel group layout from **Components** palette and drop it inside the top facet of the panel stretch layout component.

3. Change the `Layout` attribute of the newly-added panel group layout to `vertical`.

4. Change the `Halign` attribute to `center`.

5. Change the `inlineStyle` attribute to `background-color: #007294;`.

6. Drag another panel group layout and drop it inside the panel group layout we added in step 2.

7. Change the `Layout` attribute of the newly added panel group layout to `horizontal`.

8. Change the `inlineStyle` attribute to `background-color: #007b9d; border: solid 1px #006e8b; padding:20px;margin: 2.5% 0 2.5% 0;`.

9. Drag an output text component and drop it inside the horizontal panel group layout we added in step 6.

10. Change the text to `HR App` by using the **Select Text Resource** option (remember localization).

11. Change the `inlineStyle` attribute to `color:#fff; font-size:x-large;`.

12. Drag a **Spacer** component from **Components** palette and drop it inside the panel group layout that we created in step 6.

13. Change the `width` attribute of the spacer to `300`.

    Now that we have finished with the header, let's start working on the footer.

14. Drag the panel group layout component and drop it inside the bottom facet of panel stretch layout.

15. Change the `Layout` attribute to `vertical`.

16. Change the `Halign` attribute to `center`.

17. Change the `inlineStyle` attribute to `background-color: #E3E9DC;`.

18. Drag the output text component and drop it inside the panel group layout we added in the bottom facet of the panel stretch layout.

19. Change the `value` attribute to `© Hr App. All rights reserved.` using the **Select Text Resource** option.

20. Change the `inlineStyle` attribute to `color:#A6A88F; font-size:18px; display:block;margin: 1% 0 0 0;`.

21. Open the `adfc-config` unbounded task flow.

22. Drag-and-drop a **View** activity inside it.

23. Name it `employeesTable`.

24. Double-click on the newly created view to create the JSF page.

25. In the **Create JSF Page** dialog, choose **Default Hr Template** as the page template.

26. Finish the dialog by clicking on **OK**.

27. Drag **Chapter5AppModuleDataControl** and **EmployeesVO1** from the **Data Control** pane and drop it inside the center facet as an **ADF Table**.

28. Check the **Read-Only** option on the **Table Creation** dialog.

29. Close the dialog by clicking on **OK**.

30. Surround the **Table** component with the **Panel Collection** component from the **Structure** pane.

31. Select the `af:pageTemplate` node from the **Structure** pane.

32. Change the `leftColumnWidth` attribute to `0px`.

33. Change the `rightColumnWidth` attribute to `0px`.

34. Save everything.

35. Run the `employeesTable.jsf` page. You should end up with the following screenshot:

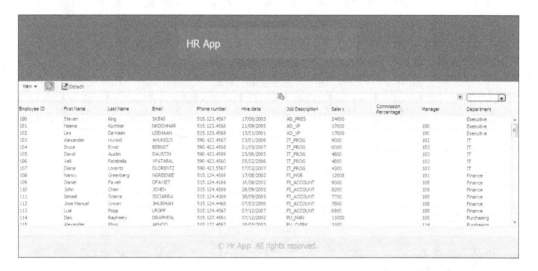

36. Examine the end result of the page and how changing the page template attribute values can change the look and feel of the page template.

How it works...

There are several ADF layout components that can be stretched and can stretch their children. These components are `panelStretchLayout`, `panelSplitter`, `panelDashboard`, `panelAccordion` with a `showDetailItem` component, and `panelTabbed` with a `showDetailItem` component. You should use these components as root components when you want to make the contents of the page fill the entire browser window, which gives you a sense of a desktop application.

In the last recipe, you added a panel stretch layout inside the page template. The panel stretch layout is one of the components that can be stretched and can also stretch their children. That's why it was picked as a root component of the page template. It has five main facets: top, bottom, start, center, and end, which perfectly fit a three-column layout structure.

 You can learn about all stretchable and non-stretchable components from the official documentation at `http://docs.oracle.com/middleware/1212/adf/ADFUI/af_orgpage.htm#CDEFAFGJ`

Another component that can be stretched but doesn't stretch its children is `PanelGroupLayout` in the vertical and scroll layout modes. That's why it's being used inside `PanelStretchLaytout` to lay down the structure of the top and bottom facets as we don't want to stretch the components inside `PanelGroupLayout`.

You started by adding a vertical panel group layout as the root of the top and bottom facets of panel stretch layout. In the top facet, we changed the `inlineStyle` of the root panel group layout to have a blue background color. You also changed the `HAlign` attribute to `center` to horizontally center any components inside of it. After that, we added another panel group layout (horizontal) component inside it. The horizontal panel group layout needs to look like a box that has a title and a menu. You added an output text with the title inside of it and a spacer to give some space between the **Title** and the **Menu** option.

In the bottom facet of the panel stretch layout component, we only needed an output text so we didn't have any nested panel groups inside the root panel group layout.

After we defined the header and the footer of your page template, we created a JSF page based on this template. You can see from the structure that you have three facets out of this template: Center, Left, and Right.

 Left and right should not be real names, since some locales have right-to-left direction. So, it is safer to have a start and end instead. However, left and right is used for clarity in order to be differentiated from the panel stretch layout facet names.

Also, we changed the page template attribute values to have a one-column layout instead of a three-column layout.

When you run your page, you will notice that everything is stretched to the max of the browser window, and if you start minimizing and maximizing the window you will see that the template will always have the same ratio, which is perfect for desktop-like applications.

Sometimes you will want to have a regular scroll without having everything stretched. In that case, you might need to consider a non-stretchable component as a root, something like panel group layout.

Creating an ADF skin for your application

An ADF skin is a collection of a special style sheet, an optional resource bundle, a name, and a base structure called the base skin.

In this recipe, we will create a custom ADF skin, remove the inline style inside the page template, and convert it to a cleaner page template.

In this recipe, it's assumed you understand native CSS and how to use it.

You can continue from the last recipe or you can grab the `ADFFacesSkinning` application from the Git repository.

How to do it...

To know how to create an ADF skin, perform the following steps:

1. Right-click on **ViewController**, navigate to **New | From Gallery | Web Tier | JSF/ Facelets | ADF Skin**, and click on **OK**.

2. Change the filename to: `hrBlue.css`.

3. Change the family to `hrBlue`.

4. Leave the **Use as the default skin family for this project** checkbox checked to change the default skin to the one we will create.

5. Click on **Next** to choose the base skin that you will extend it to.

6. Leave the **Skyros-v1.desktop** skin selected and click on **Finish** to close the dialog.

7. Examine the **Application** navigator for the new files created. You can see that four files have been generated (four will be generated only the first time, one should be generated for each new skin you create), as shown in the following screenshot:

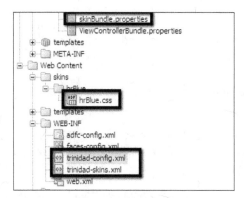

Now that we have finished creating the skin, let's start changing some styles.

8. Open the `hrBlue.css` file.

9. You can notice from the design view that there are multiple areas you can change, and you can view these changes in the sample page underneath.

10. First, let's change the **Default** font to `Ubuntu Condensed, sans-serif`. We will load this custom font later.

11. Change **Font Size** to `13.5pt`.

12. Change the default text colors **Main** and **Primary** to `#878E83`. You will also need to add some styles to the table component, so let's do that. You should end up with the following screenshot:

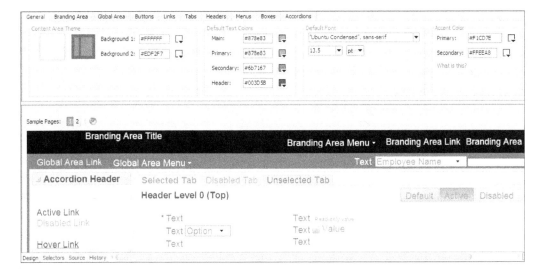

Now that we have finished the changes of the **Design Mode**, let's change to the **Selectors** mode

13. Open the **Selectors View** of `hrBlue.css`.

14. Navigate to **Global Selector Aliases | Color | Derivative Color** and click on **AFGridCellBorderColor**.

15. Change **Color** to `#FFFfff;`.

16. Navigate to **Faces Component Selectors | Column | Pseudo-Elements** and click on **column-header-cell**.

17. Change the **Background Color** to `#FFFfff` from the **Properties** pane.

18. Change the **Color** to `#007897`.

19. Change the **Border** to `0px`.

20. Change the **Border Color** to `#007897`.

21. Scroll down in the properties pane and click on the **Borders** tab (looks like a box icon).

22. Expand **Border Bottom** and change **Border Bottom** to `2px solid #007897;`.

23. Now, navigate to **Faces Component Selectors | Table | Component Selector Aliases** and click on **AFTableCellDataHGrid:alias**.

24. Change **Border** to `0px`.

25. Navigate to **Faces Component Selectors | Table | Component Selector Aliases** and click on **.AFTableCellDataVGrid:alias**.

26. Change **Border** to **0px**.

27. Navigate to **Faces Component Selectors | Table | Pseudo-Elements** and click on **data-row**.

28. Change **Height** to `30px`.

29. Click on the gear icon just beside **Height** and click on **Go to declaration** to open the Source mode of `hrBlue.css`.

30. Change the **data-row** style from `height: 30px;` to `height: 30px !important;` which will give this style a priority of execution.

    Now that we set the main styles and the table styles, let's remove the inline styles of the page template and give them style classes instead.

31. Open `defaultHrTemplate.jsf`.

32. Drag **Resource Component** from **Component Palette** (you can find it under the layout section) and drop it inside the root panel group layout inside the top facet (there can only be one main component).

33. Choose `css` as a type.

34. Change the `Source` attribute to `http://fonts.googleapis.com/css?family=Ubuntu+Condensed`. This will load the custom font from Google Font APIs and use it as the default font.

35. Click on **OK**. You should have the following source code in your page template:

```
<f:facet name="top">
 <af:panelGroupLayout id="pt_pgl1" layout="vertical"
   halign="center"
                       styleClass="background-color:
                         #007294;">
 <af:resource type="css"
   source="http://fonts.googleapis.com/
   css?family=Ubuntu+Condensed"></af:resource>
```

36. Select the root panel group layout inside the top facet from the **Structure** pane.

37. Change `styleClass` to `hr-header-wrapper`.

38. Remove what's inside the `inlineStyle` attribute.

39. Expand the selected Panel Group Layout and select the horizontal panel group layout inside of it.

40. Change the `styleClass` attribute to `hr-header-main`.

41. Remove what's inside the `inlineStyle` attribute.

42. Expand the selected horizontal panel group layout and select the output text underneath it.

43. Change the `styleClass` attribute to `hr-header-title h1`.

44. Remove what's inside the Inline Style attribute.

45. Expand the bottom facet and select the panel group layout inside it.

46. Change the `styleClass` attribute to `hr-footer-wrapper`.

47. Remove what's inside the inline style attribute.

48. Select the output text inside the panel group layout.

49. Change the `styleClass` attribute to `hr-footer-copyright`.

50. Remove what's inside the Inline Style attribute.

    Now we need to style the `styleClass` attribute that we applied for the components, so let's do that.

51. Open the `hrBlue.css` file.

52. Go to the Source mode.

53. Add the following CSS lines to the end of the `hrBlue.css` file:

```css
.hr-header-wrapper {
    background-color: #007294;
}

.hr-header-main{
    background-color: #007b9d;
    border: solid 1px #006e8b;
    padding:20px;
    margin: 2.5% 0 2.5% 0;
    border-radius: 10px;
    box-shadow: inset 0px 0px 0px 1px #12a0bf, 0px 1px 4px
      0px rgba(0,0,0,0.10);
}
.hr-header-title{
    color:#fff;
    text-decoration: none;
}
.hr-footer-wrapper{
    background: #E3E9DC;
}
```

```
.hr-footer-copyright{
    color:#A6A88F;
    font-size:18px;
    display:block;
    margin: 1% 0 0 0;
}
```

54. Run the `employeesTable.jsf` page and see the difference in the look and feel, as shown in the following screenshot:

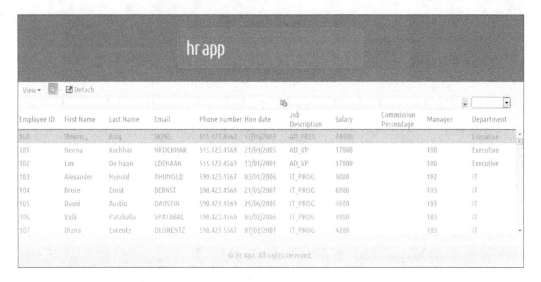

How it works...

In this recipe, you created your first ADF skin and set it as the default skin for your application.

If you examine what's created out of the ADF skin creation, you will notice that there are four files generated: `WEB-INF\trinidadad-config.xml`, `WEB-INF\trinidad-skins.xml`, `skins\hrBlue\hrBlue.css`, and `skinBundle.properties`. These are created under the main source path directory.

If you opened `trinidad-skins.xml`, you will find the skin definition inside this file. This includes the skin's family name, what base skin does it extend from, what is the resource bundle for this skin, and the skin's CSS file location. All ADF skin definitions that you create inside your application will be added inside this file. If this file doesn't exist (in case you create your first ADF skin) JDeveloper will create the file for you and fill it with the right information. One attribute worth mentioning is the base skin, which resembles the skin that inherits its properties. The most basic one is the `simple.desktop` skin which has minimal configuration. If you have something completely different from the skin that you are setting as base, it's better to use the `simple.desktop` skin as a base skin family.

The `trindad-config.xml` file is the configuration file that defines the default skin family to be used inside the application.

The `skinBundle.properties` file is the resource bundle where you can change the string text that the components generate, like the Ok dialog and Cancel labels. You can change these coded labels inside this file.

The `hrBlue.css` file is the ADF skin CSS file that should have the styles of your application components and even custom styles.

When you open the ADF skin CSS file, you open JDeveloper's skin editor. In this recipe, we dealt with different modes of the skin editor: Design mode, Selectors mode, and Source mode.

The Design mode is intended to give you an overview of the global selectors to lay down the default structure of the skin, such as default font, default text color, and so on.

The Selectors mode is perfect if you want to change what a specific component looks like. You get a tree of the components, select a specific component, and easily change its properties from there using the properties pane.

The Source mode is perfect to lay down your own layout structure if you have different variations of the same component. I personally recommend looking at the Source mode to understand what's happening when you change a certain property, even if you use it in the Selectors or the Design mode.

An ADF skin is more than just a CSS file. The skin gets parsed and obfuscated at runtime. It also generates the native CSS file for each operating system and browser. You can disable compression of the CSS-generated file to see all of the ADF styles in HTML itself by adding a Context parameter in `web.xml`. This approach is not recommended for enterprise applications as compression can affect performance greatly, but it's good if you are starting your way with ADF skinning.

```
<context-param>
  <param-
    name>org.apache.myfaces.trinidad.DISABLE_CONTENT
    _COMPRESSION</para
m-name>
  <param-value>true</param-value>
</context-param>
```

In native CSS, if you want to target a tag, you just name it. However, since ADF uses components, there is no way to target the entire component styles. That's why ADF has introduced a new additional syntax to the native CSS, which in runtime gets converted and hooked to the component at the right time.

In ADF skin CSS, if you want to target a specific component, you need to prefix it with `af|` followed by the component name (you can select it from the Selectors mode of the skin to know its name easily). When the component has multiple component parts inside of it, you can suffix it by using the `::` operator (you can also choose them by using the Selectors Mode). So, for instance, in our example we want to change the data cell of the table, which is inside the column component. So, we target the style by writing it in the `af|column::data-cell` format. This way only the data-cell will be changed. Also, if there are multiple states to the component, such as selected or hover, you can suffix it with the `:` operator. If you are targeting Right-to-Left (RTL) systems, it can be considered to be in a state. So, if you want to change what the selected data cell will look like, you will write it in the `af|column::data-cell:selected` format.

ADF skin CSS has a concept of Global Selectors (aliases). Global Selectors are selectors that affect more than one component. If the selector name ends with `:alias` pseudo-class, then the selector is most likely included in other component-specific selectors. Defining properties for a selector that ends with `:alias` will most likely affect the skin for more than one component. For example, most ADF components use the `.AFDefaultFontFamily:alias` definition to specify the font-family. If your skin overrides the `.AFDefaultFontFamily:alias` selector with a different font-family, that change will affect all the components that have included it in their selector definition.

You can create your own alias and reference it using `-tr-property-ref` to use the same style in different places. The `-tr-property-ref` reference is acting like a method, which takes two parameters. The first one is the alias that you are copying the property from. The second one is the property that you are copying; for example, if you want to have a color property based on the default text color, you define your property in the `color: -tr-property-ref(".AFTextColor:alias", "color");` format.

There is another concept of `-tr-rule-ref`, which unlike `-tr-property-ref` includes everything inside the alias defined. So, if you want to include whatever is used inside the `defaultFontFamily` alias, you can use the `-tr-rule-ref: selector(".AFDefaultFontFamily:alias")` format.

Also, in the ADF skin CSS file, you can define a specific selector for a specific browser, locale, device, accessibility profile, or operating system. For example, if you want to apply certain styles to Internet Explorer, you can use the `@agent ie{ <your styles in here> }` format. There are multiple keywords that you can use, such as `agent`, `accessibility-profile`, `locale`, and `platform`.

In this recipe, we also loaded external custom Google fonts by using the `af:resource tag`. This tag is very helpful since we don't want anything to be processed at runtime, such as custom fonts and custom styles.

Also, we extracted the inline style from the page template by using the `styleClass` attribute of the ADF components. Like native CSS, if you want to target some components by class, you use `.className`. This class name can be used inside the ADF component's `styleClass` attribute. We added these class names inside the ADF skin to target these specific components as you should avoid using `inlineStyle` at all cost.

The only time you might need to use `inlineStyle` is if you have some dynamic value that gets updated with the EL expression.

As ADF skin CSS parses its content, some styles may not work, such as `-webkit`, `-moz`, or media query since it can't recognize them. So, in order to overcome this, you should create another native CSS file and include these properties inside it by targeting components using the `styleClass` definition. However, beware not to style ADF components inside the native CSS file using `af|` as a native CSS file doesn't know how to deal with them.

See also

There are a couple of resources that you can see in order to understand skinning more:

- ▶ Check the ADF RichClient Demo application at `http://jdevadf.oracle.com/adf-richclient-demo/faces/index.jspx`.
- ▶ Also, you can use the following guide for ADF skinning and ADF skin Editor at `http://docs.oracle.com/middleware/1212/skineditor/ADFSG/index.html`

Changing skins at runtime

Having a skin for your application is great to manage how it looks and feels from a central location, but giving the user an option to change the skin at runtime is also a great feature that many applications might want to provide to their users.

In this recipe, we will know how to provide the user with the capability to change skins at runtime and swap between two skins.

You can continue from the last recipe, or you can grab the `ADFFacesSwapSkins` application from the Git repository.

How to do it...

To know how to change skins at runtime, perform the following steps:

1. Create a new skin by following steps 1 to 8 of the previous recipe with the following changes:
    - □ Name the skin `hrRed` instead of `hrBlue`
    - □ Choose the base skin `hrBlue`
    - □ Uncheck the **Use as the default skin family for this project** option

2. Open the `hrRed.css` file.

3. Open the Source mode of `hrRed.css`.

4. Add the following lines:

    ```
    .hr-header-wrapper {
        background-color: #821816;
    }
    ```

5. Create a new task flow with the name `hr-skins-menu`.

6. Change the default directory of the task flow and put it under `WEB-INF\ taskflows\common directory`.

7. Drag a View activity and change the name to `skinsMenu`.

8. Double-click on the View to create the page fragment.

9. Put the fragment under the `public_html\fragments\common` directory.

10. Drag and drop a panel group layout as the root component of the page fragment.

11. Change the **Layout** of the panel group layout to `Horizontal`.

12. Add a spacer component inside the separator facet of the panel group layout component.

13. Drag two command link components under the panel group layout.

14. Change the first link **Text** to `Blue` by using select resource text functionality.

15. Change the second link **Text** to `Red` by using select resource text functionality.

16. Click on the gear icon beside the **Action** attribute of the blue link.

17. Click on **Edit**.

18. Navigate to **Method Binding | Managed Bean** and then click on **New**.

19. Change the **Bean Name** to `userSkin`.

20. Change the **Class Name** to `UserSkinBean`.

21. Change the **Package** to `com.adffaces.chapter5.view.beans`.

22. Change the **Scope** to `Session` (more about scopes in *Chapter 7, Handling Events and Partial Page Rendering*).

23. Click on **OK** to close the dialog.

24. In the original dialog, navigate to **Method | New**.

25. Name the method `makeBlueDefaultSkin`.

26. Click on **OK** to close the dialog.

27. Repeat steps 16 to 24 for the red link.

28. Name the method `makeRedDefaultSkin`.

29. Open the `UserSkinBean` class.

30. Add the following code to the class body (make sure you include all the necessary imports):

```
String defaultSkin="hrBlue";

public void setDefaultSkin(String defaultSkin) {
    this.defaultSkin = defaultSkin;
}

public String getDefaultSkin() {
    return defaultSkin;
}

private void refreshPage() {
    FacesContext fctx = FacesContext.getCurrentInstance();
    String refreshpage = fctx.getViewRoot().getViewId();
    ViewHandler ViewH = fctx.getApplication().
getViewHandler();
    UIViewRoot UIV = ViewH.createView(fctx, refreshpage);
    UIV.setViewId(refreshpage);
    fctx.setViewRoot(UIV);
}
```

31. Add the following lines to the `makeBlueDefaultSkin` function:

```
defaultSkin="hrBlue";
refreshPage();
```

32. Add the following lines to the `makeRedDefaultSkin` function:

```
defaultSkin="hrRed";
refreshPage();
```

33. Drag the `hr-skin-menu` task flow from **Application** navigator, navigate to **defaultHrTemplate | Top Facet | Panel Group Layout vertical | Panel Group Layout Horizontal**, and drop it inside just under the spacer component and select **Region** when the **Drag and Drop** dialog appears.

34. Open `trinidad-config.xml`.

35. Change this line `<skin-family>hrBlue</skin-family>` and replace it with the following line:

    `<skin-family>#{userSkin.defaultSkin}</skin-family>`

36. Open the `hr-skins-menu` task flow and open it in the Source mode.

37. Cut the `ManagedBean` tag.

38. Paste the tag inside `adfc-config` just before `</adfc-config>`.

39. Save everything.

40. Run the `employeesTable.jsf` page. You should end up with the following screenshot, and clicking on the red button should change the color to red:

How it works...

In order to be able to grant end users the ability to change the application skin, you first need to expose a component that allows them to update the value of the `skin-family` property in the `trinidad-config.xml` file.

In this recipe, we made these changes by having two links. You can create a drop-down list or a menu for the same action, but I chose something easy to understand.

We also created a task flow to contain these links, so that when you want to change how this language looks and feels, you can do this easily afterwards without the need to change every page template that has this functionality—always remember to **Don't Repeat Yourself** (**DRY**).

We also created a managed bean in the session scope to hold this value and pointed the `trinidad-config.xml` file to that value. When you click on the link, it changes the session's variable value.

The only missing piece is a function called `refreshPage`. This function is needed since you need to refresh the entire page in order for the changes to take effect.

Also, we needed to cut the managed bean tag inside `adfc-config`. This is needed because this will be a generic managed bean, not bounded to a `hr-skins-menu` task flow, that's why we moved it from the `hr-skins-menu` task flow to `adfc-config` to make it globally accessible.

At runtime, the end user clicks on the link. The link submits the value that the end user selected to a managed bean that, in turn, sets the value of a managed bean property (`skinFamily`). At runtime, the `<skin-family>` property in the `trinidad-config.xml` file reads the value from the managed bean using an EL expression.

See also

▶   You can learn more about changing skins at runtime from the official documentation at `http://docs.oracle.com/middleware/1212/adf/ADFUI/af_skin.htm#CHDFEFCE`

Using skins like a pro by using Sass and compass

Native CSS is very static and doesn't provide much flexibility, that's why ADF skinning provided aliases, `-tr-property-ref` and `-tr-rule-ref` to make loading dynamic properties easier. However, even when you create an enterprise application with multiple components, you end up with a very big CSS file, which is very hard to maintain.

Sass is meant to help you fix this problem. It is considered the most mature and powerful CSS extension language. It is a scripting language that is interpreted into CSS. It embraces the DRY method to the fullest so that you won't have to write any redundant styles. It also makes the maintaining process of CSS much easier.

Sass provides so many features such as variables, mixin (a group of CSS styles that you want to reuse as whole, which can be parameterized), functions, and even mathematical calculations and loops so that you have a very tidy and small CSS, for instance, a syntax like the following:

```
$blue: #3bbfce;
$margin: 16px;
.content-navigation {
  border-color: $blue;
  color: darken($blue, 20%);
}
.border {
  padding: $margin / 2;
  margin: $margin / 2;
  border-color: $blue;
}
```

Is compiled to (In native CSS):

```
.content-navigation {
  border-color: #3bbfce;
  color: #2b9eab;
}
.border {
  padding: 8px;
  margin: 8px;
  border-color: #3bbfce;
}
```

Sass is great, but some standard and best practices of CSS such as box shadow, gradient, floating, and resetting styles are often used in all applications. However, they become very tedious to write every time you start creating your application. That's when compass comes into the picture.

Compass is a collection of helpful styles and best practices that every great looking application needs, which comes out of the box for you to use with Sass.

In this recipe, you will convert the `hrBlue` skin into a Sass-enabled skin and use a couple of features such as variables, mixins, and functions with the help of compass.

You can continue from the last recipe, or you can grab the `ADFFacesSkinningWithSASS` application from the Git repository.

Getting ready

Unfortunately, JDeveloper and ADF skin doesn't support Sass. That's why we need to make a couple of configurations in JDeveloper first, and also install software to convert the Sass extension `.scss` to a normal native `.css` file.

- ▸ Install the open source software Scout application from the following link: `http://mhs.github.io/scout-app/`. It is available for Mac and Windows.
- ▸ Add `scss` as a file by type by:
  - ❑ Navigating to JDeveloper's **Tools menu** | **Preferences** | **File Types**
  - ❑ Clicking on the **Add** button and writing `.scss` and changing the **File type** to `Cascading Style Sheet`
  - ❑ Restarting JDeveloper

How to do it...

To know how to apply Sass and compass, perform the following steps:

1. Open the Scout application.

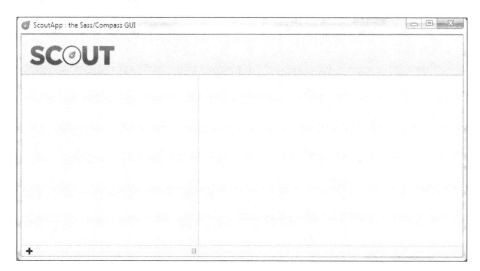

2. Click on the plus icon button in the bottom-left of the application.

3. Navigate to `ADFFacesSkinningWithSASS` under your workspace.

4. Point the input and output directories to `ViewController\public_html\skins\hrBlue`.

5. Navigate to the `hrBlue` directory and take a backup of your CSS file.

6. Open JDeveloper if it's not opened.

7. Select the `hrBlue` folder from the **Application** navigator pane and right-click on it and navigate to **New | From Gallery | General Category**, select **File**, and click on **OK**.

8. Change the file name to `hrBlue.scss`.

9. Click on the **Play** button in the Scout application to start seeing the changes.

10. Add the following lines inside `hrBlue.scss` to declare all the variables inside the .scss file:

```
@charset "UTF-8";
/**ADFFaces_Skin_File / DO NOT REMOVE**/
@namespace af "http://xmlns.oracle.com/adf/faces/rich";
@namespace dvt "http://xmlns.oracle.com/dss/adf/faces";
// Variables definition
$defaultFontSize: 13.5pt;
$defaultFontFamily: 'Ubuntu Condensed', sans-serif;
$defaultTextColor: #878e83;
$secondaryTextColor: #6B7167;
$defaultBorderColor: #fff;
$tableHeaderColor: #007897;
$tableRowHeight: 30px;
$tableBorder: 0px;
```

11. After that, we will use these variables inside our global selectors by adding the following lines:

```
// Use Variables by appending $ and the name of the variable
.AFDefaultFontFamily:alias {
    font-family: $defaultFontFamily;
}
.AFDefaultFont:alias {
    // you can use mathematical operations with your variables
    font-size: $defaultFontSize / 2 * 2;
}
.AFTextColor:alias {
    color: $defaultTextColor;
}
```

```
.AFTextTertiaryColor:alias {
    color: $defaultTextColor;
}
.AFTextSecondaryColor:alias {
    color: $secondaryTextColor;
}
.AFLabelColor:alias {
    color: $secondaryTextColor;
}
.AFTextPrimaryColor:alias {
    color: $defaultTextColor;
}
.AFGridCellBorderColor:alias {
    color: $defaultBorderColor;
}
.AFTableCellDataHGrid:alias {
    border: $tableBorder;
}
.AFTableCellDataVGrid:alias {
    border: $tableBorder;
}
```

12. Add the nested table styles inside `hrBlue.scss` by adding the following lines at the end of the file:

```
// You can use nested component
af|table{
    & af|column {
        &::column-header-cell{
            border: $tableBorder;
            border-color: $tableHeaderColor;
            border-bottom: 2px solid $tableHeaderColor;
            height: $tableRowHeight;
            color: $tableHeaderColor;
            background-color: white;
        }
    }
    &::data-row{
        height: $tableRowHeight !important;
    }
}
```

13. Save and refresh your `hrBlue.css` file by using the refresh icon in the **Application** navigator to see the result.

14. Examine the result and see what the generated CSS file looks like.

    Now you need to create another native CSS file to hold the styles that are not based on ADF components, so let's do that.

15. Navigate to **ViewController | Web Content | Skins | hrBlue** in **Application** navigator.

16. Right-click on **hrBlue** directory and select **File** under **New**.

17. Name the file `hrBlueStyles.scss`.

18. Add the variables definition by adding the following lines inside the `hrBlueStyles.scss` file (which are the missing pieces from the skin file):

```
@import 'compass'; //This imports compass framework

//Header specific Variables
$headerWrapperBackgroundStartColor: #008dab;
$headerWrapperBackgroundEndColor: #007294;
$headerMainBackgroundStartColor: #008ead;
$headerMainBackgroundEndColor: #007b9d;
$headerMainBorderColor: #006e8b;
$headerMainRadius: 10px;
$headerTitleColor: #fff;

//Footer specific Variables
$footerWrapperBackgroundColor: #E3E9DC;
$footerCopyrightsColor: #A6A88F;
$footerCopyrightsFontSize: 18px;
```

19. Add any generic styles by appending the following lines inside `hrBlueStyles.scss`:

```
// Generic styles
.h1 {
    font-size: 2.4em;
    letter-spacing: -2px;
    text-transform: lowercase;
}
```

20. Add the header styles by appending the following lines inside `hrBlueStyles.scss`:

```
.hr-header-wrapper {
    height: 150px;
    display: block;
```

```
    background-color: $headerWrapperBackgroundEndColor;
    //This is a compass mixin for making the background use
linear-gradient
    @include background(linear-gradient(top,
$headerWrapperBackgroundStartColor,
$headerWrapperBackgroundEndColor));
}
.hr-header-main {
    background-color: $headerMainBackgroundEndColor;
    border: solid 1px $headerMainBorderColor;
    padding: 20px;
    margin: 2.5% 0 2.5% 0;
    //Another useful compass mixins
    @include border-radius($headerMainRadius);
    @include background(linear-gradient(top,
$headerMainBackgroundStartColor, $headerMainBackgroundEndColor));
    @include box-shadow(inset 0px 0px 0px 1px #12a0bf, 0px 1px 4px
0px rgba(0, 0, 0, 0.10) );
}
.hr-header-title {
    color: $headerTitleColor;
    text-decoration: none;
}
```

21. Add the footer styles by appending the following lines inside `hrBlueStyles.scss`:

```
.hr-footer-wrapper {
    Height: 50px;
    background-color: $footerWrapperBackgroundColor;
}
.hr-footer-copyright {
    color: $footerCopyrightsColor;
    font-size: $footerCopyrightsFontSize;
    display: block;
    margin: 1% 0 0 0;
}
```

22. Save and refresh your **Application** navigator to see the new `hrBlueStyles.css` file generated.

    Now that we have finished creating the additional style sheets file, we need to include it in the page template, so let's do that.

23. Open the `defaultHrTemplate.jsf` page template.

24. Put `af:resource` under the resource that loads the custom font we put in the *Create an ADF skin for your Application* recipe.

25. When prompted, choose **Style Sheets** as a **Type**.

26. Change the source attribute to `/skins/hrBlue/hrBlueStyles.css`.

27. Run the `employeesTable.jsf` page. You can see now that the linear gradient is applied successfully to the header with the box radius and shadow, as shown in the following screenshot:

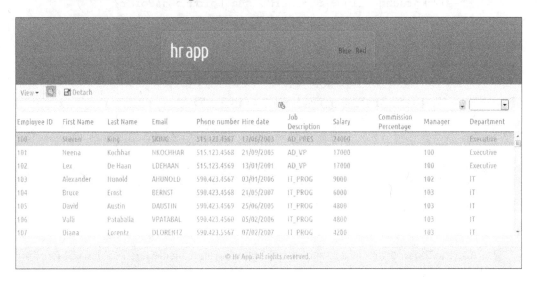

How it works...

In this recipe, we converted the ADF skin CSS file to a Sass file. We used the Scout application to watch the changes that happened to the Sass file, in order to convert it to a native CSS file, so that you can see the changes the moment you save your `.scss` file.

As you can see, you were able to define variables and use it effectively using Sass, which is a great feature. We combined this with aliases so that when we change a variable you automatically change the alias that references this variable.

We also created another `.scss` file to hold the `hrBlueStyles`. This file is specifically useful when you want to have something that is not specific to a component or a global selector, that's why we moved all of the header and footer properties inside this file. We also used it to use some features that otherwise won't be possible inside the ADF skin CSS file, like the linear gradient and any style that generate Webkit or Mozilla specific tags.

You also used mixins in `hrBlueStyles.css` by using the word `@include` followed by the mixin name, but you can notice that we didn't provide this mixin anywhere. That's because these are compass mixins, which load all of the attributes necessary to make this mixin work on multiple browsers, and this wouldn't be possible without the `@import compass` we wrote in the beginning of the `hrBlueStyles.scss` file.

The next time you work with a style sheet, you should not worry about your CSS file . Instead, you should focus on your `.scss` file, which is far more flexible and provides much more functionality out of the box.

See also

- ▸ You can learn more about Sass from the official Sass website at `http://sass-lang.com/`
- ▸ You can find out more about compass from the official compass website at `http://compass-style.org`

Using mdia queries for a responsive web design

Responsive Web Design (**RWD**) is a web design approach aimed at crafting sites to provide an optimal viewing experience, such as easy reading and navigation with a minimum amount of resizing, panning, or scrolling. RWD is meant to be used across a wide range of devices (from mobile phones to desktop computer monitors).

A site designed with RWD adapts the layout to the viewing environment by using fluid, proportion-based grids, flexible images, and CSS3 media queries, an extension of the `@media` rule.

This means in order to make your website responsive and work well with different devices, we should think about considering the RWD approach.

The key element to make your application responsive is to use media queries effectively. Unfortunately, the ADF skin CSS file doesn't support media queries tag, which means we need to work with a native CSS file to add the media queries.

In this recipe, we will create another page template, which has two facets: 1 sidebar and 1 for the content. We will copy some parts from `hrDefaultTemplate` using the structure pane's copy context menu of the component.

You can continue from the last recipe, or you can grab the `ADFFacesSkinningWithRWD` application from the Git repository.

How to do it...

To know how to use media queries for responsive UI, perform the following steps:

1. Navigate to **ViewController** | **Web Content** | **Templates** using the **Application** navigator.

2. Right-click on the `templates` directory and navigate to **New** | **ADF Page Template**. This will create the `Page Template` directory inside the `templates` directory

3. Change the file name to `responsiveHrTemplate.jsf` and click on **Next**.

4. Keep the **Blank template** option selected and click on **Next**.

5. Define two facets as defined before with the following names:

    ❑ Content

    ❑ Sidebar

6. Define one attribute with the following information:

    ❑ Name: `sidebarWidthPercentage`, type: `java.lang.String`, defaultValue: `25%`

7. Click on **Next**.

8. Check the **Create Page Definition File** option.

9. Click on **Finish** to close the dialog.

    Now that we have created the page template, we need to create the layout of the page template. We will copy a couple of things from the `hrDefaultTemplate` page template.

10. Open the `responsiveHrTemplate.jsf` page template.

11. Drag a panel group layout from **Components** palette and drop it as the root component just under `xmlContent` from the **Structure** pane.

12. Copy what's inside the top facet of the panel stretch layout of `defaultHrTemplate` and paste it inside the root panel group layout.

13. Change the `Layout` attribute of the `hr-header-wrapper` panel group layout to `scroll`.

14. Expand the `hr-header-wrapper` panel group layout.

15. Expand the `hr-header-main` panel group layout.

16. Select the output text and change the `value` attribute to `Hr App` by using the **Select Text Resource** option.

    This is required because when we copied what's inside the top facet from `defaultHrTemplate`, the resource bundle tag reference wasn't copied, so we do this to add the tag again.

17. Remove the `af:region` tag of the menu.

18. Drag the `hr-skins-menu` task flow from the **Application** navigator and drop it just after the spacer. This is also needed to copy the bindings of the region.

19. Drag another panel group layout from **Components** palette and drop it under the root panel group layout.

20. Change the `Layout` attribute to `Vertical`.

21. Change the `styleClass` attribute to `hr-main-wrapper`.

22. Drag two additional panel group layouts and drop them inside the `hr-main-wrapper` panel group layout.

23. Change their `Layout` to `vertical`.

24. Change `StyleClass` of the first one to `hr-main-sidebar`.

25. Change `StyleClass` of the second one to `hr-main-content`.

26. Select the `hr-main-sidebar` panel group layout from the **Structure** pane.

27. Change the `inlineStyle` to `width: #{attrs.sidebarWidthPercentage}`.

28. Right-click on the `hr-main-sidebar` panel group layout from the **Structure** window and navigate to **Insert Inside | ADF Faces | Facet Definition (facetRef)**.

29. Choose **Sidebar** from the combobox of the dialog when prompted.

30. Select the `hr-main-content` panel group layout from the **Structure** window, right-click on it, and navigate to **Insert Inside | ADF Faces | Facet Definition (facetRef)**.

31. Choose **Content** from the combo box when a dialog is prompted.

32. Copy the bottom facet from `defaultHrTemplate` to the root panel group layout of the `responsiveHrTemplate` page template.

33. Change the `Layout` attribute of the `hr-footer-wrapper` panel group layout to `scroll`.

34. Save everything.

    Now that we have added the Layout to the Page Template, we will create a page based on `responsiveHrTemplate`, so let's do that.

35. Open the `adfc-config` task flow file.

36. Drag a view activity from **Components** palette and drop it inside the task flow.

37. Name the view activity: `responsiveEmployees`.

38. Double-click on the newly created view activity to create the page.

39. Choose the `Responsive Hr Template` as your page template.

40. Click on **OK** to close the dialog.

41. Select the `af:document` tag from the **Structure** pane.

42. Right-click on it and navigate to **Insert inside | JSF | Facet** and click on **metaContainer** from the combo box of the dialog when prompted.

43. Change to Source mode and add the following line inside the `metaContainer` facet:

```
<meta name="viewport" content="width=device-width, initial-
    scale=1.0" />
```

44. Change back to the Design mode.

45. Navigate to **Chapter5AppModuleDataControl | EmployeesVO1** from the data control Pane and drop it inside the center facet as an ADF form.

46. Check both, the **Read-only** and **Row Navigation** options.

47. Click on **OK**.

48. Navigate to the footer facet of the panel form layout from the **Structure** pane.

49. Select the **Horizontal** panel group layout inside of it.

50. Change the `styleClass` attribute to `hr-main-content-navigation`.

51. Now navigate to **Chapter5AppModuleDataControl | EmployeesVO1** again, this time inside the Sidebar facet as an ADF Tree.

52. Change the display attributes to have only `FirstName` and `LastName`.

53. Click on **OK** to close the ADF Tree creation dialog.

    Now that we have finished the page creation, we need to add the media query tag and a few styles to the `hrBlueStyles.scss` file, so let's do that.

54. Open `hrBlueStyles.scss`.

55. Add the following lines to add a couple of styles inside the Sass file:

```
.hr-main-sidebar {
  float: left;
}
.hr-main-content {
  float: left;
}
//Hide the navigation button by default
.hr-main-content-navigation {
  display: none;
}
```

56. Now add the following media query CSS to make the application more responsive:

```
//Define media query if the maximum width is 700px
@media screen and (max-width: 700px) {
  //Hide the Sidebar
  .hr-main-sidebar {
    display: none;
  }
  //Display the navigation button
  .hr-main-content-navigation {
    display: block;
  }
}
```

57. Save everything and click on the refresh icon of the **Application** navigator.

58. Run the `responsiveEmployees.jsf` page and try to reduce the size of the browser window to see the sidebar hiding and the navigation buttons appearing, you should see something like the following screenshot:

How it works...

In this recipe, you created another page template `responsiveHrTemplate`, which embraces the RWD. This page template has a different structure compared to the `defaultHrtemplate` page template.

To make a true responsive design, you should start with a layout that doesn't stretch its children, that's why we didn't add a panel stretch layout and chose a panel group layout instead, since panel group layout doesn't stretch its children. If you choose panel stretch layout, the columns will be fixed in size and the center facet is the only facet that will act responsive. Even if the window got small enough, the two side columns will still appear.

In RWD, you might want to focus on the center content and either make the two side columns disappear or be under the main content, which cannot happen with a layout component that stretches its children (that's why panel group layout was used).

You can use media query easily by defining media screen in the following format: `@media screen|print|all and ([min-width:0px and ]max-width: 700px)`.

The browser understands this tag and observes the browser window and when the condition is met, all the styles under this `@media` tag are applied.

We also added a `viewport` meta information to the page to disable the pinch-to-zoom feature in any mobile device and to make mobile devices auto scale the content of the page. If this mobile device has a default canvas less than 700px, the media query will automatically be applied.

See also

> ▸ You can learn more about RWD by referring to the following reference at `http://coding.smashingmagazine.com/2011/01/12/guidelines-for-responsive-web-design/`

Using flat design techniques

In the last several years, there has been a rapid shift in software and application interface design, from 3D and skeuomorphic to flat and minimal.

Flat design is aimed for simplicity, clarity, and honesty of materials in the user interface.

That means getting rid of beveled edges, gradients, shadows, and reflections, as well as creating a user experience that plays to the strengths of digital interfaces, rather than limiting the user to the confines of the familiar analog world.

In web design as well, flat pages rarely introduce dimensionality, shadows, or textures into the equation, relying instead on parallax scrolling and visual clarity to communicate.

One of the most popular frontend frameworks that embrace the flat design is Twitter-bootstrap, which uses solid colors and font-icons for icons and design.

In this recipe, you are going to style the blue and red links to apply some flat design techniques and also add icons by using font-awesome icon font. You are not going to download the entire Twitter Bootstrap to only apply the buttons styles in the application design, but you can try them in your free time.

You can continue from the last recipe, or you can grab the `ADFFacesFlatUI` application from the Git repository.

How to do it...

To know how to apply Flat UI techniques, perform the following steps:

1. Open the `hrBlueStyles.scss` file.
2. Add the following lines to add different button styles. Make sure it's outside the media query tags:

```scss
//Styles for flat button styles
.btn {
  display: inline-block;
  padding: 6px 12px;
  margin-bottom: 0;
  font-size: 14px;
  font-weight: normal;
  line-height: 1.428571429;
  text-align: center;
  white-space: nowrap;
  vertical-align: middle;
  cursor: pointer;
  border: 1px solid transparent;
  border-radius: 4px;
  -webkit-user-select: none;
     -moz-user-select: none;
      -ms-user-select: none;
       -o-user-select: none;
          user-select: none;
}
.btn:focus {
  outline: thin dotted #333;
  outline: 5px auto -webkit-focus-ring-color;
  outline-offset: -2px;
}
.btn:hover,
.btn:focus {
  color: #333333;
  text-decoration: none;
}
.btn:active{
  background-image: none;
  outline: 0;
  @include box-shadow(inset 0 3px 5px rgba(0, 0, 0,
    0.125));
}
```

3. Save everything and make sure that `hrBlueStyles.css` has the new styles.

   We created a general button style, but we also need to style the ADF link component to complete the user experience.

4. Now open `hrBlue.scss` (the ADF Sass skin).

5. Add the following lines for `red-btn` and `blue-btn` styles of the ADF link.

```
af|link{
  color: #ffffff;
    &.red-button{
    background-color: #d9534f;
    border-color: #d43f3a;

    &:hover,&:focus,&:active{
      color: #ffffff;
      background-color: #d2322d;
      border-color: #ac2925;

    }
    }
    &.blue-button{
    background-color: #5bc0de;
    border-color: #46b8da;

    &:hover,&:focus,&:active{
      color: #ffffff;
      background-color: #39b3d7;
      border-color: #269abc;

    }
    }
  }
```

6. Save everything and make sure that styles are copied into the `hrBlue.css` file.

   As you can see, Sass is making things very easy for us! Now we need to add a couple of `styleClasses` to the buttons inside the page fragment, so let's do that.

7. Open the `skinsMenu.jsff` fragment file.

8. Switch to the Source mode.

   This time we will add some `.html` tags inside the `af:link` tags.

9. Change the first link (blue) to the following code to add a circle icon and convert the link to a button:

```
<af:link id="l1" action="#{userSkin.makeBlueDefaultSkin}"
  styleClass=" btn blue-button">
        <i class="icon-circle"></i>
```

```
        #{viewcontrollerBundle.BLUE}
</af:link>
```

10. Do the same for the red link and change it to the following:

```
<af:link text="" id="l2"
  action="#{userSkin.makeRedDefaultSkin}"
  styleClass="btn red-button">
    <i class="icon-circle-blank"></i>
      #{viewcontrollerBundle.RED}
</af:link>
```

11. Now let's add the font-awesome icon font to both your templates (`defaultHrTemplate` and `responsiveHrTemplate`) by dragging a Resource Component from the **Component Palette** and drop it just under the old resources in the `hr-header-wrapper` panel group layout.

12. Change the `type` to `StyleSheet`.

13. Change the source to `http://netdna.bootstrapcdn.com/font-awesome/3.2.1/css/font-awesome.css`.

14. Save everything.

15. Run both your pages (`employeesTable.jsf` and `responsiveEmployees.jsf`). You should end up with the following screenshot:

How it works...

In this recipe, you were able to see a small part of the flat design in action by applying the button styles on the skin's menu links. We started by adding some generic button styles in `hrBlueStyles.scss`.

After that we added two variations of the link component that we used inside the skins menu fragment inside the ADF skin. This variation was possible by suffixing it with the class name, that is, `.red-button` and `.blue-button`, which we added by using the `styleClass` attribute of the two links.

This urges the question when should you put the styles inside the ADF skin file and when should it be in the additional CSS file. The following table should help you answer this question.

ADF Skin CSS	Additional CSS File
The style is related to an ADF component or a variation of the ADF component.	The style is generic and not related to any ADF component.
The style is globally used and can be applied to one of the global selectors.	The style has media queries or browser specific CSS values.

You also provided the link styles with different states for active hover and focus on them by suffixing with the `:` operator.

You also used two great features of facelets:

- Using HTML tags such as the HTML `i` tag inside the ADF link component
- Using EL expressions without any tag surrounding them

By using the HTML `i` tag, we were able to load the circle icons to be inside your buttons. We also changed the structure of the link so that the icon appears before the text, not after it.

See also

- You can learn more about Flat UX and the idea behind it at `http://alistapart.com/article/material-honesty-on-the-web`
- You can learn about Twitter-bootstrap from its official website at `http://getbootstrap.com/`
- You can also learn more about font awesome, which can be used without Twitter-bootstrap from its official website at `http://fortawesome.github.io/Font-Awesome/`

6
Enriching User Experience with Visualization Components

The chapter includes the following recipes:

- ▸ Showing metrics with graphs and gauges
- ▸ Putting data on maps
- ▸ Using pivot tables instead of spreadsheets
- ▸ Showing tasks on Gantt charts
- ▸ Presenting the company's hierarchy using the Hierarchy Viewer
- ▸ Presenting historical data using the Timeline component
- ▸ Using sunburst to further show the hierarchical compositions

Introduction

In this chapter, we will address a different business requirement: a dashboard with different data visualization components such as graphs, gauges, and maps. Oracle ADF Faces provides a exhaustive set of data visualization components that cover almost all business needs. These components are called **Oracle Data Visualization** components.

Oracle ADF Data Visualization components provide significant graphical and tabular capabilities to display and analyze data. Any component that belongs to the **ADF Data Visualization Tools** (**DVT**) tag library is prefixed with dvt.

Data visualization components are usually used to create dashboards and views to provide analytical data about a business model. The recipes you are going to create in this chapter will all be created separately, but the output of these recipes will be displayed inside a single dashboard so that at the end of the chapter, you will have a single big dashboard with different components and views.

Also, in this chapter, you will be introduced to more layout components such as springboard, panel dashboard, panel tabbed, and panel splitter. You can find all the recipes of this chapter inside the Chapter 6 folder of the book's Git repository. Make sure you have already created the faceshr database schema in order for your recipes to work without problem.

All the model projects of this chapter's recipes have been created for easy access. We will not talk about how the ViewObject class is created since this book's focus is the features related to ADF Faces.

Showing metrics with graph and gauge components

The graph components are one of the greatest ADF Visualization components since they have more than 50 types of graphs, such as a bar, area, and funnel.

The gauge components are indicator measures to show a single data item (typically a number) that indicates a state represented by a color, for example, acceptable is indicated by green, average by yellow, and dangerous by red. Gauges come in three flavors: dial, status meter (vertical and horizontal), and LED.

In this recipe, you will use two graph components (bar and pie) and one dial gauge component in order to display metrics information about the departments and number of employees and compare this information with percentage of the total number of employees in the company.

In this recipe, the application and its model have been created for you. You can obtain them by cloning the ADFFacesDashboard project from the Git repository (don't forget to change the database connection to suit your needs).

Getting ready

You might need to start a Scout application as we will need to change a couple of styles inside the `hrBlue.scss` file. Make these styles point to the project as we did in the previous chapter.

How to do it...

In order to display graphs and a gauge, perform the following steps:

1. First we will create the task flow with the page fragment.

   1. Open the `ADFFacesDashboard` application.

   2. Create a new task flow inside the `ViewController` project.

   3. Rename the task flow as `employees-graph-flow`.

   4. Add a view inside the newly created task flow with the name `employeesGraphs`, which will hold both graph components.

   5. Double-click on the newly created view activity and create the page fragment under the `fragments` folder.

2. Now we will add the bar graph inside the page fragments:

   1. Open the `employeesGraphs.jsff` page fragment if it's not already opened.

   2. Insert the `panelTabbed` component as the root component of the newly created page fragment.

      The `panelTabbed` component provides a tabbed user interface to separate the views; these views are displayed inside the `showDetailItem` under the `panelTabbed` component.

   3. Change the `Text` attribute inside the first `showDetailItem` component—which was created by default when you inserted the `panelTabbed` component in the previous step—of the `panelTabbed` component to `Bar Graph`.

   4. Drag the `EmployeesCountInDepartments` view object in `HrAppModuleDataControl` from the **Data Control** pane, drop it inside the first `showDetailItem` component, and select the **Graph** option.

5. Select **Bar** from the **Categories** pane and click on **OK** as shown in the following screenshot:

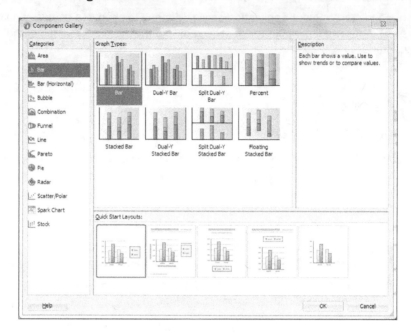

6. Drag-and-drop `EmployeesCount` inside **Bars** and `DepartmentName` inside **X Axis** as shown in the following screenshot:

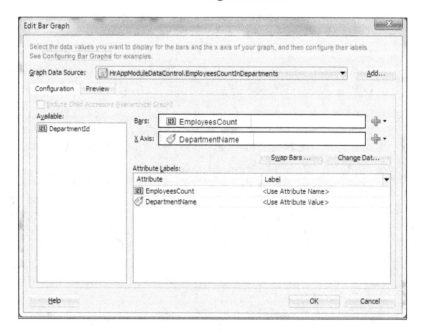

7. Click on **OK** to close the dialog.

8. Change the `threeDEffect` attribute of the graph to `true`, which will present the bar graph in 3D instead of 2D.

9. Change the `animationOnDisplay` attribute to `zoom`, this will make a zoomed animation when the graph is displayed.

10. Right-click on **BarGraph** and navigate to **Insert Inside Bar... | ADF Data Visualizations**.

11. Choose **Marker Text** from the list. This will configure what the marker text of the chart should look like.

12. Click on the **Configure Marker** combobox from the **Properties** pane and select **Y1 Format**.

    As shown in the following screenshot, **Y1 Format** is selected because the bar will be represented on the *y* axis, and we have only one bar to represent:

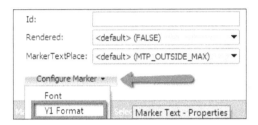

13. Select `dvt:y1Format` from the **Structure** pane and change the `AutoPrecision` attribute to `off`.

This will remove any precision and fractions of the numbers shown when you hover over the bars.

3. Now we have finished the first bar graph. Let's add a pie graph in another tab by performing the following steps:

    1. Right-click on the `panelTabbed` component from the **Structure** pane and navigate to **Insert Inside PanelTabbed... | Show Detail Item**.

    2. Select the new **Show Detail Item** option from the **Structure** pane and change the `Text` attribute to `Pie Graph`.

    3. Drag `EmployeesPercentageInDepartments` in `HrAppModuleDataControl` from the **Data Control** pane, drop it inside the newly created `ShowDetailItem` component, and select **Graph** from the list.

4. Select **Pie** from **Categories** and click on **OK** to close the dialog as shown in the following screenshot:

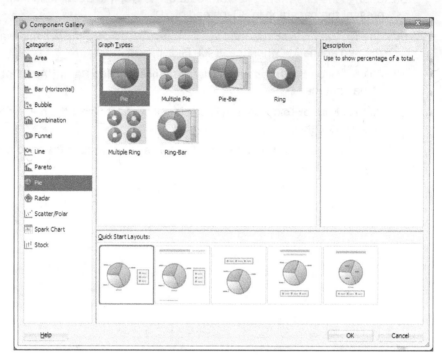

5. Choose the `EmployeesPercentage` attribute as a **Pie** attribute from the combobox.

6. Drag-and-drop the `DepartmentName` attribute inside the **Slices** attribute; you should see something like what is shown in the following screenshot:

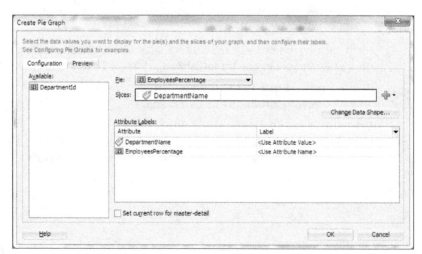

7. Select `dvt:pieGraph` from the **Structure** pane.

8. Change the `ThreeDEffect` attribute to `true` to enable the 3D effect for the pie graph.

9. Change the `animationOnDisplay` attribute to `zoom` to enable a zoomed animation when you first display the graph.

10. Change the `InteractiveSliceBehavior` attribute under the **Appearance** category to `explodeAll` and `explode` by clicking on the gear icon.

    This will make the pie slices explode on click and provide a context menu to explode all slices at once.

11. Expand **PieGraph** from the **Structure** pane and select `dvt:sliceLabel`.

12. Change the `AutoPrecision` attribute to `off`.

This will remove all the fractions and make the numbers integers.

4. We have now finished adding the bar and pie graphs. Let's create a task flow for `gauge` by performing the following steps:

    1. Create a new task flow and name the page fragment `employees-gauge-flow`.

    2. Drag-and-drop a view inside the newly created task flow; name it `employeesGauge`.

    3. Double-click on the view to create it and put it under the `fragments` folder.

    4. Open the `employeesGauge.jsff` page fragment if it's not already opened.

    5. Drag the `EmployeesPercentageInDepartments` view object in `HrAppModuleDataControl` from the **Data Control** pane and drop it under the page fragment by choosing the option **ADF Form**.

    6. Check both the **read-only** and **Row Navigation checkbox** options.

    7. Remove `DepartmentId` and `EmployeesPercentage` from the fields by clicking on the **x** icon.

    8. Click on **OK** to close the dialog.

    9. Expand the `EmployeesPercentageInDepartments` view object from the **Data Control** pane.

    10. Drag the `EmployeesPercentage` attribute from **Gauge** and drop it below the `DepartmentName` field.

11. Select **Dial with Thresholds** and click on **OK** as shown in the following screenshot:

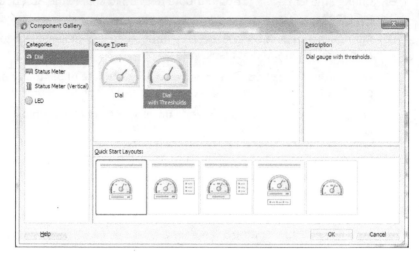

12. Change the `Metric Value` attribute to `EmployeesPercentage`, which should be selected by default.

13. Change `Minimum value` to `0` and `Maximum value` to `100`.

14. Uncheck the **Show Top Label** option.

15. Change the `Threshold` value of `threshold1` to `5` and `threshold2` to `20` as shown in the following screenshot:

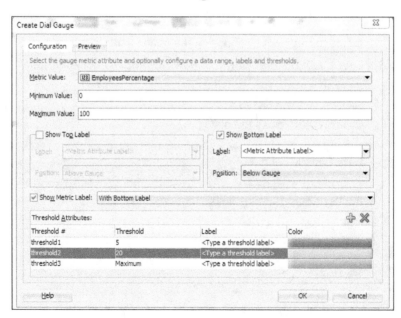

16. Click on **OK** to close the dialog.

17. Change the `AnimationOnDisplay` attribute from **Gauge** to `auto`.

5. We have finished creating the `gauge` component. Let's create the dashboard that will host both the `gauge` and `graph` components by performing the following steps:

    1. Open the `adfc-config.xml` file.

    2. Drag-and-drop a view inside it and name it `employeesDashboard`.

    3. Double-click on the newly created view to create the JSF page and base it on the `defaultHrTemplate` attribute that was created in the previous chapter.

    4. Select the `af:pageTemplate` attribute from the **Structure** pane and change the `leftColumnWidth` attribute to `0px`.

    5. Change the `rightColumnWidth` attribute to `0px`.

    6. Drag a panel springboard component and drop it inside the `Center` facet of the page template.

    7. Change the `DisplayMode` attribute to `Grid`.

    8. Right-click on `af:panelSpringboard`, go to **Insert Inside...**, and select **Show Detail Item**.

    9. Change the `Text` attribute of the newly created `showDetailItem` to `Graphs and Gauges`.

    10. Change the `Icon` attribute to point to the `pie-chart.png` image under the `images` folder using the gear icon. (If prompted to add this image to resources, click on **No**).

    11. Drag `PanelDashboard` from the **Components** palette and drop it inside `showDetailItem` of the panel springboard.

    12. Change the `columns` attribute to `2`.

    13. Change the `RowHeight` attribute to `400px`. If you have a small screen, you might need to change it to `300px`.

    14. Insert two panel boxes under **Panel Dashboard** from the **Components** palette.

    15. Change the `Text` attribute of the first panel box to `Graphs` and the second one to `Gauge`.

    16. Drag the `employees-graph-flow` task flow from the application navigator and drop it inside the first panel box as a **Region**.

    17. Drag the `employees-gauge-flow` task flow from the application navigator and drop it inside the second one as a **Region**.

18. Right-click inside the first panel box and navigate to **Insert Inside | ADF Faces | componentDragSource**.

19. Repeat the previous step for the second panel box.

    The previous two steps will enable both the panel boxes to be draggable inside **Panel Dashboard**.

20. Add the following styles under `hrBlue.scss` to format the springboard to have a color scheme similar to that of the template:

```
af|panelSpringboard {
    background-color: #007b9d;

  &:strip af|panelSpringboard::item:selected {
    background-color: #FFF;
    color: #007b9d;
  }
  &::item{
    background-color: #007b9d;
    color: #FFF;
    height: 110px;
    width: 200px;

    &:selected,&:hover{
        background-color: #FFF;
      color: #007b9d;
    }
  }
  &::item-text{
    color: #FFF;
    width: 180px;

    &:selected{
        background-color: #FFF;
      color: #007b9d;
    }
  }
}
```

21. Add the following lines to tweak some graph properties for it to look better:

```
af|dvt-gauge{   /* for the size of the gauge */
    width:300px;
}

af|dvt-sliceLabel { /* for the pie graph slice */
    -tr-font-size: 13px;
}
af|dvt-legendText { /* for all graph legend text */
    -tr-font-size: 15px;
}
```

```
af|dvt-o1TickLabel { /* for all graphs tick label */
    -tr-font-size: 15px;
}
af|dvt-pieLabel { /* for all pie graph label */
    -tr-font-size: 15px;
}
af|dvt-lowerLabelFrame { /* for the gauge */
    -tr-border-color: #006e8b;
    -tr-background-color: #007b9d;
}
af|dvt-bottomLabel { /* for the gauge */
    -tr-color: #FFF;
    -tr-font-weight: bold;
    -tr-font-size: 13px;
}
af|dvt-metricLabel { /* for all graphs */
    -tr-color: #fff;
}
```

22. Run the `employeesDashboard.jsf` page and see the `graph` and `gauge` components in action as shown in the following screenshot:

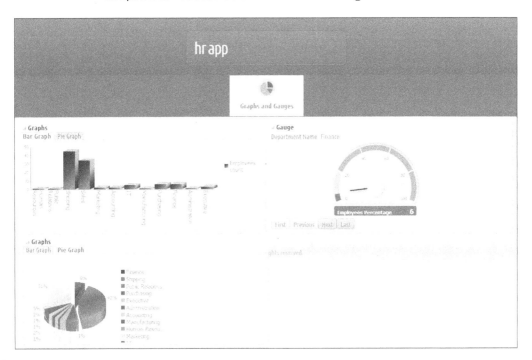

How it works...

In this recipe, you laid down your dashboard and added three visualization components: bar, pie graphs, and a dial gauge.

A bar graph represents data as a series of vertical bars. Using bar graphs, we were able to compare the count of employees as a bar to differentiate between different departments, which are represented on the x axis.

The bar's attribute that you configured when you dragged-and-dropped your data model into the page indicated the number of bars to show. The number of bars can be more than one and hence, you would have y1, y2, ...yn bars, which are all compared against the x axis.

The view object that is used in the recipe shows that the bar graph is a simple query-based view object that calculates the count of employees grouped by departments.

If you look at the page definition of the page fragment, you will see a new binding type called `graph`. This `graph` binding is what represents the graph data noce, which is populated when we configure the graph; this applies to all graph components including pie graphs.

The pie graph represents one group of data as sections of a circle causing the circle to look like a sliced pie. Using the pie graph, we were able to show the relationship between different parts in a single chart, such as the number employees from various departments.

The pie graph only represents a single set of data; that's why you were offered a combobox in the pie graph configuration instead of a multivalue attribute.

Finally, a dial gauge indicates its metric along a configurable arc value axis. Using the dial gauge, you were able to display the number of employees in each department with an indicator represented by a threshold.

A `gauge` component's data is represented by a single number; that's why you won't see any fancy binding under the page definition, just a normal `attributeValues` binding. However, when you combine it with a threshold, it gives you an indication of the state of this number and if it should be larger or smaller.

The view object that is used in the recipe to show the pie graph and the dial gauge is a simple, query-based view object that divides the count of employees over the total number of employees and multiplies it by 100 in order to derive a percentage. Also, the round function gives the output number up to two decimal places instead of having too many fractions, and the percentage is grouped by departments.

In this recipe, your were also introduced to four more layout components: `panelSpringboard`, `panelDashboard`, `panelBox`, and `panelTabbed`. The following list explains these layout components:

- `panelBox` – This is a simple layout component that represents a box with a header that can be disclosed at runtime. Also, it has a toolbar that can be useful to interact with whatever is inside the panel box.

- `panelDashboard` – This component is used to create a dashboard based on the number of columns you define in its attributes and the height of each row. When you put a panel box inside a dashboard, you will see boxes inside of it that look exactly like a dashboard. However, to use the dashboard to its highest capacity, we inserted an `af:componentDragSource` component inside the panel boxes, making them draggable inside the dashboard, which can be used to create personalized dashboards.

- `panelTabbed` – This component is used to present tabs in the user interface, and each tab is represented by a `showDetailItem` component, which can have a text and/or icon to indicate what's inside the tab.

- `panelSpringboard` – This component is used to display a set of icons, either in a grid or strip. It behaves in the same way as `panelTabbed` so that each icon and/or text is represented by a `showDetailItem` component and when the user clicks on an icon, the associated `showDetailItem` component's contents is displayed below the strip.

We styled the `panelSpringboard` component in order to have the same color scheme as our page template. Also, we changed the font size of the graph and gauges so that they look a little bit clearer. You can see that there are new attributes such as `-tr-color`, `-tr-font-weight`, and `-tr-font-size`, which are used to change the default settings of the color, font weight, and font size, respectively, for the DVT components.

See also

To know more about the `graph` and `gauge` components, refer to the official documentation at the following links:

- http://docs.oracle.com/middleware/1212/adf/ADFUI/dv_graph.htm#BABFBGI

- Jhttp://docs.oracle.com/middleware/1212/adf/ADFUI/dv_gauge.htm#BBABADCF

Putting data on maps

There are two map components inside Oracle ADF Data Visualization components—**geographic map** and **thematic map**. The following list explains them:

> ▸ **Geographic map** – This map represents business data in one or more map layers of information (themes) that is tiled on a map. In order to work with a geographic map, you require a connection to a `MapViewer` service and, optionally, a `Geocoder` service.

> ▸ **Thematic map** – This map represents business data as patterns in shapes, areas, and markers. The good thing about a thematic map is that it doesn't require a connection of any kind as its focus is more on the data and not on actual maps.

In this recipe, we will use the `Thematic Map` component to graphically display the number of employees in different regions. The model has been created for you in this recipe, so you can continue from the previous one or open the project directly by cloning the `DataOnMaps` project from the Git repository.

How to do it...

In order to add a thematic map, follow the ensuing steps:

1. Create a new task flow inside the `ViewController` project.
2. Name the task flow `employees-map-flow`.
3. Add a view activity inside the newly created task flow and name it `employeesMap`.
4. Double-click on the newly created activity to create the page fragment and put it in the `fragments` folder.
5. Drag the `EmployeesCountInRegion` view object in `HrAppModuleDataControl` and drop it inside the `employeesMap` page fragment by choosing **Thematic Map...**, as shown in the following screenshot:

6. Choose **World** from the **Base Map** pane, select **World continents** from **Area Layer**, and click on **OK** as shown in the following screenshot:

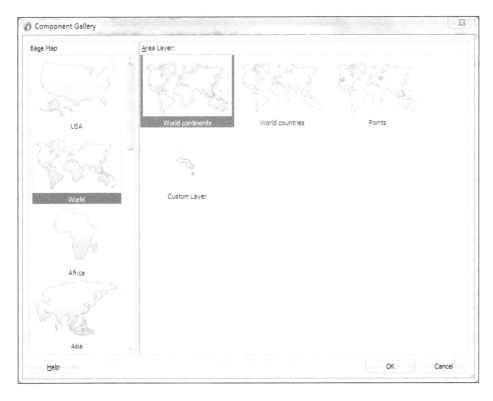

7. In the `Location` field, change the data to `RegionCode` and click on **OK**.

8. Select the `Thematic Map` component from the design mode of the page, expand `Area Layer` and `Area Data Layer`, and click on `Area - a1` and the pencil icon (used for editing), as shown in the following screenshot:

9. Switch to the **Attribute Groups** tab in the dialog box when the page opens.

10. Click on the plus icon, and in the `Group by Value` section, change the value to `NumberOfEmployees`. Do the same for `Legend Label` so that you end up with the arrangement in following screenshot:

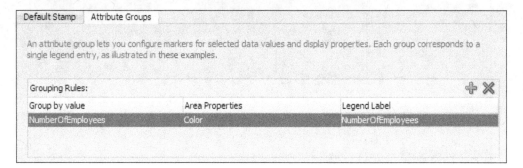

11. Click on **OK** to close the dialog.

12. Expand the `dvt:area` attribute from the **Structure** pane and select `dvt:attributeGroups`.

13. Change the `Label` attribute to `#{row.NumberOfEmployees} Employees`.

    Now you have finished creating the thematic map, let's add it to the dashboard.

14. Open the `employeesDashboard.jsf` page.

15. Select `af:PanelSpringboard` from the **Structure** pane and go to **Insert Inside... | Show Detail Item**.

16. Change the `Text` attribute to `Map`.

17. Change the `Icon` attribute to point to `location.png` under the `images` folder.

18. Drag-and-drop the panel group layout inside the `showDetailItem` component.

19. Change the `Layout` attribute to `vertical`.

20. Change the `Halign` attribute to `center`.

21. Drag the `employees-map-flow` task flow from applications explorer and drop it inside the panel group layout by choosing **Region**.

22. Run the `employeesDashboard.jsf` page and see the map in action, as shown in the following screenshot:

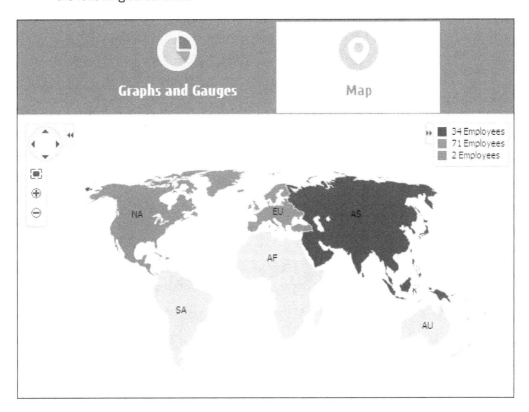

How it works...

Thematic maps display trends or patterns in data associated with a geographic shape. Data is stylized by region. We used the thematic map in this recipe to display different colors on the continent map based on the number of employees as you can see when you run the page.

You can have multiple layers inside your map that can represent data based on color, pattern, or opacity. What we did is made it based on color by adding the attribute group, which refers to the number of employees.

The view object we used to display the map is a simple query-based view object that groups the count of employees based on regions. Since this map can't understand the region's name, we provided the `RegionCode` attribute, which resembles what's written on the map itself.

The thematic maps represent a normal tree binding just like tables and trees because they deal with a tabular data form and all extra information is configured inside the `map` component itself.

Thematic maps can be very powerful. Think about a thematic map that represents a car instead of a world map, and instead of having a color layer we have a pattern. This pattern can then be used to display accidents' locations. The sky is the limit when it comes to using the thematic map.

See also

To know more about geographical and thematic maps, refer to the official documentation at `http://docs.oracle.com/middleware/1212/adf/ADFUI/dv_map.htm#CEGBGCEC`.

Using pivot tables instead of spreadsheets

Pivot tables are tables on "steroids" that can display data in a grid layout with unlimited layers of row header cells and column header cells that are hierarchically nested. Also, they can have a drilling down functionality to drill down on different groups. Similar to spreadsheets, pivot tables provide options to automatically generate subtotals and totals for the grouped data.

In this recipe, we will use the `PivotTable` and `pivotFilterBar` components to display and filter the number of employees by drilling into different regions, countries, cities, and departments with totals and subtotals. We will also get to know about a new layout component, `panelSplitter`.

In this recipe, the model has been created for you; you can continue from the previous recipe or you can open the project directly by cloning the `PivotTable` project from the Git repository.

How to do it...

In order to add a pivot table, follow the ensuing steps:

1. Create a new task flow inside the `ViewController` project.
2. Name the new task flow `employees-pivot-flow`.
3. Create a view activity inside the newly created task flow and name it `employeesPivot`.

4. Double-click on it to create the page fragment and place it inside the `fragments` folder.

5. Drag the `panelSplitter` component from the **Components** palette and drop it as the root component for the page fragment.

6. Select `af:panelSplitter` from the **Structure** pane.

7. Change the `Orientation` attribute to `Vertical`.

8. Change the `SplitterPosition` attribute to `50`.

9. Drag the `EmployeesCountInDepartment1` view object in `HrAppModuleDataControl` from the **Data Control** pane, drop it inside the `second` facet of the panel splitter, and save it as a pivot table by navigating to **Table / List View | ADF Pivot Table**.

10. Drag `NumberOfEmployees` inside the **Data Labels** pane.

11. Put the other attributes in the following order into the left column:

    1. `RegionName`
    2. `Country Name`
    3. `City`
    4. `DepartmentName`

12. If you did everything right, you should see something like what is shown in the following screenshot:

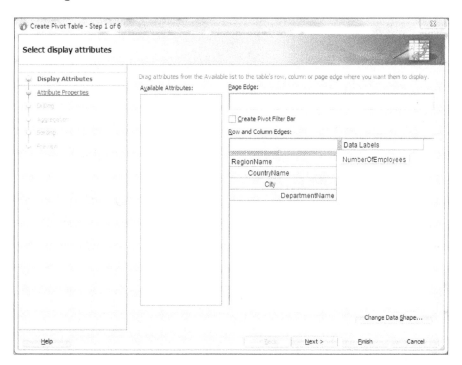

13. Click on **Next**.

14. Leave everything unchanged in the second step of creating the pivot table and click on **Next**.

15. Select the **Insert Drilling** radio button and enable all the drill paths as shown in the following screenshot:

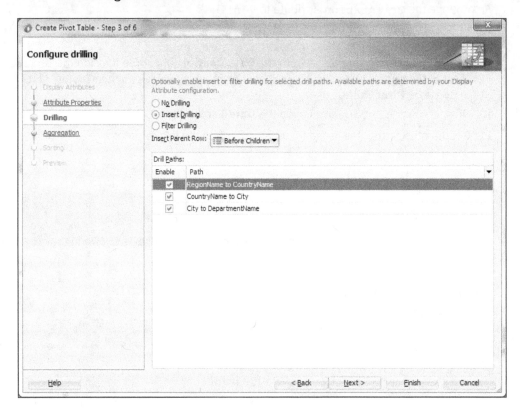

16. Click on **Next**.

17. Switch to the **Category Total** tab.

18. Click on the plus icon and change the `Attribute` value to `RegionName`.

19. Change the `Insert Total` attribute to `After`.

20. Change the `Total Label` value to `Total`.

21. Repeat the last three steps to add the `CountryName`, `City`, and `DepartmentName` attributes. You should see something similar to what is shown in the following screenshot:

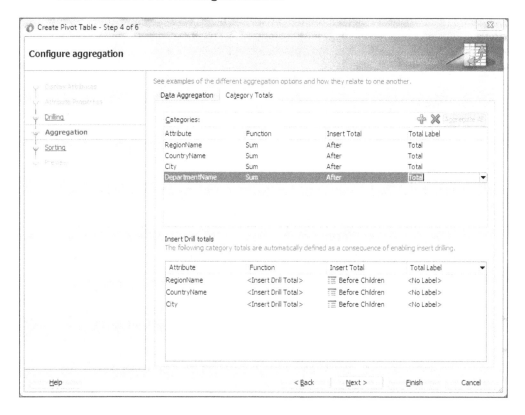

22. Click on **Finish** to close the dialog box.

23. Drag-and-drop `pivotFilterBar` from the **Components** palette to the `second` facet of the panel splitter above the pivot table. You will see a warning that says the second facet contains too many components.

> You can find the `pivotFilterBar` component by navigating to **ADF Data Visualization** | **Other Type-specific Child Tags** | **Pivot Table**, or you can directly search for `pivotFilterBar` from the **Components** palette.

24. Drag-and-drop the `af:pivotFilterBar` component from the second facet to the `first` facet.

 This is a small trick in order for JDeveloper to automatically provide the same bindings for the `pivotFilterBar` component as those for a pivot table. If you put it directly into the `first` facet, the bindings will not be populated automatically.

25. Save everything.

Now that you have finished creating the pivot table, it's time to put it inside the dashboard.

26. Open the `employeesDashboard.jsf` page.

27. Add another `ShowDetailItem` component under the panel springboard.

28. Change the `Text` attribute to `Pivot Table`.

29. Change the `Icon` attribute to point to the `trends.png` image.

30. Drag-and-drop the `employees-pivot-flow` task flow as a region under the `showDetailItem` component.

 There is a small bug in JDeveloper 12.1.2.0, bug number 17794508, which prevents the pivot table from being displayed properly under the panel springboard. This problem is addressed in the next releases and there is a good chance that you might not see it when the book is out, but if you have, you can create a small testing page to see the pivot table in action.

31. Run the `employeesDashboard.jsf` page to see the pivot table in action as shown in the following screenshot:

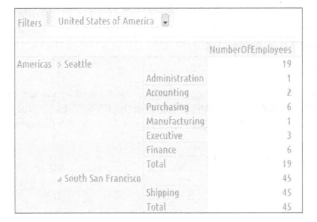

How it works...

In this recipe, we used the `PivotTable` component to show the totals of the various attributes related to employees based on different groupings. We also used a `pivotFilterBar` component to filter and change the display of the table.

As you saw, the configuration of the pivot table is too much for a tree binding. That's why there is another binding called the pivot binding, which you will find when you open your page definition. This binding has all the settings that you configured when you configured the pivot table.

The view object that has the data is a simple query that displays the number of employees grouped by `DepartmentName`, `City`, `Country Name`, and `Region Name`.

The `pivotFilterBar` component is a great component to showcase the filtering power of pivot tables. The `pivotFilterBar` component uses the same binding value as that of the pivot table; however, instead of pointing to `pivotTableModel` like the pivot table does, it points to `pivotFilterBarModel`. That's why we directly dragged-and-dropped the `pivotFilterBar` component at the top of the pivot table for this binding to be added automatically by JDeveloper.

You can also export `pivotTableData` to Excel just like you do with tables, but instead of using `af:exportCollectionActionListener`, use `dvt:exportPivotTableData` as shown in the following code snippet:

```
<af:button text="Export Pivot" partialSubmit="false" id="b1">
    <dvt:exportPivotTableData exportedId="pt2" exportedData="all"
type="excelHTML" filename="pivotData.xls" title="pivotTable data"/>
</af:button>
```

By replacing `pt2` with the pivot table ID, you get the choice to either export all of the data or a selected record by changing `exportedData` attribute to `selected` instead of `all`.

In this recipe, we also saw `panelSplitter` in action. The `panelSplitter` component is one of the stretching components that lets you create two panes separated by a splitter that can be resized at runtime. Each splitter component has two facets, `first` and `second`, which correspond to the first and second panel. Child components can reside inside the facets only. You can also create more than two panes by nesting the `panelSplitter` components.

See also

To learn more about the pivot table, refer to the official documentation at `http://docs.oracle.com/middleware/1212/adf/ADFUI/dv_crosstab.htm#BAJCIFJF`.

Showing tasks on Gantt charts

The `GanttChart` component presents a Gantt representation with three flavors—project, resource utilization, and scheduling. The following list explains them:

- **Project Gantt chart** – This component's main purpose is to show tasks and phases in a way similar to that in Microsoft Project

- **Resource utilization Gantt chart** – This component's main purpose is to show resource utilization instead of focusing on a task's progress

- **Scheduling Gantt chart** – This component's main purpose is to show schedules and resource activities similar to those in a calendar

 Another component that can display activities but has a different look is the ADF Calendar component. The Calendar component displays activities in daily, weekly, monthly, or list views for a given provider or providers (a provider is the owner of an activity).

All three flavors look similar, but have different models "behind the scenes". All of the Gantt charts are composed of two regions, a table and chart data, which can be resized based on a time scale, and both regions have a horizontal scroll bar.

In this recipe, you will use the project Gantt chart component to display employees' tasks. Again, in this recipe, the model has been created for you. You can continue from the previous recipe or you can open the project directly by cloning the `GanttChart` project from the Git repository.

How to do it...

In order to add a Gantt chart, follow the ensuing steps:

1. Create a new task flow inside the `ViewController` project.

2. Name the task flow `employees-tasks-gantt-flow`.

3. Drag-and-drop a view activity inside the task flow and name it `employeesGantt`.

4. Double-click on the view activity to create the page fragment and put it under the `fragments` folder.

5. Drag `EmployeeTasksView` in `HrAppModuleDataControl` from the **Data Control** pane, drop it inside the page fragment root, and save it as a project by navigating to **Gantt | Project**.

6. Change mappings as shown in the following table (also click on **Show more...** for the last two mappings):

Gantt Chart Field	Model Mapping
Task Id	TaskId
Start Time	StartDate
Task Type	TaskType
End Time	EndDate
% Complete	Percentage
Critical	CriticalBoolean

7. Remove all attributes from **Table Columns** except for the `Label` attribute. You should end up with what you see in the following screenshot:

8. Switch to the **SubTasks** tab.

9. Select `TasksView` from the **SubTasks Accessor** option.

10. Make the same mappings as shown in the table under step 6.

11. Switch to the **Appearance** tab.

12. Select the label `LastName`. This will show the last name along with the Gantt chart data.

13. Click on **OK** to close the dialog.

14. Select the Gantt chart from the **Structure** pane.

15. Change the `styleClass` attribute to `AFStretchWidth`. This will stretch the component to a width of 100 percent.

    Now that you have finished creating the Gantt chart, let's add it to the dashboard.

16. Open the `employeesDashboard.jsf` page.

17. Add a new `showDetailItem` component under the springboard component.

18. Change the `Text` attribute to `Gantt chart`.

19. Change the `Icon` attribute to point to the `check.png` image under the `images` folder.

20. Drag-and-drop `employees-tasks-gantt-flow` under the `showDetailItem` component.

21. Run the `employeesDashboard.jsf` page to see the Gantt chart in action as shown in the following screenshot:

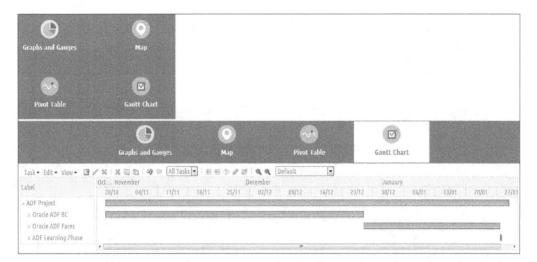

How it works...

In this recipe, the view object that our data is based on is a recursive table, which is represented by view links and has information about tasks and subtasks with details such as start and end dates with completion percentage and task type.

The Gantt chart has specific bindings called `Gantt` that provide all the mappings between Gantt data and view object data; it also provides more information about dependent tasks, split tasks, and subtasks.

See also

To know more about Gantt charts, check the official documentation at `http://docs.oracle.com/middleware/1212/adf/ADFUI/dv_gantt.htm#BABJJCJG`.

Presenting the company's hierarchy using the Hierarchy Viewer

The `HierarchyViewer` component is used to graphically display trees and hierarchical data, which usually comes from a master-details relationship, in a beautiful graphical representation. Each row is represented by a shape (node) that can be configured in order to display multiple attributes and utilized to view many attributes using the panel cards layout component. In this recipe, you will use the `HierarchyViewer` component to display an organization chart of employees.

Also, in this recipe, the model has been created for you; you can continue from the previous recipe or you can open the project directly by cloning the `HierarchyViewer` project from the Git repository.

How to do it...

In order to add the hierarchy viewer, follow the ensuing steps:

1. Create a new task flow inside the `ViewController` project.
2. Name the task flow `employees-organization-chart-flow`.
3. Add a view activity under the task flow and name it `employeesHierarchy`.
4. Double-click on it to create the page fragment and put it under the `fragments` folder.

5. Drag `EmployeesView1` in `HrAppModuleDataControl` from the **Data Control** pane and drop it inside the page fragment root by choosing **Hierarchy Viewer**.

6. Choose **Vertical Top Down** from the list of types and click on **OK** as shown in the following screenshot:

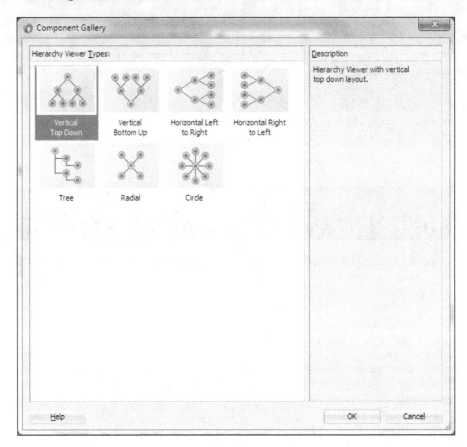

7. Change the `Image`, `FirstName`, `LastName` component's attributes to be only output text and the rest to be **ADF Output Text w/Label** from the **Node** area.

8. Check the `EmployeesView` option under **Descendants**.

9. Make order arrangements so that you end up with what is shown in the following screenshot:

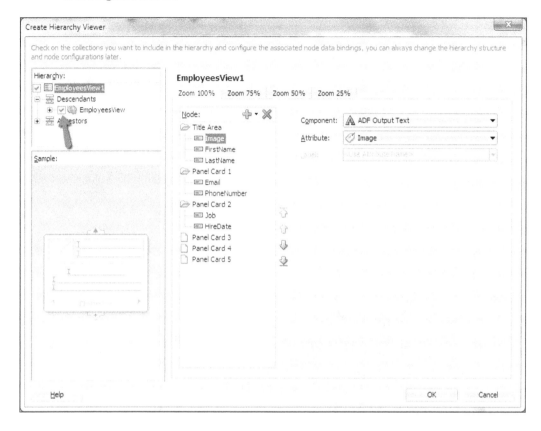

10. Remove the last three panel cards (**Panel Card 3**, **Panel Card 4**, and **Panel Card 5**).

11. Change the `Text` attribute of **Panel Card 1** to `Contact information`.

12. Change the `Text` attribute of **Panel Card 2** to `Job information`.

13. Click on **OK** to save and close the dialog.

14. Open the **Structure** pane and navigate to **dvt:hierarchyViewer | dvt:node | f:facet zoom100 | af:panelGroupLayout**.

15. Right-click on `af:outputText - #{node.Image }` and navigate to **Convert to...| Image**.

16. Click on **OK** when a dialog pops up.

17. Click on the gear icon besides the `Source` attribute and select **Expression Builder**.

18. Add the expression `/images/#{node.Image}` and click on **OK**.

19. Change the panel group layout that surrounds the `Image`, `FirstName`, and `LastName` layout attributes to `Horizontal`.

    Now that we have finished the hierarchy viewer, let's add it to the dashboard.

20. Open the `employeesDashboard.jsf` page.

21. Add a new `showDetailItem` component under the springboard component.

22. Change the `Text` attribute to `Organization Chart`.

23. Change the `Icon` attribute to point to the `stack.png` image under the `images` folder.

24. Drag `employees-organization-chart-flow` task flow from the application navigator and drop it inside the `showDetailItem` component.

25. Run the `employeesDashboard.jsf` page to see the hierarchy viewer in action as shown in the following screenshot:

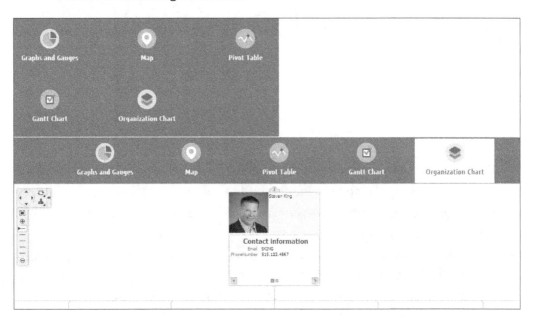

How it works...

A hierarchy viewer visually displays hierarchical data and the master-details relationships; that's why the bindings of the hierarchy viewer are the same as the tree binding because it displays master-details data.

The view object behind it is the default view object of the `Employees` table with a recursive view link to provide the master-details relationship between managers and employees.

The `HierarchyViewer` component is a great visual component that provides a range of features for end users, such as panning, zooming, and changing the layout view. It also provides a range of presentation features, such as changing node shape, lines, and labels.

Inside a single node of the hierarchical node, you can have panel cards that hold different sets of information for the nodes, which the hierarchy viewer component references. The panel card is an area inside the node element that behaves the same way as `panelTabbed` and contains one or more `showDetailItem` components. Each of the `showDetailItem` elements references a set of content. In our recipe, the `HierarchyViewer` component renders the organization chart and has contact and job information, which can be utilized using panel cards.

See also

To find out more about hierarchy viewer, refer to the official documentation at `http://docs.oracle.com/middleware/1212/adf/ADFUI/dv_hviewer.htm#BGBEDIDI`.

Presenting historical data using the Timeline component

The `Timeline` component has been newly introduced to ADF 12c; it presents interactive visualization across a date range that you can move forward or backward along the data timeline. Events (rows) are presented as nodes with lines across the data range similar to the nodes in the `HierarchyViewer` component, which can have images, links, and more.

In this recipe, we will add a timeline component to display the employees' hire history based on the hire date. Also, in this recipe, the model has been created for you; you can continue from the previous recipe or you can open the project directly by cloning the `Timeline` project from the Git repository.

How to do it...

In order to add the `Timeline` component, follow the ensuing steps:

1. Create a new task flow inside the `ViewController` project.
2. Name the task flow `employees-timeline-flow`.
3. Drag-and-drop a view activity inside the task flow and name it `employeesTimeline`.
4. Double-click on the view activity to create the page fragment and add it to the `fragments` folder.
5. Drag `EmployeesView1` in `HrAppModuleDataControl` and drop it inside the page fragment by choosing **Timeline**.
6. Choose `HireDate` as `Item Data Value`, which should be selected by.default.
7. Change the `Image` attribute to `/images/#{evt.Image}`.
8. Add the `FirstName`, `LastName`, and `Image` attributes as **OutputText**; you should end up with what is shown in the following screenshot:

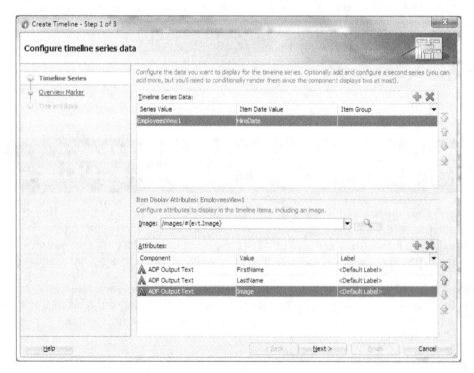

9. Click on **Next**.
10. Leave everything as default in the **Overview Marker** section (**Create Timeline - Step 2 of 3**) and click on the **Next** button.

11. Change the `start time` attribute to `2001-01-01`.

12. Click on **Finish** to close the dialog.

13. Select `dvt:timeline` from the **Structure** pane.

14. Change the `styleClass` attribute to `AFStretchWidth` under the **Styles** category.

15. Expand `dvt:timeline` and navigate to **dvt:timelineSeries | dvt:timelineItem | af:panelGroupLayout | af:panelGroupLayout**.

16. Remove the `af:outputText` component with `#{evt.Image}` as its value.

    Now that we have finished creating the `Timeline` component, let's add it to the dashboard.

17. Open the `employeesDashboard.jsf` page.

18. Add a new `showDetailItem` component under the springboard component.

19. Change the `Text` attribute to `Timeline`.

20. Change the `Icon` attribute to point to the `shoeprints.png` image under the `images` folder.

21. Drag `employees-timeline-flow` from the application navigator and drop it inside the `showDetailItem` component by choosing **Region**.

22. Run the `employeesDashboard.jsf` page to see the timeline in action as shown in the following screenshot:

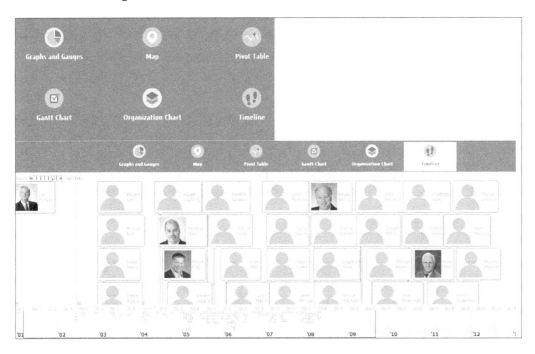

How it works...

The `Timeline` component is a simple component that displays events as timeline items along the time axis. In this recipe, we used the default `Employees` view object to show employees' hiring history in the `Timeline` component. When you drag-and-drop the view object as a timeline, you end up with a tree binding just like a hierarchy viewer and tables.

If you explore the `Timeline` component, you will realize it has a timeline series. This series has to be based on a collection model from a tree binding. Inside the timeline series, you will see a `Timeline` item, which has to be based on a `Date` value. Inside the `Timeline` item, the structure of the node is laid to view the timeline. Usually, this structure can be `PanelGroupLayout` or you can use the panel card, like in hierarchy viewer.

The `Timeline` component can be extended to have two series—a dual timeline—used to compare two series of events.

See also

To know more about the `Timeline` component, check the official documentation at `http://docs.oracle.com/middleware/1212/adf/ADFUI/dv_timeline.htm#CHDBGDJJ`.

Using sunburst to further show the hierarchical compositions

The `sunburst` and `treemaps` components are used to display quantitative hierarchical data across two dimensions, represented visually by size and color. The `treemaps` and `sunbursts` components use a shape called a **node** to reference the data in the hierarchy.

The `treemaps` and `sunburst` components are very similar when it comes to a model with small differences; so in this recipe, we will use the `sunburst` component to display the number of employees in different regions and departments based on color.

In this recipe, the model has been created for you; you can continue from the previous recipe or you can open the project directly by cloning the `Sunburst` project from the Git repository.

How to do it...

In order to use sunburst to further show hierarchical compositions, perform the following steps:

1. Create a new task flow inside the `ViewController` project.
2. Name the task flow `employees-sunburst-flow`.

3. Drag-and-drop a view activity inside the task flow and name it `employeesSunburst`.
4. Double-click on the view activity to create the page fragment and add it to the `fragments` folder.
5. Drag `EmployeesCountInRegions` in `HrAppModuleDataControl` and drop it inside the fragment by choosing **Sunburst**.
6. In the hierarchy on the top-left corner, click on the `EmployeesCountInDepartments` option.
7. Select `EmployeesCountInRegions` from the hierarchy, change the `Value` attribute to `NumberOfEmployees`, and the `Label` attribute to `RegionName`.
8. Add a grouping rule with `NumberOfEmployees` as **Group by Value**.
9. Select `EmployeesCountInDepartments` from the hierarchy and change the `Value` attribute to `EmployeesCount` and the `Label` attribute to `DepartmentName`.
10. Add the grouping rule with `EmployeesCount` as `Group by Value`.
    You should end up with what is shown in the following screenshot:

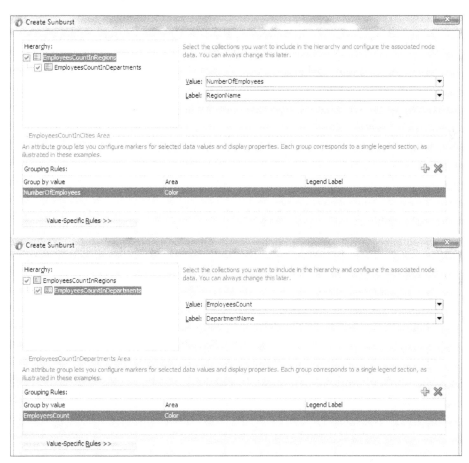

11. Click on **OK** to save and close the dialog.

12. Select `dvt:sunburst` from the **Structure** pane.

13. Change the `DisplayLevelChildren` attribute to `0`, which will make everything collapse when the sunburst graph first shows up.

14. Change `colorLabel` to `Number of Employees`.

15. Change the `legendSource` attribute to `ag1`. This is the `ID` attribute of the `dvt:attributeGroups` component; you can locate it by navigating to **dvt:sunburst | af:switcher | f:facet – EmployeesCountInRegions0 | dvt:sunburstNode | dvt:attributeGroup** from the **Structure** pane.

16. Change the `AnimationOnDisplay` attribute to `fan`, which will provide a fan animation when the graph first shows up.

17. Change the `styleClass` attribute to `AFStretchWidth`.

18. Navigate to **af:switcher | f:facet EmployeesCountInRegions0 | dvt:sunburstNode**.

19. Change the `shortDesc` attribute to `#{row.RegionName}: #{row. NumberOfEmployees} Employees`. This will create a beautiful display when you hover over slices in the sunburst at runtime.

20. The `insert` attribute will ensure provision of the details of the current node when you hover over the edge of the slice.

21. Expand the `dvt:sunburstNode` component and select `dvt:attributeGroup`.

22. Change the `attributeType` attribute to `continuous`.

23. Change the `MinValue` attribute to `1`.

24. Change the `MaxValue` attribute to `100`. By our defining these two values as `continuous`, the sunburst will know how to lay down different colors based on the numbers.

25. Change the `MinLabel` attribute to `Zero`.

26. Change the `MaxLabel` attribute to `1 Hundred`.

27. From the **Structure** pane, expand `f:facet EmployeesCountInRegions1` and select `dvt:sunburstNode`.

28. Change the `shortDesc` attribute to `#{row.DepartmentName}: #{row. EmployeesCount} Employees`. This will create a good display when you hover over slices in the sunburst at runtime.

29. Expand the `dvt:sunburstNode` component and select `dvt:attributeGroup`.

30. Change the `attributeType` attribute to `continuous`.

31. Change the `MinValue` attribute to `1`.

32. Change the `MaxValue` attribute to `50`. By our defining these two values as `continuous`, the sunburst will know how to lay down different colors based on the numbers.

    Now that we have finished creating the sunburst, let's add it to the dashboard.

33. Open the `employeesDashboard.jsf` page.

34. Add a new `showDetailItem` component under the springboard component.

35. Change the `Text` attribute to `Sunburst`.

36. Change the `Icon` attribute to `rainbow.png` under the `images` folder.

37. Drag the `employees-sunburst-flow` task flow from the application navigator and drop it inside the `showDetailItem` component as **Region**.

38. Run the `employeesDashboard.jsf` page to see the sunburst in action as shown in the following screenshot:

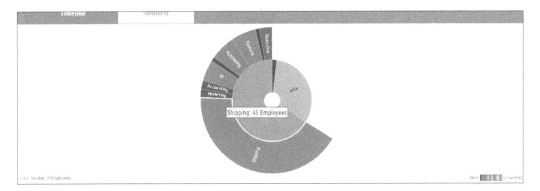

How it works...

Sunbursts display the nodes in slices much like pie charts, while `TreeMap` displays them in a rectangle-like shape. You drill down as you get away from the central circle.

When you explore the page definition, you will find that the sunburst has the same bindings as those in `Tree`, which provides master-details, and its `treeModel` component is used inside the `Value` attribute to lay down the different hierarchical data.

Note that inside the `sunburst` component structure, you have a switcher with facets equal to the number of levels the sunburst has. Inside each switcher, there is a `dvt:sunburstNode` component that has the `value` and `label` attributes, which you specified when you configured the `sunburst` component. Inside of `dvt:sunburstNode`, you can find an `attributeGroups` just like the one you saw in thematic map component, which behaves the same way. You can control the colors of the generated sunburst by adding multiple `f:attribute` components with names equal to `color1`, `color2`, and `color3`, and values equals to the hash code of the colors without the # symbol.

The difference between sunbursts and tree maps is that sunbursts can show hierarchical structure by enabling drilling unlike tree maps, which show only two metrics of data. Both of them can be used to display thousands of data rows in a small graph area, which is great to identify interesting patterns.

See also

To know more about the `sunburst` and `treeMap` components, refer to the official documentation at `http://docs.oracle.com/middleware/1212/adf/ADFUI/dv_treemap.htm#BEHHDEAF`.

7
Handling Events and Partial Page Rendering

In this chapter, we will cover the following topics:

- ▸ Using partial triggers
- ▸ Using ADF Faces server events
- ▸ Using ADF Faces client events
- ▸ Sending custom events from a client to a server
- ▸ Executing JavaScript within an event response
- ▸ Using the `scrollComponentIntoViewBehavior` tag
- ▸ Using the `target` tag to execute **Partial Page Rendering** (**PPR**)
- ▸ Using partial page navigation
- ▸ Adding drag-and-drop capabilities
- ▸ Using polling events to update pages
- ▸ Using ADF Faces **Active Data Service** (**ADS**)
- ▸ Using WebSockets for building a more interactive application

Introduction

Typical JSF applications handle events on the server. JSF event handling is based on the JavaBeans event model, where event classes and event listener interfaces are used by the JSF application to handle events generated by components. This includes clicking on a button or link, selecting an item from a list, or changing a value in an input field.

When a user clicks on a button, the button component creates an event object that stores information about the event and identifies the component that generated the event. This event then gets added to an event queue in which it gets executed at the appropriate time in the JSF life cycle.

But before talking about events, we need to first understand how different scopes are handled in Oracle ADF Faces.

Imagine that you have a bounded task flow with one of the page fragments containing a region and two instances of a declarative component (more about declarative components in *Chapter 9, Building Your Application for Reuse*). The following diagram represents the scopes available and their life span:

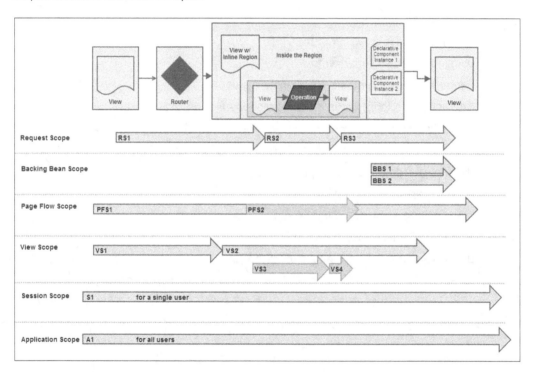

You can notice that there are three additional scopes that didn't exist in JSF. To understand the different scopes, refer to the following table:

Scope Name	Life span	Description
Request scope	This scope starts with an event that is triggered in Page A and gets destroyed once Page B is rendered. It is active during the transition from A to B.	The Request scope exists between two pages to deliver a state; once it reaches the second page, it gets destroyed and a new request is instantiated. This scope is part of JSF.
Backing Bean scope	In this scope, the event is triggered by Page A for a specific region or declarative component and gets destroyed once Page B is rendered.	This acts exactly like the Request scope. The main difference is that for different instances of regions/declarative components, separate instances of the Backing Bean scope and managed beans are created. This scope is part of ADF Faces.
Page Flow scope	This scope's life spans throughout a single task flow's lifetime.	Any managed bean that lives inside the Page Flow scope can live throughout the whole task flow, even if the task flow has more than two pages / page fragments. This scope is part of ADF Faces.
View scope	This scope's life spans until the View ID of the current view activity changes.	This is typically used to hold values that are important for a given page, while Request scope is used between two Views. The View scope will be lost once View ID changes. This scope is part of ADF Faces.
Session scope	This scope lives throughout the user session.	This is typically used to store user-related information. This scope is part of JSF.
Application scope	This scope lives through all user sessions and only gets destroyed when the application is down or undeployed.	This is typically used for application-wide variables such as application preferences. This scope is part of JSF.

Understanding scopes is essential to understand how different events live inside the ADF and JSF life cycles. In JSF, you can register an event listener, which then tells the component to broadcast the event to the corresponding listener and invokes the `listener` method that processes the event. This listener method can trigger a change in the user interface, invoke the backend application code, or do both.

ADF Faces's navigation components such as JSF components deliver the `ActionEvent` event when the components are activated, and ADF Faces's input and select components deliver the `ValueChangeEvent` event when the components' local values change.

While ADF Faces follows the standard JSF event-handling techniques, it also enhances event handling in two key ways by providing the Ajax-based functionality in the form of **Partial Page Rendering** (PPR) and a client-side event model.

In this chapter, we will get to know how ADF Faces handle PPR and server- and client-side events. We will also learn how to use some of the interesting tags such as `scrollComponentIntoViewBehavior` and `target`, and learn some great techniques for synchronous and asynchronous page updates.

You can find all the recipes of this chapter inside the `Chapter 7` folder of the book's Git repository. If you haven't already created the `faceshr` database schema, make sure you create it for your recipes to work without problem.

Using partial triggers

In order to provide a dynamic and responsive web application and make changes from the server side to the client side, a technique emerged back in 2007 called **Ajax** that is still being used up to this moment.

In ADF Faces, Ajax is implemented under a different umbrella called PPR. During PPR, the JSF page's life cycle is run only for certain components in the page and doesn't submit the whole page. The best part about it is that you can use PPR declaratively without the need for a single line of code.

In this recipe, we will create two cascading `selectOneChoice` options, which represent regions and countries respectively; when you change the region, the countries get filtered based on the region selected.

The model of this application has been created for you. You can open it by cloning the `ADFFacesPartialTriggers` application from the Git repository.

How to do it...

To learn how to use PPR, follow the ensuing steps:

1. Open the `ADFFacesPartialTriggers` application.
2. Double-click on the `adfc-config.xml` file to open it.
3. Drag a `View` attribute from the **Components** palette and drop it inside the **Diagram** mode of the `adfc-config` attribute.
4. Name the view `partialTriggers`.

5. Double-click on the **View** option to create the page and choose **Default Hr Template** as the page layout.

6. Drag a panel form layout from the **Components** palette and drop it inside the Center facet of **Page Template**.

7. Go to **Chapter7DataControl | RegionView1** and drag **RegionView1** from the **Data Control** pane and drop it inside the panel form layout by navigating to **Single Selection | ADF Select OneChoice**.

8. Select **RegionName** as a display attribute and click on **OK**.

9. Select the component from the **Structure** pane and set the AutoSubmit attribute to true.

   The previous attribute will make sure that when the value changes, it automatically submits the attribute and doesn't wait to submit the whole form.

10. Drag **CountriesView2** by navigating to **Chapter7DataControl | RegionView1** from **Data Control Pane** and drop it inside the panel form layout by navigating to **Single Selection | ADF Select OneChoice**.

11. Select **CountryName** as a display attribute and click on **OK**.

12. Select the component from the **Structure** pane and set PartialTriggers to point to the selectOneChoice component of **RegionName** that we created in step 7, like the following screenshot:

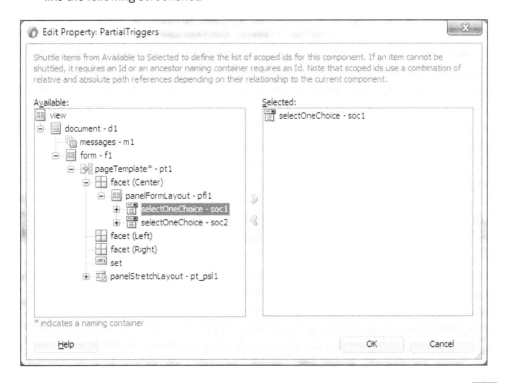

13. Save everything and run the `partialTriggers.jsf` page, and change **RegionName** to see how the names of the countries change, as shown in the following screenshot:

RegionName	Europe	▼		RegionName	Americas	▼
CountryName	Belgium	▼		CountryName	Argentina	▼

How it works...

In this recipe, we saw how to use PPR. We made sure that whenever the user selects a region from the first `selectOneChoice`, it updates the countries' values in the second `selectOneChoice`.

By changing `autoSubmit` to `true`, we made sure that the value of the region is sent back to the model so that the master-detail relationship can then filter the countries based on the region selected.

However, doing this alone won't update the countries' `selectOneChoice`, since we still need to tell the countries' `selectOneChoice` component to listen to any change that occurs in the region's `selectOneChoice`.

In order for the countries' `selectOneChoice` to see the new values from the model, we used the `partialTriggers` attribute and then pointed it to the region's `SelectOneChoice`.

If you don't want the `partialTriggers` attribute to always refer to a component, you can do it on demand programmatically from the value change listener of the region's `selectOneChoice`, as shown in the following code:

```
AdfFacesContext adfFacesContext = AdfFacesContext.
getCurrentInstance();
adfFacesContext.addPartialTarget(_countriesSelectOneChoice);
```

You still need to have a reference to the component at the server side by binding it, using the `bindings` attribute or locating it by the name using `UIViewRoot`.

Using ADF Faces server events

ADF Faces provides a huge list of server events that you can use with ADF Faces components, events such as `ActionEvent` with all navigation components, `DisclosureEvent` with tabs and accordion disclosure, `PollEvent` with poll components on each tick, `SelectionEvent` with tables, `TreeTable` with tree selections, `ValueChangeEvent` with input's value change, and more.

You can see all events from the events table in the official documentation at `http://docs.oracle.com/middleware/1212/adf/ADFUI/af_event.htm#BABHEEJJ`.

This recipe will register two listeners to listen to `ActionEvent` and `ValueChangeEvent`, and to track changes of the `Input Text` and change the `Text` attribute of a `Button`.

You can refer to the last recipe, or you can also grab this project's recipe by cloning the `ADFFacesServerEvents` application from the Git repository.

How to do it...

To learn how to use ADF Faces server events, follow the ensuing steps:

1. Open the `adfc-config.xml` file.
2. Drag `View` from the **Components** palette and drop it inside the **Diagram** mode of the `adfc-config` file.
3. Name the `View` events.
4. Double-click on `View` to create it, and choose **Default Hr Template** as the page layout.
5. Go to **Chapter7DataControl**, drag `EmployeesView1`, and drop it inside the center facet of the page template as **ADF Form**.
6. Remove all fields except for `FirstName` and `LastName`.
7. Check the **Row Navigation** and **Submit** checkboxes options and click on **OK**.
8. Select `FirstNameinputText` from the **Structure** pane.
9. Click on the gear icon beside the `ValueChangeListener` attribute and click on **Edit**.
10. Click on the **New** button beside the **Managed Bean** field.
11. Change the `Bean Name` to `eventsBean`.
12. Change the `Class Name` to `EventsBean`.
13. Change the `Package Name` to `com.adffaces.chapter7.view.beans`.
14. Leave the rest as default and click on **OK**.
15. Click on the **New** button beside the `Method` field.
16. Change the **Method Name** to `changeFirstName` and click on **OK**.

17. Open the `EventsBean` Java class and add the following code under the `changeFirstName` method:

```
System.out.println("First Name Changed from: " + valueChangeEvent.
getOldValue() + " to: " + valueChangeEvent.getNewValue());
```

> Using `System.out.println` is not a best practice and not recommended. It's used here for elaboration purposes; a better way is to use ADFLogger, which provides all the capabilities needed for logging. To learn how to use ADFLogger, refer to the series of articles at `https://blogs.oracle.com/groundside/entry/adventures_in_adf_logging_part`.

18. Open the `events.jsf` page again and select the **Submit** button from the **Structure** pane (located inside **footer Facet | Panel Group Layout**).

19. Change the `PartialTriggers` attribute to point to the **Submit** button (Reference: the PartialTrigger of the button to itself).

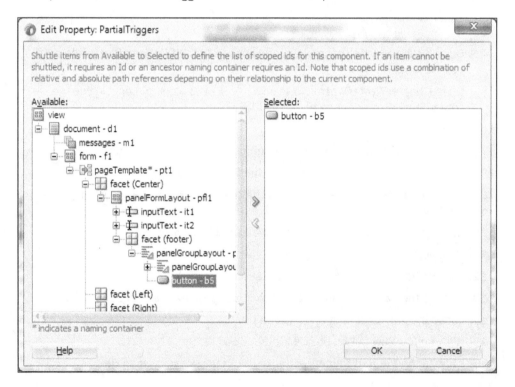

20. Click on the gear icon beside the `ActionListener` attribute and click on **Edit**.

21. Select **eventsBean** from the `ManagedBean` list.

22. Click on the **New** button beside the method name and change the method name to `submitChanges`.

23. Open the `EventsBean` Java class and add the following code under the `submitChanges` function:

```
System.out.println("All Values Submitted");
((RichButton) actionEvent.getSource()).setText("Submitted");
```

24. Save everything, run the `events.jsf` page, change the first name, and click on **Submit**.

How it works...

All server events have event listeners on their associated components. You need to follow the event signature and create a handler that processes the event and then associates that handler code with the listener on the component, as we did in step 9 for the input text and step 20 for the button.

JDeveloper makes it easy to create the managed bean and the event signature using the gear icon beside the attribute.

In this recipe, we created a managed bean with two event handlers, one for the input text and one for the button, and registered them inside their components using `valueChangeListener` and `actionListener` attributes respectively.

In the first method, namely, `changeFirstName`, we captured the old value and the new value from the `valueChangeEvent` method and displayed them on the console.

In the second method, namely, `submitChanges`, we also captured the button component and changed the `Text` attribute from `Submit` to `Submitted`.

In the button, we needed to have the partialTriggers attribute set to the button itself. As buttons have the partialSubmit attribute to true by default, which can prevent the button UI from being refreshed if we didn't add the partialTriggers attribute.

 A `partialSubmit` attribute allows form submit that doesn't require the whole page to get refreshed; unlike ADF 11g, the `partialSubmit` attribute is enabled by default in 12c.

Notice that the `changeFirstName` method only occurred on the **Submit** button because it waits for the form submit in order for the function to get executed in the JSF's life cycle; however, if you want to execute it instantly, you should set the `autoSubmit` attribute to `true`.

Also, you can notice that the `changeFirstName` method occurred before the `submitChanges` method, which makes sense as it reflects what happened; you changed the value and then clicked on the button.

ADF Faces's server events are great, but again, they need a round trip to the server, which can introduce latency, especially if you need to change something in the user interface. In the next recipe, we will see how to use different kinds of events, namely, client events.

Using ADF Faces client events

Most ADF Faces components can also work with client-side events. Handling events on the client side saves a round trip to the server. JavaScript replaces managed beans to handle client-side events. This JavaScript can be inline on the page or in a separate JavaScript file.

In this recipe, we will create a client listener to capture the change in the value of the `LastName` attribute and alert the end user about the change. You can refer to the last recipe to do this, or you can grab this project's recipe by cloning the `ADFFacesClientEvents` application from the Git repository.

How to do it...

To learn how to use ADF Faces's client events, follow the ensuing steps:

1. Open the `events.jsf` page.
2. Select the `LastName` field from the **Structure** pane.
3. Right-click on it, select **Client Attribute** by navigating to **Insert inside | ADF Faces**, and click on **OK**.
4. Change the `Name` attribute to `label`.
5. Change the `Value` field to `#{bindings.LastName.hints.label}`.
6. Right-click on the `LastName` field from the **Structure** pane, select **Client Listener** by navigating to **Insert Inside | ADF Faces**, and click on **OK**.
7. Change the `Method` field to `changeLastName`.
8. Change the `Type` field to `valueChange`.

   Now we have registered a function called `changeLastName` that will get executed on the `valueChange` event; next, we need to create the JavaScript function.

9. Select `af:document` from the **Structure** pane.

10. Right-click on it, select **Resource** by navigating to **Insert Inside | ADF Faces**, and click on **OK**.

11. Change the `Type` field to `JavaScript` and click on **OK**.

12. Open the **Source** mode of the page, and add the following code inside the `af:resource` opening and closing tags:

```
function changeLastName(valueChangeEvent){
var label = valueChangeEvent.getSource().getProperty("label");
alert(label + " Changed from: " + valueChangeEvent.getOldValue() +
" to: " + valueChangeEvent.getNewValue());
}
```

Using the JavaScript `alert` method is considered a bad practice; it was just mentioned here for elaboration purposes but should be avoided in any production application.

13. Save everything, run the `events.jsf` page, change `Last Name`, and press *Tab* to lose focus to see the alert in action.

How it works...

In this recipe, instead of registering a server listener using the component's attribute, we registered a client listener using the `clientListener` tag.

Each component has different event types that get passed to the client that you can register to. In this example, we used the `valueChange` type and registered a JavaScript function that we called to alert the user about any change. You can have mouse action types or even keyboard action types that you can register to.

We also added an additional attribute to be sent to the the JavaScript function using the `clientAttribute` tag, and we retrieved it using the first line in the JavaScript. This is important since you might have locales and retrieving their values will be different based on the locale.

The client-side action is triggered instantly and doesn't wait for you to click on the **Submit** button; this is because the actions triggered on the client side are always instant and don't need any `autoSubmit` attribute.

You can also notice that the JavaScript function also has a `ValueChangeEvent` passed to it as a parameter, and you can use it to retrieve the component itself or use some of its properties like we did in the last recipe.

 The excessive use of JavaScript is not recommended in ADF, especially if you are using external libraries and not ADF JavaScript APIs. To know more about ADF JavaScript APIs, refer to the official documentation at `http://docs.oracle.com/middleware/1212/adf/AFCJS/toc.htm`.

Since ADF Faces 12c, you can also use JSF2 Ajax tags instead of `clientListener` as shown in the following code:

```
<f:ajax event="change" onevent="function(event) { …}" render="@this" />
```

Client-side events are great and save round trips to the server, but sometimes, you want to propagate events from the client-side to the server for further actions. In the next recipes, we will see how to do that.

Sending custom events from a client to a server

In the previous recipe, we used `clientListener` and `clientAttribute` tags to call a function in JavaScript. We also had a bonus attribute accessible from the client side, but those attributes are not synchronized back to the server.

In this recipe, we will send custom data back to the server and send some payload with it. You can refer to the last recipe to do this, or you can grab this project's recipe by cloning the `ADFFacesClientServerEvents` application from the Git repository.

How to do it...

To learn how to send custom events from a client to a server, follow the ensuing steps:

1. Open the `events.jsf` page.
2. Drag the **Email** field under **Chapter7DataControl** | **EmployeesView1** and drop it inside the panel form layout by navigating to **Text** | **ADF Input Text w/ Label**.

3. Right-click on the **Email** field from the **Structure** pane and select **Client Listener** by navigating to **Insert Inside | ADF Faces**.

4. Change the `Method` field to `changeClientEmail`.

5. Change the `Type` field to `valueChange`.

6. Right-click on the `Email` field again from the **Structure** pane and select **Server Listener** by navigating to **Insert Inside | ADF Faces |**.

7. Change the `Type` field to `changeServerEmail`.

8. Select the **Server Listener** from the **Structure** pane, click on the gear icon beside the `Method` attribute, and click on **Edit**.

9. Select `eventsBean` and in the `Method Name`, click on the **New** button to create a new method and name it `changeServerEmail`.

10. Go to the **Source** mode of the page at the end of the file inside the `Resource` tag we created in the previous recipe and add the following code:

```
function changeClientEmail(valueChangeEvent){
  var component = valueChangeEvent.getSource();
  console.log("Email Changed from: " + valueChangeEvent.
getOldValue() + " to: " + valueChangeEvent.getNewValue());
  AdfCustomEvent.queue(component, "changeServerEmail", { newValue:
valueChangeEvent.getNewValue(), oldValue: valueChangeEvent.
getOldValue() }, true);
  valueChangeEvent.cancel(); //This line will prevent the input
text to propagate any events to the server.
}
```

This will capture the old and the new value, and it will call the custom function specified inside the `ServerListener` tag, which will execute the managed bean's `ChangeServerEmail` method. All we need to do now is get those values from the server side and print them out.

11. Open the `EventsBean` Java class and add the following code under the `ChangeServerEMail` method:

```
Object oldValue = clientEvent.getParameters().get("oldValue");
Object newValue = clientEvent.getParameters().get("newValue");
System.out.println("Email Changed from: " + oldValue + " to: " +
newValue);
```

12. Save everything and run the `events.jsf` page; change the `Email` value and press *Tab* on your keyboard to lose focus and see the browser and Weblogic consoles.

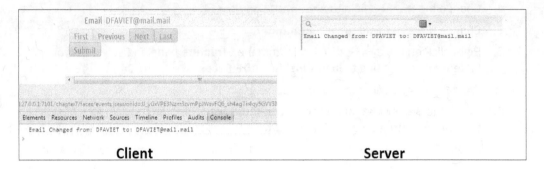

How it works...

The `AdfCustomEvent.queue()` JavaScript enables the client-side script to fire a custom event from the calling component or any component whose `clientComponent` attribute is set to `true`.

 When `clientComponent` is set to `true`, ADF JavaScript APIs create a JavaScript instance of the object to be available from the client side.

The custom event object contains information about the client-event source and a map of parameters to include on the event; also, the event can be set for immediate delivery (the Apply Request Values phase), or non-immediate delivery (the Invoke Application phase).

In this recipe, we used the `AdfCustomEvent.queue()` method to call the custom server event defined as `changeServerEmail`.

In the `AdfCustomEvent.queue()` method, we passed the component in the first parameter, the server-side event name in the second parameter, the payload in the third parameter—that is a **JSON (JavaScript Object Notation)** object with key-value mappings—and the immediate indicator as the last parameter that when set to true indicates that this function should be fired in the apply request value phase.

This is a great way to communicate with the server side from the client side without submitting the form, but let's find out whether there is any option to call JavaScript functions from the server side in the next recipe.

Executing JavaScript within an event response

Executing JavaScript within an event response can be very useful when you have a JavaScript library that does certain things on the client side, and you want to call these functions after finishing an action on the server side.

In this recipe, we will simply add a warning message to the `Phone Number` component if the user enters anything other than a number as the first letter and return the focus to the component again. You can refer to the last recipe to do this, or you also can grab this project's recipe by cloning the `ADFFacesServerClientEvents` application from the Git repository.

How to do it...

To learn how to execute a script within an event response, follow the ensuing steps:

1. Open the `events.jsf` page.

2. Drag the `PhoneNumber` field by navigating to **Chapter7DataControl | EmployeesView1** and drop it inside the panel form layout by navigating to **Text | ADF Input Text w/ Label**.

3. Select the `PhoneNumber` field from the **Structure** pane.

4. Change the `AutoSubmit` attribute to `true`.

5. Click on the gear icon beside the `ValueChangeListener` attribute and click on **Edit**.

6. Change the **Managed Bean** field to `eventsBean` by selecting it from the list.

7. Click on the **New** button beside the `Method Name` field and name the method `changePhoneNumber`.

8. Open the `EventsBean` Java class and add the following code under the `ChangePhoneNumber` method:

```
String newValue = valueChangeEvent.getNewValue().toString();
if (!newValue.matches("^\\d.*$")) {
 FacesContext context = FacesContext.getCurrentInstance();
 ExtendedRenderKitService erks = Service.
getRenderKitService(context, ExtendedRenderKitService.class);
 StringBuilder builder = new StringBuilder();
// Get the component reference in Javascript
```

```
builder.append("var component = AdfPage.PAGE.
findComponentByAbsoluteId('" +
                              ((RichInputText) valueChangeEvent.
getSource()).getClientId() + "');");
// create an ADF Faces message instance in Javascript
 builder.append("var message=new AdfFacesMessage(AdfFacesMessage.
TYPE_WARNING, 'Double Check your input', 'Are you sure you want to
enter " +
                              newValue + " as a Phone Number');");
// Add the previous message to the component
builder.append("AdfPage.PAGE.addMessage(component.
getClientId(),message);");
// Explicitly show the message of this component
builder.append("AdfPage.PAGE.showMessages(component.
getClientId());");
// Refocus on the component again
 builder.append("component.focus();");
 erks.addScript(context, builder.toString());
}
```

 Typically, you will not be hardcoding JavaScript inside your Java classes; instead, JavaScript should be already created in JavaScript files and just get called from Java. In this recipe, it was created that way for elaboration purposes.

9. Make sure you import the `org.apache.myfaces.trinidad.util.Service` class as JDeveloper might suggest other alternatives.

10. Save everything, run the `events.jsf` page, change **PhoneNumber** to anything other than a number as the first letter, and see the **Warning** message in action.

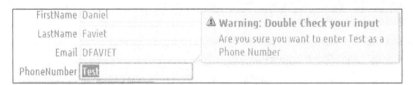

How it works...

Using the `ExtendedRenderKitService` class, we were able to add JavaScript to an event response, and we got an instance of this class using the `Service` utilities class inside the `org.apache.myfaces.trinidad.util` package. We also appended our JavaScript using the `addScript` method at the end of the `changePhoneNumber` class.

Also, make sure you understand that the script is passed as a string, so be cautious with your double quotes and quotes; luckily, JavaScript supports sending strings in single quotes.

In the JavaScript function, we used a couple of interesting ADF JavaScript API functions such as `AdfPage.PAGE.findComponentByAbsoluteId`, which retrieves an instance of the component. We also used a JavaScript class, namely, `AdfFacesMessage` that has a one-to-one correspondence to the Java class `FacesMessage`.

After creating an instance of the message, we added them to the component using the `AdfPage.PAGE.addMessage` function and showed this message using the JavaScript method: `AdfPage.PAGE.showMesssages`.

At the end of the JavaScript code, we called the `focus` method of the component to regain focus again. This method was created for clarification purposes, and the same result can be achieved by using a regular expression validator (more on this in *Chapter 8, Validating and Converting Inputs*).

You can also notice that we had to use the `autoSubmit` attribute in order for these changes to get effected immediately instead of waiting for the **Submit** button.

Using the scrollComponentIntoViewBehavior tag

The `scrollComponentIntoViewBehavior` tag is an interesting client behavior tag that can be used to enable the user to jump to a particular component on a page similar to an anchor in HTML.

In this recipe, we will use `scrollComponentIntoViewBehavior` to jump to the submit button at the end of the page. You can refer to the last recipe, or you can grab this project's recipe by cloning the `ADFFacesScrollComponentTag` application from the Git repository.

This is a very good use case since forms can grow big, and providing the end users with the option to jump to the **Submit** button directly can be a time saver.

 Note that this is a client-side component, so there are no actions submitted on the server side, which means no server round trips.

How to do it...

To learn how to use the `scrollComponentIntoView` tag, follow the ensuing steps:

1. Open the `events.jsf` page.
2. Drag a button inside the panel form layout just under the `Phone Number` input text.
3. Change the `Text` attribute to the text `Go to Bottom`.

4. Right-click on the button and navigate to **Insert Inside | ADF Faces | Scroll Component Into View Behavior**.

5. Click on the gear icon beside the `ComponentId` field and select the **Submit** button from the page structure.

6. Select the `af:scrollComponentIntoViewBehavior` tag and change the `Focus` attribute to `true`.

7. Drag the `Spacer` component inside the panel form layout just under the button we created in step 2.

8. Change the `Height` attribute to `600`.

9. Save everything, run the `events.jsf` page, and click on the **Go to Bottom** button to see it in action, as shown in the following screenshot:

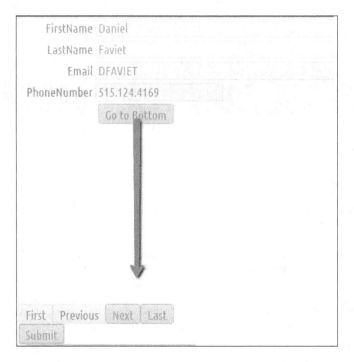

How it works...

This is a very simple recipe that makes jumping between different components of a page a breeze; we used it to directly gain focus on the submit button at the bottom of the form.

This can be useful for data-intensive forms and especially useful for data entry users.

Not only the component allows scrolling to a specific component, but also to subareas of the component. By making use of the `SubTargetId` attribute, you can target subareas of the component.

For example, if you have a rich text editor component that has multiple headings and paragraphs, you can target a specific heading inside the rich-text editor by providing the heading ID inside the `SubTargetId` attribute. Consider that you have a heading defined inside the rich-text editor like the following code:

```
<h2><a id="Summary"></a>Summary</h2>
```

If you have such a heading, you can use `Summary` inside the `SubTargetId` attribute to go to that location instead of navigating to the top of the rich-text editor component.

Using the target tag to execute PPR

Using PPR makes it really easy to render parts of your page on demand; however, in some use cases, it can become very hard to manage the PPR, especially with validations around.

For example, if you have a `selectOneChoice` component that refers to a lookup table, you may want to provide the end user with a create button to create a new row in the lookup table, if it doesn't exist. Now that is a great feature, but if `selectOneChoice` is the required field, then the create button will not be triggered unless the user selects a value of `selectOneChoice` first.

Setting the `immediate` attribute to `true` will not solve the problem either, because it'll not change or execute the update model phase, which may be required.

ADF 12c provides a great solution to this problem by providing the `Target` tag in which can be used to control the life cycle execution and rendering.

In this recipe, we have a very simple use case to be able to click on **First**, **Previous**, **Next**, or **Last** buttons without the need to validate the required fields. It gets validated only on the **Submit** button. You can refer to the last recipe, or you can grab this project's recipe by cloning the `ADFFacesTargetTag` application from the Git repository.

How to do it...

To learn how to use the `Target` tag, follow the ensuing steps:

1. Open the `events.jsf` page.
2. Locate the **First** Button from the **Structure** pane (located at **Panel Form Layout | Footer Facet | Panel Group Layout (Vertical) | Panel Group Layout (Horizontal)**).

3. Right-click on the button and select **Target** by navigating to **Insert Inside | ADF Faces**.

4. Select the newly created **Target** tag from the **Structure** pane.

5. Change the `Execute` attribute to `@this`.

6. Change the `Render` attribute to `it1 it2 it3 it4` (these are the IDs of the four input texts; if you have different ids, choose them instead).

7. Repeat the last 4 steps on the **Previous**, **Next**, and **Last** buttons.

8. Save everything and run the `events.jsf` page, then remove one of the required values and try to submit; after that, click on **Next** and see if it goes to the next record.

How it works...

By placing the `Target` tag as a child on the component whose event will cause the PPR, you are making sure that you capture this component's event and act towards it, similar to the JSF2 `Ajax` tag. After you put it as a child component, you specify the following three attributes:

- ▶ **Events**: This attribute will define all events (space delimited) that you need to capture out of this component such as `action`, `valueChange`, and `selection`; if you didn't specify any, it'll listen to all the events, that is, to the `@all` keyword.

- ▶ **Execute**: In this attribute, place component IDs (space delimited) for the components that are executed as a part of the life cycle in response to the event that occurred in the component. You can also use the `@this` keyword for the containing component and `@all` for all components inside the form tag; if you leave it empty, it'll be `@default`, which will be handled by the event root.

- ▶ **Render**: In this attribute, place component IDs (space delimited) for the components that are re-rendered as part of the life cycle in response to the event that occurred in the component. You can also use the `@this` keyword for the containing component and `@all` for all components inside the form tag; if you leave it empty, it'll be `@default`, which will be handled by the event root.

Using partial page navigation

Sometimes you might be interested to avoid making a full page transition each time you navigate to a different page, and you may wonder if you can apply the same PPR technique on navigation as well.

ADF Faces applications can be configured to have the navigation triggered through a PPR request.

In this recipe, we will enable partial page navigation to enable PPR navigation between pages and see it in action. You can refer to the last recipe, or you can grab this project's recipe by cloning the `ADFFacesPartialNavigation` application from the Git repository.

How to do it...

To learn how to use partial page navigation, we will first need to enable partial page rendering. Follow the ensuing steps to do this:

1. Open the `web.xml` file under the `Web Content/WEB-INF` folder.
2. From the overview mode, click on the plus icon in the **Context initialization parameters** category.
3. Change the `Name` attribute to `oracle.adf.view.rich.pprNavigation.OPTIONS`.
4. Change the `Value` attribute to `on`.
5. Open `adfc-config.xml`.
6. Drag `Wildcard Control Flow` from the **Components** palette and drop it inside the **Diagram** mode.
7. Drag `Control Flow Case` from the wildcard to the `events` page and name it `events`.
8. Do the same to the `partialTriggers` page and name it `partialTriggers`.
9. Open the `partialTriggers.jsf` page.
10. Drag a button from the **Components** palette and drop it inside the panel form layout.
11. Change the `Text` attribute to `Go to Events page`.
12. Change the `Action` attribute to `events`.
13. Open the `events.jsf` page.
14. Drag a button inside the panel form layout.
15. Change the `Text` attribute to **Go to Partial Triggers Page**.
16. Change the `Action` attribute to **Partial Triggers**.

17. Save everything, run the `partialTrigger.jsf` page, and open the browser console to verify that only a single GET request is obtained even if you navigate to the `events.jsf` page.

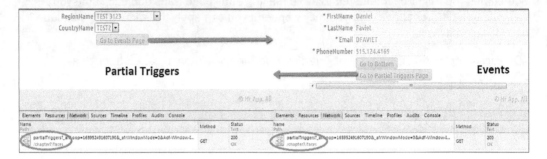

How it works...

In this recipe, we enabled partial page navigation by simply adding a new context parameter. This parameter has two possible options:

- ▶ `on`: This parameter enables partial page navigation.
- ▶ `onWithForcePPR`: This parameter enables partial page navigation and tells the framework to use PPR on all action events, even those that don't result in navigation.

When using partial page navigation, you should make sure that the buttons and links have `partialSubmit` equals to `true` or else they'll re-render the entire document again. When partial page navigation is used, ADF Faces can keep track of the location (for bookmarking purposes or when a page is refreshed) using the hash portion of the URL.

There is a reason that this feature is disabled by default and that is to make sure you are fully aware of the following points before enabling it:

- ▶ In order for PPR navigation to work efficiently, all pages involved in this navigation must use the same CSS skin.
- ▶ You can only use the `resource` tag to include JavaScript or CSS; other uses such as `verbatim` and `trh:stylesheet` will not work.
- ▶ If you are depending on the JavaScript global variables page being unloaded in each navigation, with PPR navigation, this will not happen since the JavaScript window object survives the navigation transition; however, you can utilize the `AdfPage.getPageProperty()` and `AdfPage.setPageProperty()` methods to store and retrieve these global variables.

Adding drag-and-drop capabilities

One of the events that we can use in ADF Faces is drag-and-drop.

The ADF Faces framework provides the ability to drag-and-drop items from one place to another on a page. Drag-and-drop provides users with a richer user experience that can make the user's task easier and more relevant.

In this recipe, we will implement two variations of the drag-and-drop functionality and see them in action. You can refer to the last recipe, or you can grab this project's recipe by cloning the `ADFFacesDragAndDrop` application from the Git repository.

How to do it...

To learn how to add drag-and-drop capabilities, we will first need to create a simple drag-and-drop attribute. Follow the ensuing steps to do this:

1. Open the `adfc-config.xml` file.
2. Drag a `View` component from the **Components** palette and drop it inside the **Diagram** mode.
3. Name the view `dragAndDrop`.
4. Double-click on the newly created view to create the page and choose the **Default Hr Template** page template.
5. Drag a **Panel Group Layout** inside the center facet.
6. Change the `Layout` attribute to `vertical`.
7. Drag an `outputText` component from the **Components** palette and drop it inside the **Panel Group Layout**.
8. Change the `Value` attribute to `Drag me`.
9. Right-click on the `outputText` component from the **Structure** pane and select **Client Attribute** by navigating to **Insert Inside | ADF Faces**.
10. Change the `Name` attribute to `name`.
11. Change the `Value` attribute to `John Smith`.
12. Right-click on the `outputText` component from the **Structure** pane and select **Attribute Drag Source** by navigating to **Insert Inside | ADF Faces**.
13. In the `Attribute` field, enter a name to capture the name value in the drag source.
14. Now drag an input text from the **Components** palette and drop it inside the **Panel Group Layout**.

15. Change the `Label` attribute to `Drop inside me`.

16. Right-click on the `inputText` from the **Structure** pane and select **Attribute Drop Target...** by navigating to **Insert Inside | ADF Faces**.

17. In the `Attribute` field, enter a value to put the dragged attribute inside the input text's `value` attribute.

18. Drag a `Separator` component and add it inside the **Panel Group Layout**.

    We have finished the simple drag-and-drop process; let's make things more interesting by dragging an array of strings inside a panel box. This time we will start with the drop target.

19. Add a panel box inside the **Panel Group Layout**.

20. Change the `Text` attribute to `Drop in here`.

21. Right-click on the panel box and select **Drop Target** by navigating to **Insert Inside | ADF Faces**.

22. In the drop listener, click on the gear icon and click on **Edit**.

23. In the `ManagedBean` field, click on the **New** button.

24. Change `Bean Name` to `dragAndDropBean`.

25. Change `Class Name` to `DragAndDropBean`.

26. Change the `Package` name to `com.adffaces.chapter7.view.beans` and click on **OK**.

27. Click on the **New** button in the `Method` field, name it `handleDrop`, and click on **OK**.

28. In the **Insert Data Flavor** dialog, enter `java.lang.Object[]` and click on **OK**.

29. Open the `DragAndDropBean` Java class.

30. Add the following code inside the `handleDrop` method:

```
//Get the object that gets tranfered
Transferable dropTransferable = dropEvent.getTransferable();
//We are expecting it to be of flavor Object array so we can
retrieve the data itself
Object[] drinks = dropTransferable.getData(DataFlavor.OBJECT_
ARRAY_FLAVOR);
if (drinks != null) {
  UIComponent dropComponent = dropEvent.getDropComponent();
  // Update the specified property of the drop component with the
Object[] dropped
  dropComponent.getAttributes().put("text", Arrays.
toString(drinks));
  // Return a copy operation
  return DnDAction.COPY;
```

```
} else {
// No Drag and Drop should occur
return DnDAction.NONE;
}
```

31. Now we have the method that copies the object array from an attribute and changes the text of our panel box; however, we are missing the drinks array itself, so let's create a simple method inside the class to return some drinks:

```
public String[] getDrinks() {
return new String[] { "Orange Juice", "Apple Juice", "Tomato
Juice" };
}
```

32. Drag an `output text` component and drop it just above the panel box.

33. Change the `Value` attribute to `Drag me`.

34. Right-click on the `outputText` component from the **Structure** pane and select **Client Attribute** by navigating to **Insert Inside | ADF Faces**.

35. Change the `Name` attribute to `drinks`.

36. Change the `Value` attribute to `#{dragAndDropBean.drinks}`.

37. Right-click on the `outputText` component from the **Structure** pane and select **Attribute Drag Source** by navigating to **Insert Inside | ADF Faces**.

38. In the `Name` attribute, enter `drinks` to capture the drinks value in the drag source.

39. Save everything, run the `dragAndDrop.jsf` page, and observe what happens when you drag-and-drop.

How it works...

ADF Faces supports adding many types of the drag-and-drop functionality. In this recipe, we only saw two types: Attribute Drag & Drop and Attribute Drag & Object Drop.

There are other types of drag-and-drop functionalities such as collection items drag-and-drop, calendar activity drag-and-drop, and more.

For more information about all the possible types of drag-and-drop functionalities, refer to the table in the official documentation at `http://docs.oracle.com/middleware/1212/adf/ADFUI/af_dnd.htm#CIHHDHDI`.

You can see from the first part of the recipe that we didn't need any Java code since, with it's drag-and-drop attribute, you specified what kind of attribute you wanted to drag from and what attribute you wanted to drop to. For this, you used `attributeDragSource` and `attributeDropTarget`; you can make use of `clientAttribute` to define more customized attributes.

In the second part of the recipe, since we are transferring an object, we can't really use the `attributeDropTarget` tag; hence, it is replaced with `dropTarget`. The `dropTarget` tag specifies a method that will get executed once you perform the drop and accepts an optional `dataFlavor` tag that filters and discriminates the objects dragged into this component to a specific type of data.

The `handleDrop` method is another ADF Faces server event that can be used to retrieve all the information about the data transferred and the component to which it's transferred. We do this by getting a `Transferable` object and transferring all the data inside this object.

After retrieving the data, we changed the panel box's `Text` attribute to this object. We hooked this object with a `clientAttribute` in the output text; if you try to drag the first output text inside the panel box, it'll not succeed since we only expect an array of objects.

See also

To know more about the drag-and-drop functionality and how to use it inside different components, refer to the official documentation at `http://docs.oracle.com/middleware/1212/adf/ADFUI/af_dnd.htm`.

Using polling events to update pages

ADF Faces provides the poll component that have both server and client side events, namely, `pollEvent`, which can be used to communicate with the server at specified intervals. This can be useful to provide updates to certain components at a fixed interval, and by decreasing this interval, you are getting close to providing live updates.

In this recipe, we will refresh the employees table every 5 seconds to see the changes in the table, and we will mimic this change by editing values in the database directly and see how it gets reflected on the page. You can refer to the last recipe, or you can grab this project's recipe by cloning `ADFFacesPolling` application from the Git repository.

How to do it...

To learn how to use the poll component, follow the ensuing steps:

1. Open the `adfc-config.xml` file.

2. Drag a view from the **Components** palette and drop it inside the **Diagram** mode.

3. Name the view `pollEmployees`.

4. Double-click on the newly created view to create the page and choose the **Default Hr Template** page template.

5. Drag a **Panel Group Layout** from the **Components** palette and drop it inside the center facet.

6. Drag **EmployeesView1** under **Chapter7DataControl** and drop it inside the **Panel Group Layout** created in the previous step by navigating to **Table/List View | ADF Table**.

7. Show only `EmployeeId`, `FirstName`, `LastName`, `Email`, and `Phone Number` and remove all other attributes.

8. Check the **Read-Only Table** option and click on **OK**.

9. Select `af:PanelGroupLayout` from the **Structure** pane.

10. Right-click and select **Poll** by navigating to **Insert inside | ADF Faces**.

    Now we need to make sure we refresh the table by calling the view object's `Execute` function again after polling is finished. So let's do that.

11. Drag the `Execute` function under **Chapter7DataControl | EmployeesView1 | Operations** and drop it above the **ADF Button** table.

12. Select the button from the **Structure** pane.

13. Change the `clientComponent` attribute to `true`.

    Now we have the function that we will be executing; we will create a client listener for the poll to invoke the `button` action on the client side.

14. Right-click on the poll component and select **Client Listener** by navigating to **Insert Inside | ADF Faces**.

15. Change the `Method` attribute to `refreshTable`.

16. Change the `Type` attribute to `poll`.

17. Select the `af:document` node from the **Structure** pane.

18. Right-click and select **Resource** by navigating to **Insert Inside | ADF Faces**.

19. Change the `Type` attribute to JavaScript and click on **OK**.

20. Open the **Source** mode of the page, and add the following code inside the `af:resource` opening and closing tags:

```
function refreshTable(pollEvent){
  var button=pollEvent.getSource().findComponent('b1');//The button
  var actionEvent = new AdfActionEvent(button);
  actionEvent.queue(true);//Execute the button action immediately
}
```

Now we have finished the `client` action; let's make sure that the table listens to these changes.

21. Select `af:Table` from the **Structure** pane.

22. Change the `partialTriggers` attribute to point to the poll component and the button.

23. Save everything, run the `pollEmplopyees.jsf` page, and change some of the records in the database to see the changes after 5 seconds.

How it works...

In this recipe, we used a poll component that has a 5-second interval by default and made sure that on each poll, we refresh the database table to check for changes by executing the `EmployeesView1` view object's `Execute` function, which refreshes the result list.

We can use the poll component with either a server- or client-side event.

In this recipe, I used a client-side event to mimic the pressing of the **Execute** button we had on the page. This button already executes the `Execute` method that refreshes the table. We also made sure that the table is listening to the poll component by adding the poll component ID inside the `partialTriggers` attribute.

You can specify the timeout for the poll, which is defaulted to 10 minutes; this timeout will occur when there are no keyboard or mouse activities on the page itself. You can also specify a global timeout, which can be determined by having a context variable, namely, `oracle.adf.view.rich.poll.TIMEOUT`, and each poll component can override it by specifying its own timeout using the `timeout` attribute in the component.

When you set the interval to `-1`, you stop the poll, which can be useful if you want to enable and disable polling on demand.

You can notice that this is not an optimized solution since you don't know if every 5 seconds there would be a change, and that it actually has a server round trip and can execute a SQL query as well. If you have a very high change rate, such as graphs or charts, 5 seconds might not be sufficient, and you have to decrease it to 1 second; however, you might hit a state when 1 second would not be enough to retrieve the information, which can make your application hard to predict.

One way to overcome this problem is, instead of polling for changes, waiting for these changes to be pushed to you instead. In the next recipe, we will have a simple use case of pushing data using ADS.

See also

To know more about poll components, refer to the official documentation at `http://docs.oracle.com/middleware/1212/adf/ADFUI/af_event.htm#CIHIIBEC`.

Using ADF Faces Active Data Service (ADS)

ADS is a server-side push framework that allows you to provide real-time data updates for ADF Faces components. You can bind ADF Faces components to a data source, and ADS pushes data updates to the browser when it receives new data without requiring the browser client to request it.

You can typically use this when there is a change in the database or **Java Message Service** (**JMS**) to receive these changes once the ADS receives them.

In this recipe, we will create a random generator to generate random numbers between 0 and 300, and we will see these values pushed dynamically into the browser. There is no model for this project, and this is a separate application from previous recipes. So, you should grab the `ADFFacesActiveData` application from the Git repository directly.

How to do it...

To learn how to use ADS, we need to enable it first because it is disabled by default. Follow the ensuing steps to do this:

1. Open the `ADFFacesActiveData` application.

2. Open the `adf-config.xml` file by expanding **Application Resources (Under applications navigator) | Descriptors | ADF META-INF**.

3. Add the following ADS `xmlns` at the end of the root `adf-config` tag:

   ```
   xmlns:ads="http://xmlns.oracle.com/adf/activedata/config"
   ```

4. Add the following tag at the end of the `adf-config.xml` file:

   ```
   <ads:adf-activedata-config xmlns="http://xmlns.oracle.com/adf/
   activedata/config">
           <transport>long-polling</transport>
           <latency-threshold>10000</latency-threshold>
           <keep-alive-interval>10000</keep-alive-interval>
           <max-reconnect-attempt-time>90000</max-reconnect-attempt-
   time>
           <reconnect-wait-time>8000</reconnect-wait-time>
   </ads:adf-activedata-config>
   ```

   Now that we have enabled ADS, let's create our managed bean that extends the `BaseActiveDataModel` class.

 The `BaseActiveDataModel` class is a basic implementation of the `ActiveDataModel` interface that you need to implement in order to listen to data change events and interact with the events manager. You can also register listeners by simply calling the `fireActiveDataUpdate` method in the `BaseActiveDataModel` class.

5. Right-click on the `ViewController` project and select **Java Class** by navigating to **New | From Gallery... | General**.

6. Change the `Class Name` to RandomNumberBean.

7. Change the `Package Name` to com.adffaces.chapter7.view.beans.

8. Click on the magnifying glass, search for `BaseActiveDataModel`, select the first result in the list, and click on **OK**. You should end up with your class looking like the following screenshot:

9. Click on **OK** to close the `creation` class dialog box.

10. Mark this class as a `ViewScoped` managed bean by adding the following annotations above the class declaration:

```
@ManagedBean(name = "randomNumberBean")
@ViewScoped
```

11. Create two fields at the class level, `counter` and `random`, using the following code:

```
private final AtomicInteger counter = new AtomicInteger(0);
private final Random random = new Random();
```

12. Create a method to retrieve the random value by adding the following method inside the class:

```
public String getRandomValue(){
   return String.valueOf(random.nextInt(301));
}
```

13. In the override function, getCurrentChangeCount, replace the content with the following code:

```
return counter.get();
```

14. Create a method that'll be called every 5 seconds by adding the following method:

```
public void updateRandomValue() {
 counter.incrementAndGet();
 //Creating an ADS event by defining (ChangeType, changeCount, key,
 insert key(only valid for insert ChangeType, names and values)
  ActiveDataUpdateEvent event = ActiveDataEventUtil.buildActiveData
 UpdateEvent(ActiveDataEntry.ChangeType.UPDATE, counter.get(), new
 String[0], null, new String[] { "randomValue" }, new Object[] {
 getRandomValue() });
 //Fire this event
  fireActiveDataUpdate(event);
 }
```

This method will increment the counter and create a new instance of ActiveDataUpdateEvent that returns the new random value that gets fired at the end.

15. Now we need to add randomValue to ActiveDataModel and create a scheduler that gets refreshed every 5 seconds by adding the following code inside the constructor class:

```
ActiveModelContext context = ActiveModelContext.
getActiveModelContext();
context.addActiveModelInfo(this, new String[0], "randomValue");
ScheduledExecutorService ses = Executors.
newSingleThreadScheduledExecutor();
ses.scheduleAtFixedRate(new Runnable() {
 public void run() {
   updateRandomValue();
 }
}, 5 /*Initial Delay*/, 5 /*Delay between updates*/, TimeUnit.
SECONDS);
```

Now everything is ready; let's go and create our page.

16. Open the `adfc-config.xml` file.

17. Drag a `View` from the **Components** palette and drop it inside the **Diagram** mode.

18. Name the view `random`.

19. Double-click on the newly created `View` to create the page, select **Oracle Three Column Layout** as a page template, and click on **OK**.

20. Drag `Output Text (Active) [af:activeOutputText]` by navigating to **Components Palette | Text and Selection** and drop it inside the center facet.

21. Change the `Value` attribute to `#{randomNumberBean.randomValue}`. (You can also use expression builder to get this value by navigating to JSF managed beans.)

22. Change the `inlineStyle` attribute to `font-size:xx-large`.

23. Save everything and run the `random.jsf` page.

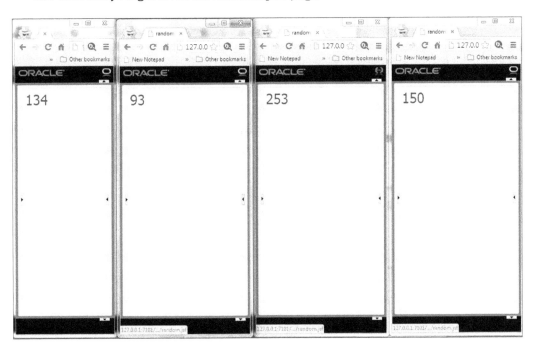

How it works...

ADS is used as an alternative approach to the automatic PPR; while PPR requires user input, ADS will always get the component's updates automatically.

Any ADF Faces components can use ADS, but `ActiveData` can only be configured with the components `activeOutputText`, `activeImage`, `table`, `treeTable`, and `tree`, and most of the DVT components. This means that you can still work with other ADF Faces components, but you have to proxy them; for example, if you want the ADF list view to provide updates automatically, you could create a `propertyChange` client listener on `activeOutputText` and trigger a server-side or client-side event to refresh the list view.

In this recipe, we first enabled ADS by adding a custom tag for ADS, defining some of the basic attributes such as transport mechanism (long polling, streaming, or poll) and other timeout and latency parameters. Then, we created a managed bean to pass an ADS event to the page by extending from `BaseActiveDataModel` and creating a method to fire the `ActiveData` event, which in our case gets called every 5 seconds. In a real application scenario, instead of manually firing the event every 5 seconds, we can use a database change listener or a JMS Message-Driven Bean.

In the page, we passed the `randomValue` attribute that will get changed every 5 seconds, and you can see that this is reflected in the page.

There are two overridden methods that we didn't manipulate, namely, `startActiveData` and `stopActiveData`, which get executed when a new listener registers itself for `ActiveData` or deregisters itself respectively. You can use them if you want to limit the number of threads to a certain number using `ActiveData`.

You can utilize ADS to create a simple chat application by storing the messages inside the `ApplicationScoped` managed bean and registering `table` instead of using `activeOutputText` to see these changes. Also, whenever the user presses the button to send a message, you fire this event to all the `ActiveData` listeners for all of them to see the chat messages in real time.

 If you want to explore the chat example using ADS, refer to the Git repository under the `AdditionalRecipes` folder to learn how to create the chat application in ADS; make sure you read the `README` file for instructions.

Since ADF 12c, you have the option to have real-time updates not only by using ADS but also WebSockets. In the next recipe, we will see how to create a simple chat application using WebSockets.

To know more about Active Data Service, refer to the official documentation at `http://docs.oracle.com/middleware/1212/adf/ADFUI/af_ads.htm#BABDHBJD`.

Using WebSockets for more interactive applications

WebSocket is a new protocol that was standardized in 2011 and provides two-way communication channels over a single TCP connection. It is designed to work with web browsers and web servers, and it has native JavaScript APIs in all modern browsers. The WebSocket protocol is totally independent from the HTTP protocol, and it can have a secured and unsecured layer just like the HTTP protocol. Starting with Weblogic 12c, it supports the WebSocket APIs fully, and we are going to use it in this recipe to create a small, anonymous chat client.

There is no model for this project, and this is a separate application from previous recipes. So, you should grab the `ADFFacesWebSockets` application from the Git repository directly.

How to do it...

To learn how to use ADF Faces with WebSockets, we first need to include the weblogic library inside our application. Follow the ensuing steps to do this:

1. Open the `ADFFacesWebSockets` application.
2. Right-click on `ViewController` and select **Libraries and Classpath** under **Project Properties**.
3. Click on **Add Library**, select the Weblogic 12.1 API library from the extension libraries, and click on **OK**.

    Now that we have finished importing the library, let's create the WebSocket adapter to receive and send messages through WebSocket.

4. Create a new class by right-clicking on the `ViewController` project and selecting **Java Class** by navigating to **New | From Gallery... | General**.
5. Change the `Class Name` to `WebsocketChatMessages`.
6. Change the `Package Name` to `com.adffaces.chapter7.view.ws`.
7. In the **Extend** field, search for `WebSocketAdapter` and select the only result in the list, that is, `weblogic.websocket.WebSocketAdapter`.
8. In the **Implements** field, click on the plus icon, search for `WebSocketListener`, and select the only result in the list, that is, `weblogic.websocket.WebSocketListener`.

9. Click on **OK** to close the Java class creation dialog.

10. Add the WebSocket annotation by adding the following line at the top of the class declaration:

```
@WebSocket(pathPatterns = { "/chat/*" }, timeout = -1)
```

This annotation will make this class listen to the `/chat/*` URL pattern from JavaScript clients. Because this class is created by the Weblogic server itself, we need to capture the last object created in Weblogic. So let's go ahead and do that.

11. Create an instance of the class itself as a member by adding the following code to the class body along with a variable to hold all messages:

```
private static WebsocketChatMessages ws;
private List<String> messages=Collections.synchronizedList(new
ArrayList<String>());
```

12. In the `Constructor` method, add the following code:

```
ws = this;
```

13. Add two public methods to retrieve the last object instance, and retrieve all messages by adding the following two methods to the class body:

```
public static WebsocketChatMessages getWs() {
  return ws;
}
public List<String> getMessages() {
  return messages;
}
```

Since we only use the server to send messages, we do not handle received messages. We need to add a method to broadcast these messages, so let's do that.

14. In the class body, add the following function:

```
public void broadcastChatMessage(String message) {
 messages.add(message);
 for (WebSocketConnection conn : getWebSocketContext().
getWebSocketConnections()) {
   try {
    System.out.println("Sending the message: "+message);
    if (conn.isOpen()) {
      conn.send(message);
    }
   } catch (Exception ex) {
    ex.printStackTrace();
   }
 }
}
```

With this, we created the WebSocket adapter. Now it's time to create the managed bean that will work with the WebSocket adapter by performing the following steps:

15. Create a new class as in step 4 and change the `Class Name` to `ChatBean`.

16. Change the `Package Name` to `com.adffaces.chapter7.view.beans`.

17. Add two annotations to mark the class as a `SessionScoped` managed bean by adding the following code above the class declaration:

```
@ManagedBean(name="chatBean")
@SessionScoped
```

Now we have a list of messages in the chat that will be presented in a table and one input text that should have a `valueChangeListener` class to broadcast the new message to all users. We also need to refresh the table by having a server listener that will be called from the server side (remember the *Sending custom events from a client to a server* recipe). Let's implement these functionalities.

18. Add the following function to present the chat messages list:

```
public List<String> getChatMessages(){
  if(WebsocketChatMessages.getWs().getMessages()==null){
     return new ArrayList<String>();
  }
  return WebsocketChatMessages.getWs().getMessages();
}
```

19. Create the `ValueChange` listener for the input text by adding the following code:

```
public void newChatMessage(ValueChangeEvent valueChangeEvent) {
  String newValue=valueChangeEvent.getNewValue().toString();
  WebsocketChatMessages.getWs().broadcastChatMessage(newValue);
}
```

20. Create a `refreshTable` method to refresh the table for new messages by adding the following code:

```
public void refreshTable(ClientEvent clientEvent) {
  String clientId=clientEvent.getParameters().get("clientId").
toString();
  UIViewRoot root = FacesContext.getCurrentInstance().
getViewRoot();
  AdfFacesContext.getCurrentInstance().addPartialTarget(root.
findComponent(clientId));
    }
```

Now we are ready to create our page.

21. Open the `adfc-config.xml` file.

22. Drag a `View` from the **Components** palette and drop it inside the **Diagram** mode of the `adfc-config` file.

23. Name the view `chat`.

24. Double-click on the **View** to create the page and choose **Oracle Three Column Layout** as the page layout.

25. Drag a panel splitter from the **Components** palette and drop it inside the center facet of the page template.

26. Change the `Orientation` attribute to `vertical`.

27. Change the `PositionFromTheEnd` attribute to `true`.

28. Change the `SplitterPosition` attribute to `20`.

29. Change the `DimensionFrom` attribute to `parent`.

30. Drag a table inside the first facet of the panel splitter.

31. Check on the **Bind Data Row** checkbox, click on **Browse**, and enter `#{chatBean.chatMessages}` into the **Table Data Collection** textbox.

32. Remove all the columns except for one and remove the column header text and change the value to `#{row}`. You should end up with the following screen:

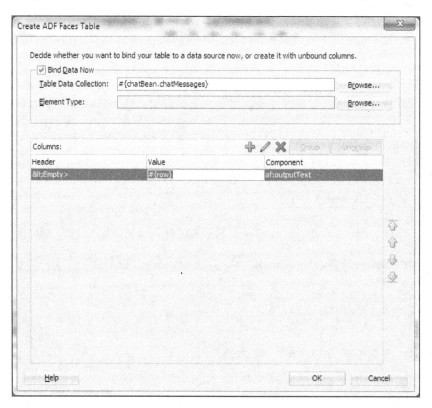

33. Click on **OK** to close the dialog.

34. Select the table from the **Structure** pane.

35. Change the `clientComponent` attribute to `true`.

36. Change the `ColumStretching` attribute to `last`.

37. Drag a **Panel Group Layout** and drop it inside the second facet of the panel splitter.

38. Change the `Layout` attribute to `horizontal`.

39. Drag an input text component and drop it inside the **Panel Group Layout**.

40. Change the `ValueChangeListener` attribute to `#{chatBean.newChatMessage}`.

41. Change the `Simple` attribute to `true`.

42. Change the `Columns` attribute to `100`.

43. Change the `PlaceHolder` attribute to `Add Chat Message`.

44. Drag a button and drop it inside the **Panel Group Layout**.

45. Change the `Text` attribute to `Send Message`.

    Now, to create the page, we need to create a JavaScript function to open the connection and listen to changes.

46. Select the `af:document` tag from the **Structure** pane.

47. Right-click and select **Resource** by navigating to **Insert Inside | ADF Faces**.

48. Change the `Type` attribute to JavaScript and click on **OK**.

49. Add the following code inside the `af:resource` tag:

```
var wsURL = "ws://127.0.0.1:7101/wschat/chat";

var websocket = new WebSocket(wsURL);

websocket.onmessage = function(evt){
    console.log("Recieved "+evt.data);
    handleMessage(evt.data);
    evt.preventDefault();
}

function handleMessage(message){
var table = AdfPage.PAGE.findComponentByAbsoluteId("pt1:t1");//
pt1:t1 is page template id combined with table id
AdfCustomEvent.queue(table, "refreshTable", {clientId: table.
getClientId()}, true);
}
```

50. Save everything, run the `chat.jsf` page, and start chatting.

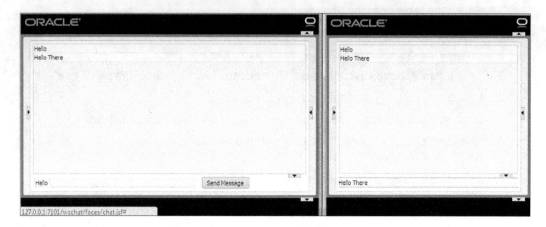

How it works...

WebSocket is a two-way communication channel that requires a server and a client.

In this recipe, the server is the `WebsocketChatMessages` class that we created. This is why we needed to use the WebSocket annotation, then extend it from the `WebSocketAdapter` class, and finally implement a `WebSocketListener` interface.

In the `WebsocketChatMessages` class, we maintained a list of messages sent to clients, and we created a custom function, namely, `broadcastChatMessage` to broadcast a message to all open connections. We also created a static variable of the adapter to retrieve the runtime object. You can extend the `WebsocketChatMessages` class by overriding other functions such as `onMessage` or `onOpen` of the `WebSocketAdapter` class to listen to received messages or react to a new connection respectively.

The WebSocket client in our case is the JavaScript code in the chat page; it opens a connection to the WebSocket server that matches the pattern in the annotation. Then, we registered the `onMessage` function to start listening to any broadcasted messages and reacting to it by refreshing the table **t1** inside the chat page.

The table value refers to the managed bean we created that has references to the `messages` list of the `WebsocketChatMessages` class. So, refreshing the table will show all the new messages to all the connections (users).

We also implemented a `valueChangeListener`, namely, `newChatMessage`, to call the `broadcastChatMessages` method on new messages.

8
Validating and Converting Inputs

This chapter will cover the following topics:

- Adding conversion
- Creating a custom converter
- Adding client-side capabilities to the converter
- Adding validation
- Creating a custom JSF validator
- Adding client-side capabilities to the validator
- Enhancing the Faces messages user experience

Introduction

Taking input from users is risky, and without the right validation and conversion you won't be able to verify the data entered by users. Validation is understandable, but what is conversion? In order to understand converters, let's get back to the JSF lifecycle.

Any web application stores data of many object types, such as numbers and dates, in the model layer. When this data is viewed in a client browser, the user interface needs to present this data in a manner that can be read or modified by the end user. For instance, when you want to represent a `java.util.Date`, you need to first convert this object as a text string in the format mm/dd/yyyy. When a user edits this field and submits the form, this string needs to be converted back to the `java.util.Date` type that is required by the application. After this, the validation can be applied against other rules and conditions. Conversely, data stored as something other than a string type can be converted to a string to display and update it.

ADF Faces inputs provide converter and validator capabilities by extending the original JSF validators and converters. ADF Faces also extends the default behavior of validation so the validation can take place on the client side and save the round trip to the server side.

Validation can be as simple as marking a field attribute `required` to `true`, or defining the `columns` attribute to limit the number of letters.

There are also more complex scenarios like checking validation by using the database or web services connection.

These validations can be applied both on the business service layer of the application or on the view layer. If you are using ADF BC, you can apply validation on entity objects directly. When you drag-and-drop it in your pages, ADF takes care of creating the appropriate validators that apply the model validations. However, in this chapter we will focus more on how ADF Faces handles validations.

 To know more about applying validation over ADF business service, check the official documentation at `http://docs.oracle.com/ middleware/1212/adf/ADFFD/bcvalidation.htm#sm0231`.

In this small chapter, we will discuss the Process Validations and explore how to add and create custom validators and converters in the view layer, as shown in the following figure:

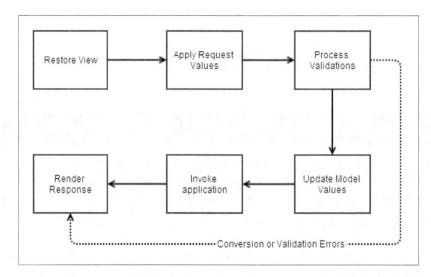

You can find all of the recipes of this chapter inside `Chapter 8` folder of the book's Git repository. If you haven't already created the database, make sure to create it for your recipes to work flawlessly. Also, don't forget to change the database connection with the right information pointing to your local database settings.

Adding conversion

In order to provide conversion from user string inputs to other object data types, ADF Faces input needs to be converted from string to the data type object and vice versa.

ADF Faces provides many converters out of the box so the developer doesn't need to create his own. Every input can be assigned to only one converter.

In this recipe, we will create an employee form that converts from `java.util.Date` to `java.lang.String` and from any number like `double` to `java.lang.String` and vice versa.

The application for this recipe and its model has been created for you. You can see it by cloning the `AddingConversion` application from the Git repository.

How to do it...

To know how to add conversions, perform the following steps:

1. Open the `AddingConversion` application.

2. Double-click on `adfc-config.xml` to open it.

3. Drag `view` from **Components** palette and drop it inside the **Diagram** mode of `adfc-config`.

4. Name the view `employees`.

5. Double-click on `view` to create it, and then choose **Default Hr Template** as a page layout.

6. Go to **Chapter8DataControl**, drag **EmployeesVO1** from the **Data Control** pane, and drop it inside the center facet of the page template as **ADF Form**.

7. Remove all of the fields except **FirstName**, **LastName**, **HireDate** and **Salary**.

8. Check the **Row Navigation** option.

9. Click on **OK** to close the dialog box.

10. Examine the source mode of the page.

If you open the source mode of the page, you can see that the `af:convertDateTime` and `af:convertNumber` tags are inside the **HireDate** and **Salary** fields. These tags are used to convert from user input to dates and numbers, respectively. It does this automatically so that the model will have dates and numbers, and the developer does not need to explicitly do the conversion himself.

You can change the date pattern or the number pattern by customizing the following two tags.

1. Select `af:convertDateTime` by expanding the **HireDate** field from the **Structure** pane.

2. Change the `Pattern` attribute to `dd MMMM yyyy`.

 This pattern will show something like 27 November 2011, in which `dd` (small letter) represents day, `MMMM` (capital letter) represents month (when you put 4 consecutively, you want to display the full name of the month), and `yyyy` (small letter) represents year. To know more about date patterns in Java, check the following link `http://docs.oracle.com/javase/7/docs/api/java/text/SimpleDateFormat.html`.

3. Change the `HintDate` attribute to `"Enter date in the format 27 November 2011"`.

4. Select `af:convertNumber` by expanding the **Salary** field from the **Structure** pane.

5. Change the `Type` attribute to `currency`.

6. Change the `CurrencyCode` attribute to `GBP`.

7. Change the `CurrencySymbol` attribute to `£`.

8. Change the `GroupingUsed` attribute to `true`.

   This attribute is used to group large numbers and provide a comma between them, for example, 10000 will be displayed as 10,000.

9. Save everything, run the `employees.jsf` file, and see the hints and error message when you give a wrong date or number, as shown in the following screenshot:

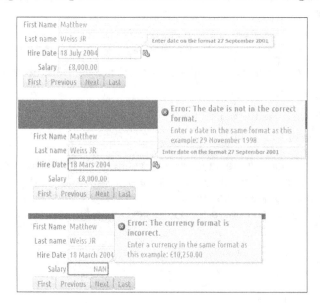

How it works...

Many ADF Faces components such as `af:inputDate` automatically provide a conversion capability. However, even if you don't want to use `af:inputDate` and want to use `af:inputText` instead, you can still use Oracle ADF Converters such as `af:convertDateTime` to provide the conversion capabilities.

In this recipe, we saw two of these converters in action, namely `af:convertDateTime` and `af:convertNumber`, we also saw how we can customize them to provide a different look to how dates and salaries are presented to the end user. If you look at any of the input components, you would find the `converter` attribute which can be used to specify the converter name that should be used. However, using a `converter` tag provides much more flexibility to how the converter behaves.

Also, notice that we didn't have any validations, and yet we got validation errors when we entered a wrong date or a wrong salary. This confirms that the conversion takes place in the Process Validations step of the JSF lifecycle. Meaning, if the converter cannot convert this input it'll throw an error just like the validation does.

ADF provides three converter tags: `DateTimeConverter`, `NumberConverter` and `ColorConverter`, which convert from `java.lang.String` to `java.awt.Color` to be used with the input color component. Other converters provided by JSF are as follows:

- `BigDecimalConverter`
- `BigIntegerConverter`
- `BooleanConverter`
- `ByteConverter`
- `CharacterConverter`
- `DateTimeConverter`
- `DoubleConverter`
- `EnumConverter`
- `FloatConverter`
- `IntegerConverter`
- `LongConverter`
- `NumberConverter`
- `ShortConverter`

You can use them by using the `converter` attribute of your input field.

> To know more about standard JSF converters, check the documentation at `http://download.oracle.com/otn_hosted_doc/jdeveloper/j2ee101302/jsf_apps/eventvalidate/sf_avc_converters.html`.

This list is big and surely covers most of the use cases of any application. However, sometimes the developer needs to create a custom converter in order to convert from other data types that are not in the aforementioned list. In the next recipe, we will learn how to do exactly that.

See also

To know more about adding conversion in ADF Faces, refer to the official documentation at `http://docs.oracle.com/middleware/1212/adf/ADFUI/af_validate.htm#BABHICGB`.

Creating a custom converter

When you create a custom converter, this converter will need to run on the server as per the JSF lifecycle.

In this recipe, we will create a custom converter to convert from `oracle.jbo.domain.ClobDomain` class to `java.lang.String` class and vice versa, which will be represented by the employee's `Biography` attribute.

In this recipe, the model has been created for you. You can continue from the previous recipe, or you can grab this project's recipe by cloning the `CreatingCustomConverter` application from the Git repository.

Getting ready

In order to create a custom JSF converter, we need to perform the following steps:

1. Create a class that implements the `javax.faces.convert.Conveter` interface.
2. Implement the following two methods: `getAsObject` and `getAsString`.
3. Register this class as a converter inside the `faces-config.xml` file.
4. Apply the converter on input components.

How to do it...

To know how to create a custom converter, perform the following steps:

1. Right-click on the `ViewController` application, select **Java Class**, and navigate to **New | From Gallery | General**.

2. Change the `Class name` to `ClobConverter`.

3. Change the `Package name` to `com.adffaces.chapter8.view.converters`.

4. Click on the plus icon inside the implements section, search for the converter, and choose the `javax.faces.convert.Converter` interface from the list, as shown in the following screenshot:

5. Click on **OK** twice to close the dialog box.

   Now that we have created the class, let's implement the `getAsObject` and `getAsString` methods.

6. Open the `ClobConverter` class.

7. Add the following code inside the `getAsObject` method:

```
if (string == null) { //Sanity check
  return null;
}
```

```
try { //ClobDomain is the official implementation of Oracle Clob
data type
  return new ClobDomain(string);
} catch (Exception ex) {
  String message =
              String.format("Unable to convert String value
\"%s\" into a oracle.jbo.domain.ClobDomain", string);
          throw new ConverterException(message, ex);
}
```

8. Add the following code inside the `getAsString` method:

```
return object.toString();
```

It's now time to register this class as a converter inside the `faces-config.xml` file.

9. Open the `faces-config.xml` file under the `WEB-INF` folder.

10. Switch to **Overview mode** of the file.

11. Select **Converters** from the left menu and click on the plus button.

12. Change the `ID` to `com.adffaces.ClobConverter`.

13. Change the `Class` to `com.adffaces.chapter8.view.converters.ClobConverter`, as shown in the following screenshot:

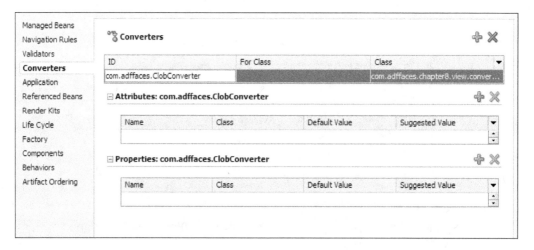

To apply this converter, perform the following steps:

1. Open the `employees.jsf` page.

2. Drag the `Biography` attribute by navigating to **Chapter8DataControl | EmployeesVO1** and drop it inside the `af:panelFormLayout` by navigating to **Text | ADF Input Text w/ Label**.

3. Right-click on `Biography` field from the **Structure** pane and click on **Rich Text Editor** by navigating to **Convert to...**.

4. Click on **OK** again when a dialog box appears.

5. Change the `Conveter` attribute to `com.adffaces.ClobConverter`. (You should be able to select it from the choice list.)

6. Save everything and run the `employees.jsf` page and edit the biography. Also, try to remove the `converter` attribute and see the errors you get.

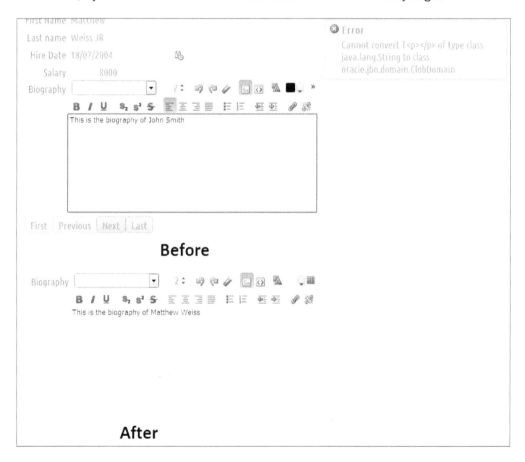

How it works...

In this recipe, we created a small custom JSF converter to convert from the `oracle.jbo.domain.ClobDomain` class, which is responsible of understanding Oracle database clob type, to `java.lang.String`. This was done by using the implementation of the `getAsObject` and `getAsString` methods that were provided by the `javax.faces.convert.Converter` interface.

When the end user first sees the page, the component calls the `getAsString` method to show the end user the string value of the result. When the user submits the page containing this converter, the ADF lifecycle calls the converter's `getAsObject` method to convert the string value to the `ClobDomain` object. When there are no converters attached to the component, then ADF will check the model's data type and it tries to find the appropriate converter. If the conversion fails, the component will be marked as not valid and JSF adds an error message to a queue that is maintained by `FacesContext`. However, if the conversion is successful, the converted value is passed to the validators.

Another famous converter, which we used in *Chapter 4, Using Common ADF Faces Components*, is `FileUploadConverter`.

The `FileUploadConverter` custom converter converts from the `UploadedFile` class that is saved inside the request scope, and it can be accessed through `FacesContext` and it extracts `FileName` from it.

You can check the source code of this converter in the `Chapter 4` folder of the Git repository.

As you can see, we were able to convert types in the server side. However, still this might not be sufficient and we might need to implement a way to convert it on the client side and save this round trip to the server. In the next recipe, we will know exactly how to do that.

See also

To know more about creating custom converters, refer to the official documentation at `http://docs.oracle.com/middleware/1212/adf/ADFUI/af_validate.htm#BABGIEDH`.

Adding client-side capabilities to the converter

ADF Faces converters are JSF converters with client-side capabilities that can save a round trip to the server if not converted correctly.

In this recipe, we will create a new converter with client-side capabilities to check whether the value is a valid XML syntax or not. Then, we will apply this on the `CodeSample` attribute. You can continue from the previous recipe, or you can grab this project's recipe by cloning the `CreatingCustomCSConverter` application from the Git repository.

Getting ready

In order to create a converter with client-side capabilities, we need to do two things:

1. Create a JavaScript version of the converter following the Trinidad documentations.
2. Create a class that implements `javax.faces.convert.Converter` and `org.apache.myfaces.trinidad.validator.ClientConverter` interfaces and override its methods.
3. Register the converter inside the `faces-config.xml` file.
4. Apply the converter on input components.

The second step is important since even though we are creating a client-side converter, we need to have server-side code in case someone tries to mimic a POST operation. So, we need to create a new class that will extend the original `ClobConverter` class and add support to the client-side functionality.

How to do it...

To know how to create a custom client-side converter, perform the following steps.

First, we will create a JavaScript file that represents the validation logic, so let's start doing that:

1. Right-click on the `ViewController` project, navigate to **New | From Gallery | Web Tier | HTML**, and select the JavaScript file.
2. Name the file `XmlConverter.js` and make sure you put it inside the `resources\js` directory.

3. Add the following code inside the newly created JavaScript file:

```
//Acts as a constructor
function XmlConverter() {}
//Tells that XmlConverter extends the TrConverter
XmlConverter.prototype = new TrConverter();

//Implements the getAsString function just like server side
XmlConverter.prototype.getAsString = function (value, label) {
    return value;
}
//Implements the getAsObject function just like server side
XmlConverter.prototype.getAsObject = function (value, label) {
    if (!value) {return null;} //Sanity Check
    try {
        var parser = new DOMParser();
        var xmlDoc = parser.parseFromString(value, "application/
xml");
        if (xmlDoc.getElementsByTagName("parsererror").length > 0)
{
            sendError(label);
        }
        return value;
    }
    catch (err) { sendError(label);}
}
//Helper method to send the exception
function sendError(label) {
    var fm = new TrFacesMessage("Convertion Error", label + " is
not in XML format", TrFacesMessage.SEVERITY_ERROR);
    throw new TrConverterException(fm);
}
```

After creating the JavaScript, let's extend `ClobConverter` and implement the `org.apache.myfaces.trinidad.convert.ClientConverter` interface and its methods.

4. Right-click on the **ViewController** application and select **Java Class** by navigating to **New | From Gallery | General**.

5. Change the `Class` name to `XMLConverter`.

6. Change the `Package` name to `com.adffaces.chapter8.view.converters`.

7. Click on the **Magnifier glass** inside the **Extends** section. Then, search for `ClobConverter` and select the `com.adffaces.chapter8.view.converters.ClobConverter` class from the list.

8. Click on the plus icon inside the **Implements** section, search for the converter, and choose the `org.apache.myfaces.trinidad.convert.ClientConverter` interface from the list. You should end up with the following screenshot:

9. Open the `XmlConverter` class if it's not already opened.

10. Inside the `getClientLibrarySource` method, add the following code:

    ```
    return facesContext.getExternalContext().getRequestContextPath() +
    "/resources/js/XmlConverter.js";
    ```

    It's now time to register this class as a converter inside the `faces-config.xml` file.

11. Open the `faces-config.xml` file under the `WEB-INF` folder.

12. Switch to the overview mode of the file.

13. Select **Converters** from the left-hand side menu and click on the plus button.

14. Change the `ID` to `com.adffaces.XmlConverter`.

15. Change the `Class` to `com.adffaces.chapter8.view.converters.XmlConverter`.

    Now, we need to create a new instance of the JavaScript class we created inside our JavaScript file in the third step. To do this, we need to change the body of the `getClientConversion` method.

16. Inside the `getClientConversion` method, insert the following code:

    ```
    return "new XmlConverter()";
    ```

    Now, all that we need to do is add the `CodeSample` attribute into the `employees.jsf` page.

17. Open the `employees.jsf` page.

18. Drag the **CodeSample** attribute by navigating to **Chapter8DataControl | EmployeesVO1**. Then, drop it inside the `af:panelFormLayout` because there is no navigation. A pop up appears and the user selects it from the small pop up. This is explained in greater details in *Chapter 3, Presenting Data Using ADF Faces*, so the reader should already have the experience to do that. Navigate to **Text | ADF Input Text w/ Label**.

19. Change the `Conveter` attribute to `com.adffaces.XMLConverter`. (You should be able to select it from the choice list.)

20. Change the `Columns` attribute to `40`.

21. Change the `Rows` attribute to `10`.

22. Save everything, run the `employees.jsf` page, and edit the first letter of the first name or the e-mail. Instantly, you'll see the error in action, as shown in the following screenshot:

How it works...

In order to add the client-side capabilities, we first created a JavaScript version of the converter, that is a JavaScript class that extends a `TrConverter` class and overrides the `getAsString` and `getAsObject` methods inside this JavaScript.

After creating the JavaScript class inside the `XMLConverter.js` file, we created a class to implement the `org.apache.myfaces.trinidad.convert.ClientConveter` interface methods.

We referred to the JavaScript source file by using the `getClientLibrarySource` method. Also, we created a new instance of the JavaScript class by passing the required constructor arguments by using the `getClientConversion` method.

In runtime, once we edit the field that has the client-side converter, this JavaScript instantiates a call that will occur on the client-side and a new instance of `XmlConverter` will be returned.

After that, the `getAsString` JavaScript method will be called if there is an original value in the field. Once the end user edits something in the field, the `getAsObject` JavaScript method will be called.

If no errors were found, then this field will be valid. However, if an error is thrown, namely `TrConverterException`, then this field will be marked as invalid and the `FacesMessage` will be shown.

This client-side converter will not prevent the server-side validation from happening. When the form is submitted, the `getAsObject` method inside the `XmlConverter` class will be fired normally like in the previous recipe. In this case, it will call the same `getAsObject` method of the `ClobConverter` class.

See also

To know more about creating custom ADF Converter, refer to the official Trinidad documentation at `http://myfaces.apache.org/trinidad/devguide/clientValidation.html#Client-side_Converters`.

Adding validation

The JSF lifecycle provides a validation mechanism that when you add validation to a component and a user edits or enters data in fields and submits the form, the data is validated against any set rules and conditions. If validation fails, the application displays an error message. This entire process happens at the server side.

ADF Faces provides client-side capabilities that can be used inside the component itself or that uses specific validation tags that provides client-side validation and saves a round trip to the server. Attributes such as `required` and `columns` can be used to provide another layer of validation that can be used to further instruct the user to enter the right data. ADF also provides multiple validator tags that can be used with input fields to add extra layer of validation.

In this recipe, we will get to know two of these validators in action by applying them on `PhoneNumber` and `Salary` attributes in our `employees` page. You can continue from the previous recipe or you can grab this project's recipe by cloning the `AddingValidation` application from the Git repository.

How to do it...

To know how to add ADF validators, perform the following steps:

1. Open the `employees.jsf` page.

2. Select the **Salary** field from the **Structure** pane.

3. Right-click on **Salary** field from the **Structure** pane and select on **Insert Inside... | ADF Faces | Validate Double Range**.

4. Select `af:validateDoubleRange` from the **Structure** pane.

5. Change the `Minimum` attribute to `500`.

6. Change the `Maximum` attribute to `100000`.

7. Change the `HintNotInRange` attribute to `"Valid number from 500 to 100,000"`.

8. Change the `MessageDetailNotInRange` attribute to `"Not valid number, the valid number should be from 500 to 100,000"`.

   Now that we have finished adding validation to **Salary**, it's time to add validation to **PhoneNumber**.

9. Drag the **PhoneNumber** attribute by navigating to **Chapter8DataControl | EmployeesVO1** and drop it inside `af:panelFormLayout` by navigating to **Text | ADF Input Text w/ Label**.

10. Right-click on the **PhoneNumber** field from the **Structure** pane, and then navigate to **Insert Inside... | ADF Faces | Validate Regular Expression**.

11. Select the `af:validateRegExp` file from the **Structure** pane and change the `Pattern` attribute to `\d{3}\.\d{2,3}\.\d{4}(\.\d{6})?`.

You need to make sure that the pattern looks exactly the same, as JDeveloper will try to append an extra forward slash before each \. In order to prevent that, use this formula directly in the source mode of the page.

12. Change the `Hint` attribute to "The valid formats are either: 123.12.1234.123456 or 123.123.1234".

13. Change the `MessageDetailNoMatch` attribute to "You didn't enter a valid format, the valid formats are either: 123.12.1234.123456 or 123.123.1234".

14. Save everything and run the `employees.jsf` page and change the salary outside the range or change phone number to see the error message, as shown in the following screenshot:

How it works...

In this recipe, we saw two of the ADF validators in action, namely `af:validateRegExp` and `af:validateDoubleRange`. As you can see, these validations occur immediately on the client side, without the need to submit the form. This is shown clearly as you lose focus, the error message appears and you won't be able to submit your form.

Using these validators' tag, we were able to customize the behavior of the validation and add extra information to instruct the user about the proper format of the fields by utilizing the `hint` attribute. We also controlled the error message shown by editing the `MessageDetail*` attributes.

Unlike the JSF validators, ADF provides client-side support for all its tags, and they are as follows:

- ▸ `ByteLengthValidator`
- ▸ `DateRestrictionValidator`
- ▸ `DateTimeRangeValidator`
- ▸ `LengthValidator`
- ▸ `LongRangeValidator`
- ▸ `RegExpValidator`
- ▸ `DoubleRangeValidator`

 To know about these validators, check the table in the official documentation at `http://docs.oracle.com/middleware/1212/adf/ADFUI/af_validate.htm#CIHEBFFD`.

As you can see in most cases, these validators will be more than sufficient. However, sometimes you may want to have a specific kind of validation that requires more than what ADF provides. In this case, you need to create your own custom validator. In the next recipe, we will know just how to do that.

See also

To know more about adding validations in ADF Faces, refer to the official documentation at `http://docs.oracle.com/middleware/1212/adf/ADFUI/af_validate.htm#BABHAHEI`.

Creating a custom JSF validator

JSF provides an easy way to create custom validation logic to meet your business needs.

If this validation only occurs in a single page, then you may consider using validation inside the page-managed bean. However, if you want this validation to be used in different components or in different pages, consider creating a JSF validator.

In this recipe, we will create a custom validator for the employee's `email` attribute that needs to start with the first letter of his first name. You can continue from the previous recipe, or you can grab this project's recipe by cloning the `CreateCustomJSFValidator` application from the Git repository.

Getting ready

In order to create custom JSF validator, we need to perform the following steps:

1. Create a class that implements the `javax.faces.validattor.Validator` interface.
2. Implement the `validate` method.
3. Register this class as a validator inside the `faces-config.xml` file.
4. Apply the validator on input components.

How to do it...

To know how to create custom JSF validator, perform the following steps:

1. Right-click on the `ViewController` application and select the **Java Class** by navigating to **New | From Gallery | General**.
2. Change the `Class name` to `EmailValidator`.
3. Change the `Package name` to `com.adffaces.chapter8.view.validators`.
4. Click on the plus icon inside the implements section, search for `Validator`, and choose the `javax.faces.validator.Validator` interface from the list.
5. Click on **OK** twice to close the dialog box.

   We have created the class, now we will implement the `validate` method.

6. Open the `EmailValidator` class.
7. Add the following code inside the `validate` method:

```
String firstName = uIComponent.getAttributes().get("firstName").
toString().toUpperCase();
if(!object.toString().toUpperCase().startsWith(firstName.
charAt(0)+"")){
```

```
     throw new ValidatorException(new FacesMessage(FacesMessage.
SEVERITY_ERROR,"Validation Error","Email address should start with
First Letter of the First Name"));
}
```

Now, its time to register the validator inside the `faces-config.xml` file.

8. Open the `faces-config.xml` file under the `WEB-INF` folder.

9. Switch to the overview mode of the file.

10. Select **Validators** from the left-hand side menu and click on the plus icon button.

11. Change `ID` to `com.adffaces.EmailValidator`.

12. Change `Class` to `com.adffaces.chapter8.view.validators.EmailValidator`, as shown in the following screenshot:

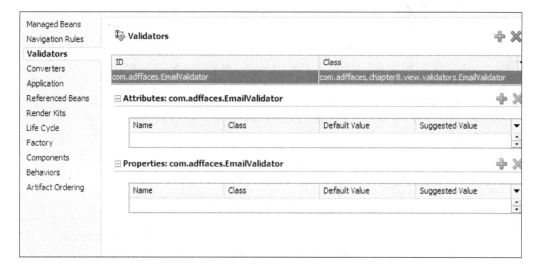

13. Open the `employees.jsf` page.

14. Select the **First Name** field from the **Structure** pane.

15. Change the `AutoSubmit` attribute to `true`.

16. Drag the `Email` attribute by navigating to **Chapter8DataControl | EmployeesVO1** and drop it inside the `af:panelFormLayout` attribute by navigating to **Text | ADF Input Text w/ Label**.

17. Expand the **Email** field from the **Structure** pane and select the `f:validator` tag inside it.

18. Change the `ValidatorId` attribute to `com.adffaces.EmailValidator`.

19. Right-click on the **Email** input text and select **Attribute** by navigating to **Insert Inside | JSF**.

20. Change the name of the attribute to `firstName`.

21. Change the value of the attribute to `#{bindings.FirstName.inputValue}`.

22. Save everything, run the `employees.jsf` page, edit the first letter of the **First Name** or the **Email**, and submit the form to see the error in action, as shown in the following screenshot:

How it works...

In this recipe, we created a custom validator that validates the e-mail's first letter against the first name's first letter when the user submits the page at the process validation phase and after ADF Faces checks the conversion. The converted value is then passed to the `validate` method that checks first whether the value is empty. The `required` attribute of the component is checked and an error message is generated if indicated.

If the submitted value is not empty, the validation process continues to call the `EmailValidator` class's `validate` method. This method checks the first letter of the value against the first name value that is passed as an attribute inside the component.

If the validation failed with the `ValidatorException`, the `FacesMessage` attribute gets queued and the render response phase is executed. If the validation is passed without throwing any exceptions, then the next phase is to be executed.

As you can see, unlike the default ADF validators, this validation takes place on the server side and therefore needs a submit. That's why we changed the `AutoSubmit` value of the **First Name** field to `true` to capture the new value before going inside the validation. However, this might not be sufficient, and we might need to implement a way to do this validation on the client side and save this round trip to the server. In the next recipe, we will know exactly how to do that.

See also

To know more about creating custom JSF validators, refer to the official documentation at `http://docs.oracle.com/middleware/1212/adf/ADFUI/af_validate.htm#BABEIIDD`.

Adding client-side capabilities to the validator

Adding client-side capabilities to the validator can save a round trip to the server, which can greatly improve performance.

In this recipe, we will add client-side capabilities to the `EmailValidator`. You can continue from the previous recipe, or you can grab this project's recipe by cloning the `CreatingCustomCSValidator` application from the Git repository.

Getting ready

In order to add the client-side capabilities to the validator, we need to do two things:

1. Create a JavaScript version of the validator following the documentations.
2. Implement the `org.apache.myfaces.trinidad.validator.ClientValidator` interface and override its methods.

The second step is important since even though we are creating a client-side validator, we need to have server-side code in case someone was trying to mimic a POST. So, we need to extend the original `EmailValidator` class to support the client-side functionality and add the necessary JavaScript at runtime.

How to do it...

To know how to create custom client-side validator, we will create a JavaScript file that represents the validation logic. Follow the ensuing steps to do this:

1. Right-click on the `ViewController` project and select **JavaScript File** by navigating to **New | From Gallery | Web Tier | HTML**.
2. Name the file `EmailValidator.js` and make sure you put it inside the `resources\js` directory.
3. Add the following code inside the newly created JavaScript file:

```
//Acts as a constructor which takes the FirstName field id
function EmailValidator(field) {
    this.firstNameField = field;
}
//Tells that EmailValidator extends the TrValidator
EmailValidator.prototype = new TrValidator();
```

```
//Implements the Validate function just like server side
EmailValidator.prototype.validate = function (value, label,
converter) {
    //Get the FirstName component reference
    var compareAgainst = AdfPage.PAGE.findComponent(this.
firstNameField);
    if (value.indexOf(compareAgainst.getValue().toUpperCase().
charAt(0)) != 0) {
        var fm = new TrFacesMessage("Validation Error", "Email
address should start with First Letter of the First Name",
TrFacesMessage.SEVERITY_ERROR);
        throw new TrValidatorException(fm);
    }
}
```

After creating the JavaScript according to the document, let's implement the `org.apache.myfaces.trinidad.validator.ClientValidator` interface and its methods.

4. Open the `EmailValidator` class that we created in the previous recipe.

5. Extend the class by implementing the `org.apache.myfaces.trinidad.validator.ClientValidator` interface.

    First, we need to point the JavaScript file created. To do that we need to change the body of the `getClientLibrarySource` method.

6. Inside the `getClientLibrarySource` method, add the following code:

    ```
    return facesContext.getExternalContext().getRequestContextPath() +
    "/resources/js/EmailValidator.js";
    ```

    Now, we need to create a new instance of the JavaScript class that we created inside our JavaScript file at the third step. To do this, we need to change the body of the `getClientValidation` method.

7. Inside the `getClientValidation` method, add the following code:

    ```
    String firstNameField = uIComponent.getAttributes().
    get("firstNameField").toString();
    return "new EmailValidator('"+firstNameField+"')";
    ```

    Now, we have added the client-side capabilities, all that we need now is to add another attribute to hold the reference of absolute ID of the `FirstName` field and make the `FirstName` field accessible from JavaScript.

8. Open the `employees.jsf` page.

9. Select the **First Name** field from the **Structure** pane.

10. Change the `clientComponent` attribute to `true`.

11. Remove the `AutoSubmit` attribute and return it back to default `false`.

12. Select the **Email** field from the **Structure** pane.

13. Right-click on the **Email** input text and select **Attribute** by navigating to **Insert Inside | JSF**.

14. Change the name of the attribute to `firstNameField`.

15. Change the value of the attribute to `pt1:t1`.

    The absolute ID is the combination of the `pageTemplateId` attribute and `FirstNameId` attribute.

 Using the absolute ID like this can be very hard and not best practice. You can replace this by having a reference of the `firstName inputText` bindings in your managed bean and use the `getClientId()` method.

16. Save everything and run the `employees.jsf` page and edit the first letter of the first name or the e-mail. You will see the error in action instantly, as shown in the following screenshot:

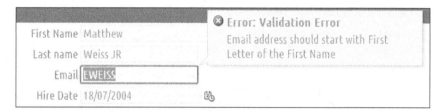

How it works...

In order to add the client-side capabilities, we should create a JavaScript version of the validation, that is a JavaScript class that extends a `TrValidator` class and overrides the `validate` method inside this JavaScript.

After creating the JavaScript class inside the `EmailValidator.js` file, we implemented the `org.apache.myfaces.trinidad.validator.ClientValidator` interface method.

We referred to the JavaScript source file by using the `getClientLibrarySource` method and we created a new instance of the JavaScript class by passing the required constructor arguments by using the `getClientValidation` method.

In this recipe, this constructor takes one argument, that is, the ID of the `FirstName` field passed through an attribute inside the component. Once we edit the field that has the client-side validator, this JavaScript instantiates a call which will occur on the client side, a new instance of this validator will be returned, and the JavaScript `validate` function will be called. If no errors thrown, then this field will be valid. However, if an error is thrown, namely `TrValidatorException`, then this field will be marked as invalid and the `FacesMessage` will be shown.

This client-side validation will not prevent the server-side validation from happening. When the form is submitted, the `validate` method inside the `EmailValidator` class will be fired normally like in the previous recipe.

From this recipe, you can imagine how you can add the client-side capabilities to your converter. However, in case of the converter, instead of having only one method to implement in your JavaScript file you will need to implement two methods `getAsObject` and `getAsString`, which will be called by the ADF JavaScript engine appropriately.

See also

To know more about creating custom ADF validators, refer to the official Trinidad documentation at `https://myfaces.apache.org/trinidad/devguide/clientValidation.html#Client-side_Validators`.

Enhancing the Faces messages user experience

All application messages are thrown as a dialog to the end user, which can be irritating sometimes. Oracle ADF Faces provides a great way of customizing this behavior by using the `af:messages` component.

In this recipe, we will edit the page template and add `af:messages` inside it. Then, we will add some CSS styles in the `hrBlue.css` skin file to enhance how messages look. Finally, we will add a button inside the `employees.jsf` to showcase different message types.

You can continue from the previous recipe, or you can grab this project's recipe by cloning the `EnhancingFacesMessageUX` application from the Git repository.

How to do it...

To know how to enhance the Faces messages experience, first we will add the `af:messages` component inside the page template, and then we will perform the following steps:

1. Open the `defaultHrTemplate.jsf` page template from the application navigator.

2. Go to **af:panelStretchLayout | f:facet – center** and select **af:facetRef – Center** from the **Structure** pane.

3. Right-click on it and navigate to **Surround with | Panel Group Layout**.

4. Drag `Messages` by navigating to **Components Palette | Text and Selection** and drop it inside the **Panel Group Layout** just before **af:facetRef – Center**.

5. Change the `Inline` attribute to `true`.

   Now that we have added the `af:messages` component, let's add a couple of styles inside the skin CSS file.

6. Open the `hrBlue.css` skin from the application navigator.

7. Switch to the source mode.

8. Add the following styles at the end of the file:

```
af|messages{
    padding: 15px;
    margin-bottom: 20px;
    border: 1px solid transparent;
    border-radius: 4px;
}
af|messages.p_AFError{
    background-color: #f2dede;
    border-color: #ebccd1;
    color: #a94442;
}
```

   This will add style to the messages component in general, and to the error messages specifically. Now, let's add a button to the `employees.jsf` page to showcase it.

9. Open the `employees.jsf` page from the application navigator.

10. Drag a button from **Components** palette and drop it inside the center facet just before the `af:panelFormLayout`.

11. Change the `Text` attribute to `Show messages`.

12. Click on the gear icon near the `Action` attribute and click on **Edit**.

13. Click on the **New** button to create a new managed bean.

14. Change the `Bean name` to messagesBean.

15. Change the `Class name` to MessagesBean.

16. Change the `Package` to com.adffaces.chapter8.view.beans.

17. Click on **OK** to close the dialog.

18. In the `Method` field, click on **New**.

19. Change the `Method name` to showMessages.

20. Click on **OK** to close the dialog box.

    Now that we have created the button, let's make the button to send multiple messages and see how they look.

21. Open the `MessagesBean` class from the application navigator.

22. Add the following code inside the `showMessages` method:

```
FacesMessage infoMsg = new FacesMessage(FacesMessage.SEVERITY_
INFO, "Information", "An Information Message");
FacesMessage warnMsg = new FacesMessage(FacesMessage.SEVERITY_
WARN, "Warning", "A Warning Message");
FacesMessage errorMsg = new FacesMessage(FacesMessage.SEVERITY_
ERROR, "Error", "An Error Message");
FacesContext ctx = FacesContext.getCurrentInstance();

ctx.addMessage(null, infoMsg);
ctx.addMessage(null, warnMsg);
ctx.addMessage(null, errorMsg);
return null;
```

23. Save everything, run `employees.jsf` page, and click on the **New** button to see the different messages, as shown in the following screenshot:

How it works...

In this recipe, we saw how to represent different message types inside the page which replaces the default behavior of showing them as a pop up.

We first added the `af:messages` component, which is the component responsible for showing Faces messages, and we set the `Inline` attribute to `true`. This is very important to replace the default behavior of showing messages.

We then styled the `af:messages` component to show it as a box with a radius of four, and had a specific style for error message by adding `.p_AFError` at the end.

After that, we added a button inside the `employees.jsf` page and created its action method to show different `FacesMessage` types inside the page. There are five different message severity types:

- Fatal
- Error
- Warning
- Information
- Confirmation

All of these types have corresponding style classes in the ADF skin CSS file that can be combined with the `af|messages` style:

- `p_AFFatal`
- `p_AFError`
- `p_AFWarning`
- `p_AFInfo`
- `p_AFConfirmation`

When the messages are shown inside the page, they'll be arranged in a descending order based on the severity type, as you can see in the previous screenshot.

9

Building Your Application for Reuse

In this chapter, we will cover the following topics:

- ▸ Creating a task flow template for your repetitive tasks
- ▸ Handling general exceptions using task flow templates
- ▸ Using task flow parameters
- ▸ Adding events to your task flow through contextual events
- ▸ Creating a declarative ADF Faces component
- ▸ Packaging your ADF Faces resources as an ADF Library
- ▸ Preserving user preferences using MDS

Introduction

Sometimes when you build your application pages, it can become very complex and hard to edit and maintain, while other pages may always contain a specific number of components that have the same structure and layout. Sometimes, you just want to share some parts of a page or entire pages with other developers in your team. Then there are times when you have a change in the UI. In these cases, you might end up replicating your changes in many places and pages.

Building and maintaining these changes can be a very tedious and troublesome process. ADF provides great reusability of your ADF Faces resources such as task flows, data controls, ADF task flow template, ADF page template, skins, and declarative components.

In this chapter, we will see how to optimize everything for reuse instead of recreating your skins every time in every project. It should be created once and applied everywhere so that when a change happens to the skin, every application that uses it gets effected.

You can find all the recipes of this chapter inside the `Chapter 9` folder of the book's Git repository. If you haven't already created the database, make sure to create it for your recipes to work flawlessly. Also, don't forget to change the database connection with the right information pointing to your local database settings.

Creating task flow template for your repetitive tasks

The smallest logic in your application should be inside your task flow. However, sometimes the task flow itself is repeated in the same way with minor differences but shares the same structure. ADF Faces introduces the concept of an ADF task flow template to eliminate this repetition and automate the task flow creation process to focus more on your business logic and less on your development time.

In this recipe, we will create a task flow template to perform simple CRUD (Create/Retrieve/Update/Delete) operations over employees. In order to do this effectively, we will create one task flow template for these operations and then create a solid task flow to implement it for employees, which can be used again for departments, regions, and more.

In this recipe, the application and its model have been created for you. You can grab this project's recipe by cloning the `CreatingTaskFlowTemplate` application from the Git repository.

How to do it...

To know how to create a task flow template, perform the following steps:

1. Open the `CreatingTaskFlowTemplate` application.

2. Right-click on **ViewController**, navigate to **New | From Gallery | Web Tier | JSF/Facelets**, and click on **ADF Task Flow Template**.

3. Name the file `hr-crud-template`.

4. Add this task flow template to the `templates` directory under `WEB-INF`.

5. Click on **OK** to close the dialog and open the ADF task flow template.

6. Drag the `View` activity from **Components** palette, drop it inside the task flow template, and name it `viewAll`.

7. Drag the `Method Call` activity from **Components** palette, drop it inside the page template, and name it `createNew`.

8. Drag **Control Flow Case**, drop it from `viewAll` to `createNew`, and name it `create` instead of `*`.

9. Drag another `View` activity and name it `newHrRecord`.

 Notice that we picked generic activities' names, because it might be used for more than one business object.

10. Drag another **Control Flow Case**, drop it from `createNew` to `newHrRecord`, and leave the default name as is.

11. Navigate to **Data Controls Pane | Chapter9AMDataControl | Operations**.

12. Drag the **Commit** operation and drop it inside `hr-crud-template`.

13. Drag the **Rollback** operation and drop it inside `hr-crud-template`.

14. Drag **Control Flow Case**, drop it from the `Commit` activity to the `ViewAll` activity, and leave the default name as is.

15. Drag **Control Flow Case**, drop it from the `Rollback` activity to the `ViewAll` activity, and leave the default name as is.

16. Drag **Control Flow Case**, drop it from the `newHrRecord` activity to the `Commit` activity, and name the case `save`.

17. Drag **Control Flow Case** from `newHrRecord` to `Rollback` and name it `cancel`.

    You should end up with the following screenshot. Notice the pink square that indicates an activity without implementation, which can be created inside a concrete task flow.

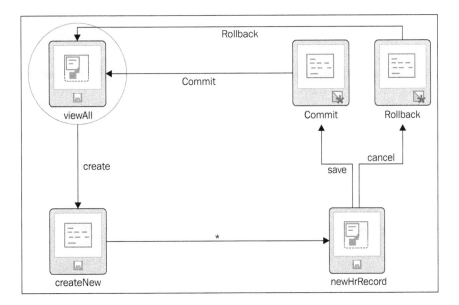

18. The next step is to create a concrete task flow for the employees table, so let's do that by performing the following steps:

    1. Navigate to **ViewController | New** and select **ADF Task Flow**.

    2. Change the task flow filename to `employees-crud-flow`.

    3. Check the **Based on Template** option and select **hr-crud-template** from the list.

    4. Make sure that the **Update the Task Flow when the Template Changes** option is checked as well.

    5. Click on **OK** to save and close the dialog.

19. You can see the same structure as in `hr-crud-template`, but everything is grayed out. In order to override the template, perform the following steps:

    1. Right-click on the `viewAll` activity and select the **Override inherited Activity** option from the context menu. This will make this view accessible in order to be created.

    2. Double-click on the `viewAll` activity to create it.

    3. Name the page fragment `viewAllEmployees`.

    4. Put the page fragment inside the `fragments` folder instead of the default one under `public_html`.

    5. Click on **OK** to close the dialog.

    6. Navigate to **Chapter9AMDataControl | Employees1** and drag **Employees1** from the **Data Controls** pane and drop it as **ADF Table** under **Table/List View**.

    7. Make sure that you check both the **Read only** and **Single Row** selection options.

    8. Remove all attributes except for the first five attributes, namely: `EmployeeId`, `FirstName`, `LastName`, `Email`, and `PhoneNumber`. Next, click on **OK**.

    9. Surround the table with an ADF panel collection by right-clicking on the **Surround by** context menu.

    10. Create a toolbar inside the toolbar facet of the ADF panel collection by dragging the toolbar component from **Components** palette.

    11. Drag a button and drop it inside the toolbar.

    12. Change the `Text` attribute to `Add new Employee`.

    13. Change the `Action` attribute to `create`.

    14. Save everything and return to the `employees-crud-flow` task flow.

20. Now that we have finished implementing the `viewAll` activity, we need to do the same for the `newHrRecord` activity as well by performing the following steps:

    1. Right-click on the `newHrRecord` activity and click on the `Override inherited` activity. This will make this view accessible in order to be created.

    2. Double-click on the `newHrRecord` activity to create it.

    3. Name the page `createEmployee` and put the page fragment under the `fragments` folder.

    4. Click on **OK** to close the dialog.

    5. Navigate to **Chapter9AMDataControl** and drag **Employees1** from the **Data Controls** pane and drop it as an ADF form.

    6. Leave the **Read-only** option unchecked.

    7. Remove all of the attributes except for the first six attributes: `EmployeeId`, `FirstName`, `LastName`, `Email`, `PhoneNumber`, and `HireDate`.

    8. Click on the **Submit** option checkbox.

    9. Click on **OK** to close the dialog.

    10. Click on the **Submit** button from the **Structure** pane.

    11. Change the `Action` attribute to `save`.

    12. Add another button beside the **Submit** button.

    13. Change the `Text` attribute of the new button to `cancel`.

    14. Change the `Action` attribute to `cancel`.

    15. Change the `Immediate` attribute in the **behavior** section to be `immediate`. This will make sure that validation is not triggered when you cancel the activity.

    16. Save everything and return to the `employees-crud-flow` task flow.

21. Now that we have finished implementing the `newHrRecord` activity, the last thing we need to implement is the `createNew` method. So, let's do that by performing the following steps:

    1. Right-click on the `createNew` activity and click on the **Override inherited Activity** option.

    2. Navigate to **Data Controls Pane | Chapter9AMDataControl | Employees1 | Operations**.

    3. Drag the **CreateInsert** operation and drop it inside the `createNew` activity until white turns yellow.

    4. This will make the implementation of the `createNew` activity to be the `CreateInsert` operation of the `Employees1` view object.

5. Save everything. You have now finished creating the employees CRUD flow.

6. Open the `adfc-config.xml` file.

7. Drag a view from **Components pallete** and change the name to `employeesCrud`.

8. Double-click on the newly created activity to create it and format it based on the `Default Hr` template.

9. Drag the `employees-crud-flow` task flow from the **Application** navigator and drop it inside the center facet.

10. Run the `employeesCrud.jsf` page and test it by creating a new record and check it in the database to make sure everything works fine, as shown in the following screenshot:

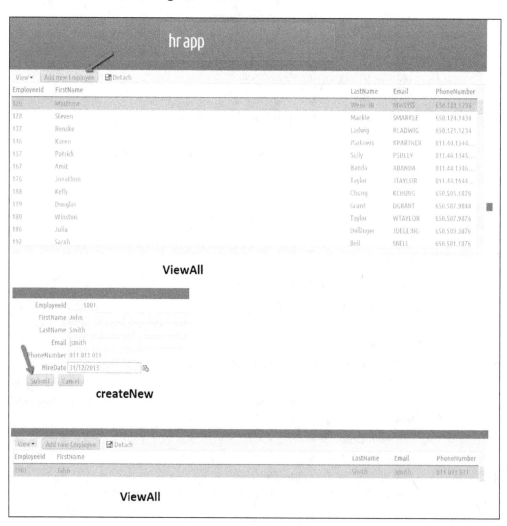

How it works...

In this recipe, you used one of the greatest reusable components, namely, the ADF task flow template.

By creating the ADF task flow template, we created a structure that multiple concrete ADF task flows can follow to have the same logic for different business entities.

Just by overriding a few activities, we were able to generate concrete task flows that perform CRUD operations without any problem.

When we created the task flow template, we ended up with the same interface as that of creating a normal task flow, which means we have all of the activities that a task flow has. The only difference in this case is that it's okay to have unimplemented activities with a pink square.

In this recipe, the task flow template has two page fragments and one `Method` activity that needs to be overridden; other than this, it has two implemented operations, namely, `commit` and `rollback` operations. This is because these two operations are shared for all of the business objects.

After we finished creating the task flow template, we started building the concrete task flow based on it.

When we created the task flow, we had two options to choose from, either getting updates from the template when the template changes or just copying them. If you are thinking about the **Don't repeat yourself** (**DRY**) principle, you should always have the **Update the Task Flow when the Template changes** option checked. In some cases though, you may just want to copy the structure and thereby change every activity in the template. In this case, you can uncheck it, but note that if you have a method call activities such as `Commit` and `Rollback`, you will have to bind them again. This is because the copy operation is just a shallow copy that copies the structure of the task flow template without copying the underlying bindings.

After we created the concrete task flow, we started overriding the unimplemented activities, which in this case were `viewAll`, `newHrRecord`, and `createNew` method, and creating the underlying pages the same way that we did in the last chapter. We also mapped the control flow rule as a button with the action mapped to the text on the control flow. After this is done, everything works great automatically.

The ADF task flows template itself can be based on other ADF task flow templates. This allows you to have a flexible structure of your task flows, which can be great if you have reusable shared libraries.

See also

Oracle provides a great video from the ADF Architecture TV channel that describes ADF task flow templates in a great and easy way. You can check the video at `http://www.youtube.com/watch?v=izTLTGDSo18`.

Handling general exceptions using task flow templates

One of the great benefits of having a task flow template is to handle general and unhandled exceptions. This can be implemented once you are inside the task flow template, and it'll be included inside any concrete task flow that extends the task flow template.

In this recipe, we will extend the `hr-crud-flow` task flow to handle a runtime exception that will be thrown by a new button which will be added inside the `viewAllEmployees.jsff` page fragment. This exception will be handled by an exception handler class, which we will create in this recipe. You can continue from the last recipe, or you can grab this project's recipe by cloning the `HandlingExceptionsUsingTFTemplates` application from the Git repository.

How to do it...

To know how to handle unhandled exceptions with task flow templates, perform the following steps.

First, we will add a step inside the task flow template to throw the exception by performing the following steps:

1. Open the **hr-crud-flow** task flow template from the **Application** navigator.

2. Navigate to **Chapter9AMDataControl**, drag **throwRuntimeException** from the **Data Control** pane, and drop it inside the **Diagram** mode of the task flow template.

3. Drag **Control Flow Case**, drop it from the `ViewAll` activity to the `ThrowRuntimeException` activity, and change the name to `throwError`.

4. Drag another **Control Flow Case**, drop it from the `ThrowRuntimeException` activity to `ViewAll`, and leave the default name as is.

Now we should add a button inside the `viewAllEmployees.jsff` page fragment to throw this exception by performing the following steps:

1. Open the `viewAllEmployees.jsff` page fragment from the **Application** navigator.

2. Drag a button and drop it inside **af:toolbar** by navigating to **af:panelCollection | f:facet – toolbar | af:toolbar**.

3. Change the `Text` attribute to `Throw Exception`.

4. Change the `Action` attribute to `throwError`.

Now let's create the exception handler class that handles the exception by performing the following steps:

1. Right-click on the **ViewController** project and navigate to **New | From Gallery | General | Java Class**.

2. Change the class name to `ExceptionHandler`.

3. Change the package name to `com.adffaces.chapter9.view.handlers`.

4. Click on **OK** to close the dialog and open the Java class.

5. Add the following method inside the class:

```
public void handleException() {
  //Get the Controller Context to access the View Port
        ControllerContext context =
    ControllerContext.getInstance();

      //Get the current root View Port Context
    ViewPortContext viewPortContext =
      context.getCurrentRootViewPort();

      //Check if Exception occurs
        if (viewPortContext.isExceptionPresent()) {
            //Clear The Exception from View Port Context
            viewPortContext.clearException();
            //Create a Faces message and display it instead
    FacesContext ctx = FacesContext.getCurrentInstance();
    FacesMessage message =
      new FacesMessage(FacesMessage.SEVERITY_ERROR,
        "UnExpected Exception occured", "I've recovered
        from Unhandled Exception");
    ctx.addMessage(null, message);
    }
  }
}
```

Now we are done with the exception handler class. The method created inspects any exception inside the controller and wraps it inside a static Faces message. Now let's create a data control out of the `ExceptionHandler` class and add it to the page template as an error handler by performing the following steps:

1. Right-click on the `ExceptionHandler` class and select the **Create Data Control** option, as shown in the following screenshot:

2. Click on **Next** and then click on **Finish** to close the dialog without changing any setting.

3. Open the **hr-crud-flow** task flow template from the **Application** navigator.

4. Navigate to **ExceptionHandler | handleException()** and drag **handleException()** from the **Data Control** pane and drop it inside the **Diagram mode** of the task flow template.

5. Right-click on it and the `handleException` activity and navigate to **Mark Activity | Exception Handler**; you should end up with something like the following diagram:

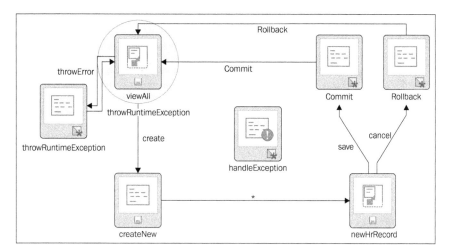

6. Save everything and run `employeesCrud.jsf`, then click on the **Throw Exception** button to see the exception handling in action, as shown in the following screenshot:

How it works...

In this recipe, we saw how to extend the task flow template to handle unhandled exceptions.

In this recipe, this exception was thrown from a custom service method inside the `Application Module Implementation` class.

 To know more about publishing custom service methods, refer to the official documentation at `http://docs.oracle.com/middleware/1212/adf/ADFFD/bcservices.htm#sm0212`.

We created a custom class with a method. This method retrieved the exception by navigating to the current view root port, then accessing any exception thrown from the controller layer, and then wrapping it inside the Faces message.

We then created a data control out of this class, added this method as the `Method-Call` activity inside the task flow template, and marked this activity as an exception handler.

Marking a `Method-Class` activity as an exception handler will tell the task flow template to automatically call this method when exceptions occur.

Looking at the previous screenshot, you can see the difference it has when you have an exception handler as compared to the way it was before.

Using task flow parameters

Task flows are great when you want to wrap small business units together. However, sometimes the business logic can change based on certain states and variables. Instead of creating multiple task flows with small changes, you can use task flow parameters to change the behavior of the task flow when it's being added as a region.

In this recipe, we will change the `employees-crud-flow` task flow to accept a parameter and to show an extra column in the employee's table based on this parameter. You can continue from the last recipe, or you can grab this project's recipe by cloning the `UsingTaskFlowParameters` application from the Git repository.

How to do it...

To know how to use parameters with task flows, perform the following steps:

1. Double-click on the `employee-crud-flow` task flow.
2. Switch to the **Overview** mode and select the **Parameters** menu from the left navigation pane.

3. Click on the plus icon to the right of **Input Parameter Definitions**.

4. Change `Name` to `showSalary`.

5. Change `Class` to `boolean`, as shown here:

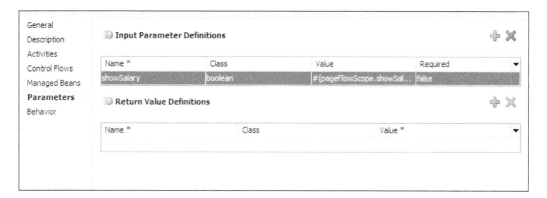

6. Open the `viewAllEmployees.jsff` page fragment.

7. Select the table component from the **Structure** pane and click on the pencil icon in the **Properties** pane.

8. Add the **Salary** column to the table, select **ADF Output Text**, and click on **OK**.

9. Select the **Salary** column, click on the gear icon besides the `Rendered` attribute, and click on **Expression Builder**.

10. Navigate to **ADF Managed Beans | pageFlowScope**, select **showSalary**, and click on **OK**.

    This is the map of the parameter that will be passed on the task flow region.

11. Open the `adfc-config.xml` file.

12. Drag a view from **Components pallete** and change the name to `employeesCrudWithSalary`.

13. Double-click on the newly created activity to create it and make it based on `Default Hr` template.

14. Drag the `employees-crud-flow` task flow from the **Application** navigator and drop it inside the center facet.

15. In the pop-up window, change the **showSalary** value to `true`.

16. Save everything, run the `employeesCrudWithSalary.jsf` page, and compare this page with the `employeesCrud.jsf` page, as shown in the following screenshot:

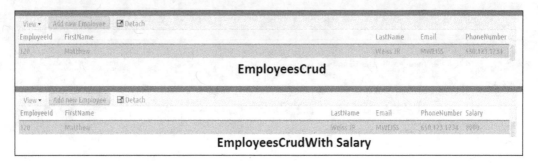

How it works...

In this recipe, we saw how we can use parameters to change how the task flow view looks. In this recipe, we created an extra column that would be visible if it is specified in the region parameter: `showSalary`.

In another scenario, you can utilize these parameters using a `Router` activity (a `Router` activity is used to declaratively route control to activities based on a logic specified in an EL expression) inside the ADF task flow to change the direction, which can create very dynamic task flows and can change their behavior based on the parameters specified.

Also, parameters can be either required or optional. When parameters are required and you haven't specified them, the task flow will throw an exception. When optional, the developer should make sure that he can cover the parameter that is missing.

Parameters in a task flow are very important when it comes to reusability, since these gives a way for the consumer page to control how the task flow behaves and looks.

Adding events to your task flow through contextual events

Task flow parameters can be used to customize how the task flow behaves, but once the task flow is loaded, how can we interact with it?

Also, how can we communicate between two task flows, or between a task flow and its page container? The answer to all these questions is in **contextual events**. Contextual events help to solve these questions in an event-driven fashion.

The idea is that one task flow publishes an event and another task flow consumes this event and reacts on it. So, when this event occurs, the other task flow or page can change its behavior without the need to refresh or reload.

You may wonder why this is not mentioned as part of *Chapter 7, Handling Events and Partial Page Rendering*, since it's an event. The reason is that even though this is an event, it can be utilized greatly for reusable applications, so it's worth mentioning here.

In this recipe, we will first publish an event in the `employees-crud-flow` task flow when a new employee is selected from the table. This event will provide us with the department ID.

Then, we will create another task flow to show details of the departments so that the new task flow can subscribe to the event to show details of this department ID.

You can continue from the last recipe, or you can grab this project's recipe by cloning the `AddingContextualEvents` application from the Git repository.

How to do it...

To know how to add contextual events, perform the following steps.

First, we need to publish an event when a user selects an employee from the `viewAllEmployees.jsff` page fragment by performing the following steps:

1. Open the `viewAllEmployees.jsff` page fragment.
2. Open the **Bindings** view of the page.
3. Click on the plus icon on the **Bindings** box.
4. Select **attributeValues** and click on **OK**.
5. Change **Data Source** to `Chapter9AMDataControl.Employees1`.
6. Change **Attribute** to `DepartmentId` and click on **OK**.

   This attribute value represents a department ID that will get changed every time a new row is selected and will always represent the current row's department ID.

7. Switch back to the **Design** view and select **af:table** from the **Structure** pane.
8. In the **Properties** pane, navigate to **Behavior | Contextual events** and click on the plus icon on the **Published Event** section.
9. Change the `Name` attribute to `selectDepartment`.
10. Check the **Pass Custom Value from:** checkbox option.
11. Select **DepartmentId** from the **Available Data Bindings** section and click on **OK**.

12. You should end up with the following screenshot:

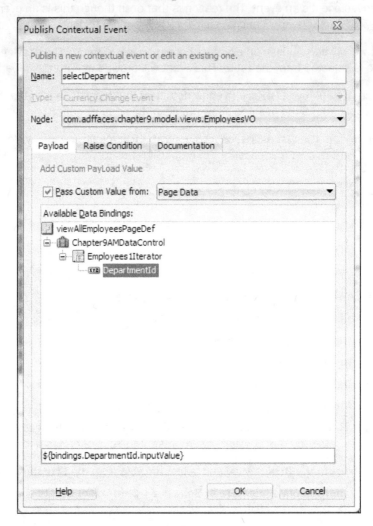

Now that we have finished publishing an event, we need to create a task flow that will consume this event, so let's do that.

13. Right-click on the **ViewController** project and navigate to **New | ADF Task Flow**.

14. Change the filename to show the department info and click on **OK**.

15. Drag a view from **Components** palette inside the task flow and name it showDepartmentInfo.

16. Double-click on the newly created view and put the page fragment under the fragments folder.

17. Navigate to **Data Controls pane | Chapter9AMDataControl | Departments1** and drag **Employees3** inside the page fragment as **ADF Master Form, Detail Table** in **Master-Detail**.

18. Change the `Text` attribute of the first panel header to `Department Info`.

19. Change the `Text` attribute of the second panel header to `Department Employees`.

20. Switch to the **Bindings** view of the page.

21. Click on the plus icon on the **Bindings** box.

22. Select **action** and click on **OK**.

23. Navigate to **Chapter9AMDataControl | Departments1 | Operations**, select **setCurrentRowWithKeyValue**, and click on **OK**.

 The `setCurrentRowWithKeyValue` operation is used to select a row by its primary key.

We have now finished creating the action that will be consuming the published event. This method is `setCurrentRowWithKeyValue` and the method's parameter will be passed by the published event custom payload that we specified. Next, we need to wire them together by putting the two task flows in a single page.

24. Open the `adfc-config.xml` file.

25. Drag a view from **Components pallete** and change the name to `employeesWithDept`.

26. Double-click on the newly created activity to create it and model it based on `Default Hr Template`.

27. Select `af:pageTemplate` from the **Structure** pane.

28. Change the `leftColumnWidth` attribute to `0px`.

29. Change the `rightColumnWidth` attribute to `300px`.

30. Drag the `employees-crud-flow` task flow from the **Application** navigator and drop it inside the center facet as `region`.

31. Change the `showSalary` attribute to `false` and click on **OK**.

32. Drag the `show-department-info` task flow from the **Application** navigator and drop it inside the right facet as `region`.

33. Open the **Bindings** view of the page.

34. Click on the **Contextual Events** tab and then click on the **Subscribers** tab.

35. Click on the plus icon underneath the **Subscribers** tab.

36. In the `Event` attribute, click the magnifier glass icon, select the `selectDepartment` event, and click on **OK**.

37. Change the publisher from the combobox to start with
    `employeesWithDeptPageDef`.

38. On the `Handler` attribute, press the magnifier glass icon and select the
    `setCurrentRowWithKeyValue` method from the list.

39. Click on the plus icon on the **Consumer Parameters** section.

40. Change the `Name` attribute to `rowKey`.

41. Change the `Value` attribute to `#{payLoad}` and click on **OK**. You should end up
    with the following screenshot:

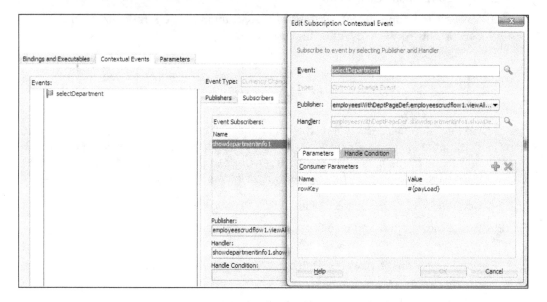

42. Save everything, run the `employeesWithDept.jsf` page, and select a different
    row and see the changes in action, as seen in the following screenshot:

View ▾ | Add new Employee | 🗗 Detach

EmployeeId	FirstName	LastName	Email	PhoneNumber
120	Matthew	Weiss JR	MWEISS	650.123.1234
128	Steven	Markle	SMARKLE	650.124.1434
137	Renske	Ladwig	RLADWIG	650.121.1234
146	Karen	Partners	KPARTNER	011.44.1344...
157	Patrick	Sully	PSULLY	011.44.1345...
167	Amit	Banda	ABANDA	011.44.1346...
176	Jonathon	Taylor	JTAYLOR	011.44.1644...
188	Kelly	Chung	KCHUNG	650.505.1876
...				

Department Info

DepartmentId 50
DepartmentName Shipping
ManagerId
LocationId 1500

First | Previous | Next | Last

Department Employees

EmployeeId	FirstName	LastNam
120	Matthew	Weiss JR
128	Steven	Markle
137	Renske	Ladwig
188	Kelly	Chung
...	...	...

View ▾ | Add new Employee | 🗗 Detach

EmployeeId	FirstName	LastName	Email	PhoneNumber
120	Matthew	Weiss JR	MWEISS	650.123.1234
128	Steven	Markle	SMARKLE	650.124.1434
137	Renske	Ladwig	RLADWIG	650.121.1234
146	Karen	Partners	KPARTNER	011.44.1344...
157	Patrick	Sully	PSULLY	011.44.1345...
167	Amit	Banda	ABANDA	011.44.1346...
176	Jonathon	Taylor	JTAYLOR	011.44.1644...
188	Kelly	Chung	KCHUNG	650.505.1876
...				

Department Info

DepartmentId 80
DepartmentName Sales
ManagerId
LocationId 2100

First | Previous | Next | Last

Department Employees

EmployeeId	FirstName	LastNam
146	Karen	Partners
157	Patrick	Sully
167	Amit	Banda
176	Jonathon	Taylor
...	...	...

How it works...

In this recipe, we saw how to utilize contextual events in a task flow to establish communication between two different task flows.

The first thing we did was to publish an event. Some components such as a table can publish events based on the table selection, or it can be triggered by a button method action.

When we defined a published event, we also specified an optional custom payload that will be sent with it. In that case, it was the current row's department ID.

In the `show-department-info` task flow, we created a binding for an action, namely `setCurrentRowWithKeyValue`, which takes the primary key of the table and sets the current row as this record. This method only has a single parameter with the name `rowKey`. However, this method cannot be wired from the task flow itself. The one that is responsible for the wiring is the host page, and that's what we did by adding both task flows inside the `employeesWithDept.jsf` page.

We added a subscriber to the published method and wired the
`setCurrentRowWithKeyValue` method's parameter, `rowKey`, to the custom payload
that is sent with the published event.

This allowed us to create an asynchronous communication between two task flows that
required no extra refreshes.

See also

▶ To know more about contextual events, refer to the official documentation at
  `http://docs.oracle.com/middleware/1212/adf/ADFFD/contextual_`
  `events.htm#ADFFD22333`

Creating declarative ADF Faces component

Declarative components are reusable, composite UI components that are made up of other
existing ADF Faces components.

When you have a common component that you want to use multiple times consistently,
declarative components can be of great help and can be useful instead of copying and
pasting the same components over and over again and risk change management.

In this recipe, we will create two components, namely, a red button and a blue button.
You can continue from the last recipe, or you can grab this project's recipe by cloning
the `CreateDeclarativeComponent` application from the Git repository.

How to do it...

To know how to create declarative ADF Faces component, perform the following steps:

1. Right-click on the **ViewController** project, select **New** by navigating to
   Gallery | JSF/Facelets | ADF Declarative Component, and click on **OK**.
2. Change `Declarative component name` to `blueButton`.
3. Change the path of the directory to be placed inside the `components` directory
   under `public_html`.
4. Change `Declarative component package` to `com.adffaces.chapter9.`
   `components`.
5. Click on the **Add Tag Library** button.
6. Change `Tag Library Name` to `FlatUI`.
7. Change `Tag Library URI` to `http://components.chapter9.adffaces.com`.
8. Change `Tag Library Prefix` to `FlatUI` and click on **OK**.

9. Inside the **Facet definitions** tab, add a facet with the name `buttonBody`.

10. Switch to the **Attributes** tab and add the following attributes:

Name	Type	Default Value	Required
text	java.lang.String	Button1	false
inlineStyle	java.lang.String		false
disabled	java.lang.Boolean	false	false

11. Switch to the **Methods** tab and add the following methods:

Name	Method Signature	Required
action	java.lang.String method()	false
actionListener	void method(javax.faces.event. ActionEvent)	false

12. You should end up with the following screenshot:

13. Click on **OK**.

14. Drag a **Link** component from **Components** palette and drop it inside the
    blueButton.jsf page.

15. Change the Text attribute to #{attrs.text}.

 You can also use an expression builder to construct this
expression by navigating to **Scoped Variables | attrs | text**.

16. Change the inlineStyle attribute to #{attrs.inlineStyle}.

17. Change the Disabled attribute to #{attrs.disabled}.

18. Change the Action attribute to #{comp.handleAction} by using the gear icon,
    and click on **Edit** and select **action** from **Declarative component method**.

19. Change the ActionListener attribute to #{comp.handleActionListener}
    as done in the previous step.

20. Change styleClass to btn blue-button.

21. Switch to the **Source** mode of the page.

22. Add the following code inside the af:link opening and closing tag:

    ```
    <af:facetRef facetName="buttonBody" />
    ```

    Now that we have finished creating the first component, let's create the second
    declarative component.

23. Repeat steps 1 to 22, but change the following:

    ❑   Change Declarative component name to redButton.

    ❑   Change styleClass to btn red-button.

    You should end up with a similar creation of the blueButton component, as shown
    in the following screenshot:

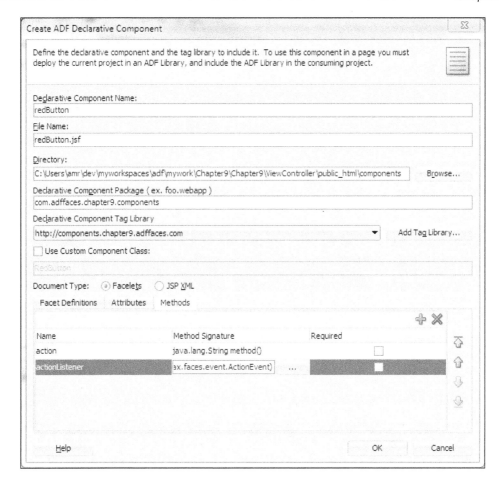

24. Save everything.

In the next recipe, we will see this component in action.

How it works...

In this recipe, we created two simple declarative components that represent two flat UI buttons: red and blue.

In order to create these two components, we created a declarative component and wrapped a `link` component to show all of the button attributes such as `text`, `inlineStyle`, and `disabled`.

We also specified two methods, `action` and `actionListener`, for the button to be able to execute as a function.

We also created a facet where if you want to add any component inside the link, it should be placed inside this facet. This will make it easier for the component to be reusable and customizable the way the component consumer sees fit.

In the **Declarative Component creation** dialog, you can spot a similarity between it and the creation of a page template, except for a couple of things:

- In the page template, there are no tabs for methods.
- Declarative components can be added to a tag library along with other declarative components.

In order to use these declarative components, we must first package these resources, which we will see in the next recipe.

Packaging your ADF Faces resources as an ADF Library

Being able to reuse your application resource in other applications is essential.

ADF provides this feature by providing developers the option to package all of the application resources from data controls, task flows, task flow templates, declarative components, skins, and more into an ADF JAR library that can be used inside other applications.

In this recipe, we will see how to package these resources and use them in another application.

In order to complete this recipe, we will need to work with two applications. One of them can be taken from the last recipe, or you can grab it by cloning the ADFFacesLibrary application from the Git repository. The other application will be created from scratch.

How to do it...

To know how to package your ADF application, perform the following steps:

1. Right-click on the **ViewController** project and select **Project Properties**.
2. Select the **Deployment** menu from the left pane and click on the **New** button.
3. Select **ADF Library Jar File** as **Profile Type**.
4. Change **Deployment Profile Name** to HRCommonResources and click on **OK**, and you should end up with the following screenshot:

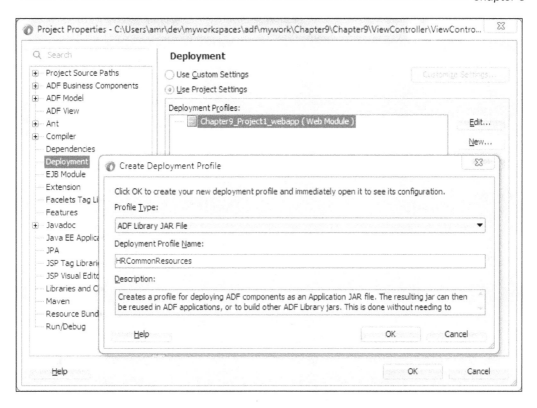

5. A pop-up will appear. Select **JAR Options** from the left menu, save **JAR file location** for future use, and click on **OK**.

6. Right-click on the **ViewController** project and navigate to **Deploy** | **HRCommonResources**.

7. Select **Deploy** for the ADF Library JAR file and click on **Finish**.

    Now that we have deployed our resources, it's time to create a new fusion web application to consume these resources.

8. In the JDeveloper file toolbar navigate to **File** | **New** | **Application**.

9. Select **ADF Fusion Web Application** from the items and click on **OK**.

10. Change **Application Name** to HrConsumerApp.

11. Change **Application Package Prefix** to com.adffaces.hrconsumer and click on **Finish**.

    We need to create a connection that monitors our ADF Library to consume it, so let's do that now.

12. In the **Resources** pane, click on the catalog icon and navigate to **IDE Connections |
File System...,** as shown below:

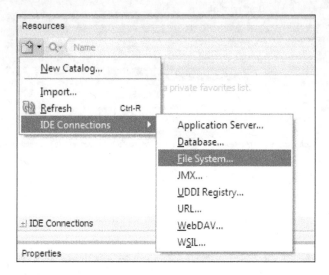

13. Change **Connection Name** to HRCommonResources.

14. Change the directory to point to the HRCommonResources JAR directory from
the path we saved in step 5.

15. Click on the **Test Connection** button to make sure everything is correct.
If it is, you should receive a success message in the status area.

16. Click on **OK** to save and close the dialog.

17. Expand **IDE Connections** from the **Resources** pane. You should see the library
as it appears in the following screenshot:

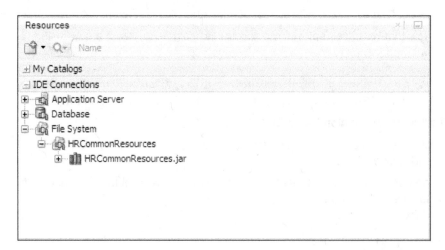

18. Right-click on `HRCommonResource.jar` and click on the **Add to Project** option.

19. When a pop up appears, click on the **Add Library** button.

20. Make sure that the database connection is established successfully by navigating to **Application Resources | Connections | Database | FacesHr** and checking the properties. If the password is missing, add it.

    Now that we have added all the resources to the new application, we can test it by first changing the default skin.

21. Double-click on the `trinidad-config.xml` file under the `WEB-INF` folder.

22. Change the `skin-family` tag from `skyros` to `hrBlue`.

23. Remove the `skin-version` tag.

    Now that we are using the `hrBlue` skin we created in *Chapter 5*, *Beautifying Application Layout*, for great user experience, let's create a page and use the task flows and declarative components.

24. Open the `adfc-config.xml` file.

25. Drag a view from **Components pallete** and change the name to `employees`.

26. Double-click on the newly created activity to create it and model it based on `Default Hr` template (it should be available).

27. Drag a panel group layout and drop it inside the center facet.

28. Change the **Component palette** resources from **ADF Faces** to **FlatUI**, as shown in the following screenshot:

29. Drag the `BlueButton` component inside the panel group layout.

30. Change the `Text` attribute to `Hello Blue`.

31. Drag the `RedButton` component inside the panel group layout.

32. Change the `Text` attribute to `Hello Red`.

33. Change the **Component palette** resources from **FlatUI** to **HrCommonResources.jar** and expand **Regions** area, as shown in the following screenshot:

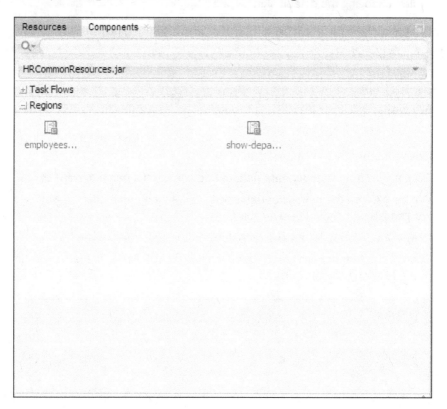

34. Drag `employees-crud-flow` inside the panel group layout as a region.

35. Change the `ShowSalary` attribute to `true` and click on **OK**.

36. Save everything and run the `employees.jsf` page. You should get something like the following screenshot:

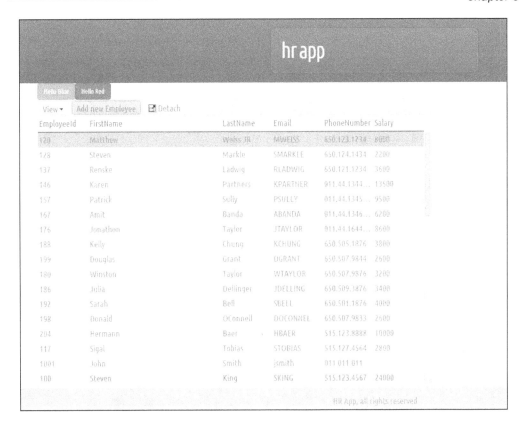

How it works...

We have created multiple reusable ADF Faces components. In order to use them, we need to first package those in an ADF Library JAR file.

When we deployed the ADF Library JAR, JDeveloper did three things for us as follows:

- ▶ It packaged all of the necessary resources and configurations
- ▶ It added the appropriate control files
- ▶ It generated the JAR file

This made all of the resources created inside the project available and accessible from different applications.

There are different ADF Faces components that are reusable as follows:

- Data controls
- Task flows
- Task flow templates
- Page templates
- Declarative components
- Skins
- Page fragments

All of these can be reused to make sure you don't repeat yourself. In this recipe, we created an extra deployment profile for the **ViewController** project and issued a deploy command to generate the ADF Library JAR file.

After that, we created a new filesystem connection to point to the ADF Library JAR file directory and added it to the newly created application by using the **Add to Project** option. This allowed the previous list of resources to be available from the ADF Library JAR file to the current application. A good strategy is to create a common application that hosts all of the main resources and templates and uses them within all of the applications that needs these resources.

Preserving user preferences using MDS

Another aspect of reusability is end user reusability. While we made sure that the ADF developer can reuse other developer assets, an end user can store his preferences in a specific store that can be reused and tailored for this user's experience.

The **Oracle Metadata Services** (**MDS**) framework allows this functionality to work, and with it, you can create applications that your end users can customize without touching the source code or affecting the ability of the application to be patched or updated.

You should grab this project's recipe by cloning the UsingMDS application from the Git repository.

Getting ready

In order to implement this functionality, we need to have security first. So, if you want to resume from the last recipe, you first need to implement security in your application for this recipe to work effectively. To know how to implement security, follow the official documentation at http://docs.oracle.com/middleware/1212/adf/ADFFD/adding_security.htm#ADFFD19890.

How to do it...

To know how to preserve user preferences, perform the following steps:

1. Right-click on the **ViewController** project node and select **Project Properties**.

2. Select the **ADF View** option.

3. Check the **Enable User Customizations** option and also check the **Across sessions using MDS** option. You should end up with the following screenshot:

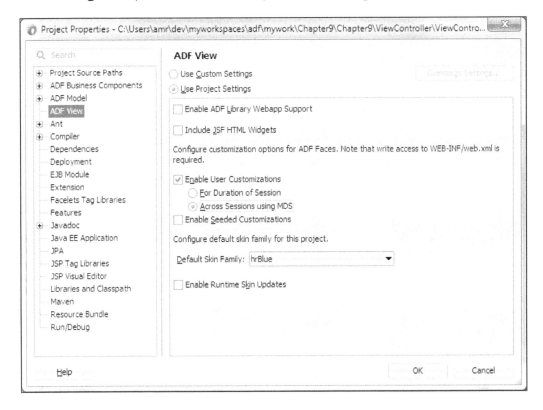

With this, we enabled user customization for the project. We need to further configure the `adf-config.xml` file, so let's do that.

4. Navigate to **Applications Navigator | Application Resource | Descriptors | ADF META-INF** and double-click on `adf-config.xml` to open it.

5. Click on **MDS** from the left menu.

6. Click on the plus icon. It will open a window to search for the customization class. Since we want customization to be saved for the user, we should search for UserCC.

7. Select **oracle.adf.share.config.UserCC** from the list of matching classes. You should end up with the following screenshot:

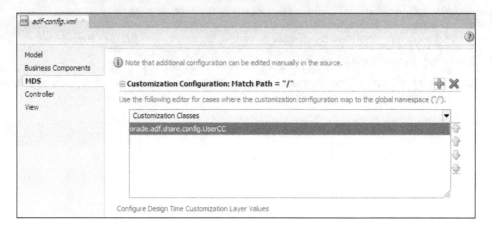

8. Click on the **View** menu from the left menu.

9. Choose **ADF Faces Components** from the **Tag Persistence** section.

10. Click on the plus icon to add the following components:

   ❑ Table

   ❑ Column

   You should end up with the following screenshot:

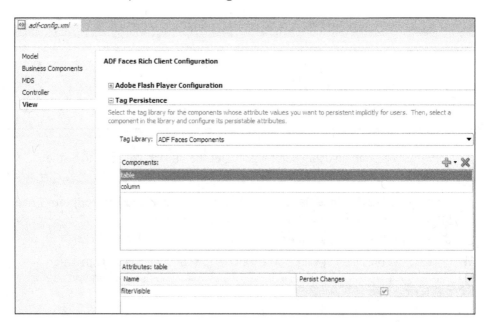

Adding these two components will save any preferences action inside MDS that the user makes on any ADF table or column.

11. Run the `employees.jsf` page, log in with the default web logic user, and change the order of the columns. See if logging out and logging in again shows the changes.

How it works...

MDS can save the user's customization data either in a filesystem or database.

In a development environment, like in this example, customization is saved in the filesystem, and you can see its path by navigating to **Application menu | Application Properties | Run | MDS**.

The next time the user logs in with a username, he should find everything as he left it. In this recipe, it was only enabled for a table and column, but you can add more ADF Faces components. Always try to limit what you want to reserve for a more performing application.

There are three customization classes for MDS:

► **User Customization Class** (**UserCC**) identifies specific users and creates customizations for each one of them. This is why you need to have security implemented in order for UserCC to work properly.

► **Security Roles Customization Class** (**SecurityRolesCC**) is based on user role memberships from the security context. Here, if multiple users share the same role and one of them changes some aspect of the customization, the rest will view the same customization.

► **Site Customization Class** (**SiteCC**) is for the entire site, so when someone applies this customization, all other users using the application will see the changes.

MDS can make the ADF application highly customizable and provide more personalization to the user so he/she can find what he/she is looking for quickly and easily.

MDS is widely used in other Oracle Middleware fusion products such as WebCenter Portal and Oracle SOA suite.

10
Scaling your ADF Faces Application

This chapter will cover the following topics:

- ▶ Applying general advices regarding performance
- ▶ Applying configuration performance recommendations
- ▶ Applying ADF Faces component's attributes recommendations
- ▶ Using **Content Delivery Network** (**CDN**) to load your static resources
- ▶ Using ADF caching to cache and compress static resources

Introduction

In this final chapter, we want to provide you with some guidelines and recommendations on how to maximize the performance and scalability of an ADF application. Always consider these recommendations in a production environment.

There are two types of changes that can be applied to an ADF application to tune it for performance and scalability. These types are as follows:

- ▶ **Configuration settings tuning**: This means using different contextual parameters in the web.xml file or in any configuration file to tune different settings of your ADF application.
- ▶ **Component level tuning**: This means using a component's attributes properly to increase its performance and minimize its load time.

Most of the recipes in this chapter are recommendations and will not need any application running; however, a few recipes have step-by-step procedures, which you can find inside the Chapter 10 folder of the book's Git repository.

Applying general advices regarding performance

There are several general advices to look at when you want to maximize the performance and scalability of your application. In this recipe, we will have a spotlight over them.

These are the first things you want to look at when you start planning your application for production. Once these recommendations are applied, rest assured that you have followed the best practices for performance tuning and scalability. This recipe doesn't require an application.

How to do it...

In order to understand different general optimization recommendations, perform the following steps:

1. Avoid adding inline JavaScript in the JSF or JSPX pages.

2. Whenever you have a custom servlet, configure the JSP timeout parameter for it by applying the following syntax in `web.xml`:

```
<servlet>
 <servlet-name>
   MyCustomServlet
   <init-param>
     <param-name>jsp_timeout</param-name>
     <param-value>10</param-value>
   </init-param>
 </servlet-name>
</servlet>
```

3. Avoid displaying pop ups on hover overs for navigation links or buttons.

4. Consider using partial page navigation.

5. Avoid using long IDs in your ADF components.

6. Optimize your page templates by avoiding the usage of the `<f:subview>` tags and use the `<jsp:include>` tags instead. However, be careful with duplicate IDs.

7. Consider using **partial page rendering** (**PPR**) whenever possible.

8. Use the `resources` servlet to cache static content such as custom JavaScript, CSS, and image files by adding the following in `web.xml`:

```
<servlet-mapping>
    <servlet-name>resources</servlet-name>
```

```
        <url-pattern>/js/*</url-pattern>
    </servlet-mapping>
    <servlet-mapping>
        <servlet-name>resources</servlet-name>
        <url-pattern>/images/*</url-pattern>
    </servlet-mapping>
```

The servlets in the following screenshot will be visible in the **Servlets** tab of
the web.xml file:

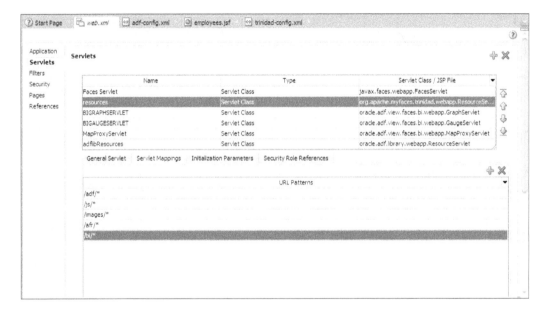

9. Consider disabling animations for your Oracle ADF DVT components by adding the
    following line inside your trindad-config.xml file:

    ```
    <animation-enabled>false</animation-enabled>
    ```

10. Always consider minifying the JavaScript and CSS files.

11. Create a JavaScript feature for your custom ADF components by performing the
    following steps:

    1. Create a file called adf-js-features.xml and save it under the META-
        INF directory of your ViewController project.

    2. Add the following XML code inside the file:

        ```
        <features xmlns="http://xmlns.oracle.com/adf/faces/feature">
          <feature>
        ```

```
      <feature-name>HrButtons</feature-name>
       <feature-class>
         com/adffaces/hrComponents/js/component/hrBlueButton.js
       </feature-class>
       <feature-class>
         com/adffaces/hrComponents/js/component/hrRedButton.js
       </feature-class>
      <!-- Example Dependency -->
      <feature-dependency>AdfRichPopup</feature-dependency>
    </feature>
```

3. Save the file.

12. Consider removing the components you are not using from the partition.

13. Consider using performance testing tools such as JMeter or **Oracle Application Test Suite (OATS)**.

How it works...

To understand what each one does, let's take it one-by-one.

By avoiding inline JavaScript in your pages, make sure of the following:

▸ Your JavaScript files can be cached in the browser and used with the `resources` servlet.

▸ Your page payload is less in size, which means there is less traffic.

Some servlets when defined are not used that much, and by setting a timeout for them, you can make sure that they get flushed from the cache.

Displaying pop ups on hover overs for navigational links can distract the end user completely and will not allow him/her to click on the link.

Partial page navigation will increase the performance rapidly since the entire page does not get re-rendered every time and only portions of the page are updated (see *Chapter 7, Handling Events and Partial Page Rendering*).

Longer IDs can have a performance impact on the server side and client processing. Always try to set your components with a minimum of three characters and a maximum of seven characters.

By using `<jsp:include>` instead of `<f:subview>`, make sure that you don't add an extra scoping layer, which results in longer IDs.

Using PPR instead of full-page rendering will use asynchronous (AJAX) requests instead of making a full server-side round trip.

Whenever you use JavaScript, CSS, or image files, mapping the `resources` servlet to their relative path enables these resources to be cached properly.

Animation is good for user experience, but sometimes all you need is speed, so disabling animations can be a good solution to speed up the performance.

Using any online or offline tools to minify your JavaScript and custom CSS files—not skins—can save the size by approximately 20 percent.

When you create a custom ADF component, creating a JavaScript feature is a good practice since it'll tell the ADF framework what kind of JavaScript files to load with the component and what the dependency of other ADF components is. If you examine the `adf-js-features.xml` file, you can see it's a definition of the component's JavaScript files or JavaScript classes, which together make a feature, and a feature can depend on other features, as you can see from the semantics of the XML.

 To know more about creating your own component features, refer to the official documentation at `http://docs.oracle.com/middleware/1212/adf/ADFUI/af_arch.htm#ADFUI10195`.

By default, ADF provides a partition for its component. A partition is multiple JavaScript features that are constructed and loaded together to save the server from round trips. Sometimes, these partitions load more stuff than you need, so it can be a good practice to create your own `adf-js-partitions.xml` file under the `WEB-INF` folder of your `ViewController` project. At runtime, the ADF Faces framework will search for this file. If it is not found, it'll use the default ADF Faces partition file.

 To know more about configuring ADF JavaScript partitions, refer to the official documentation at `http://docs.oracle.com/middleware/1212/adf/ADFUI/af_arch.htm#ADFUI10196`.

Testing will remain the best approach to analyze the application's performance. Using performance testing tools such as JMeter can help you identify your application's bottlenecks and performance issues.

 To know more about testing ADF applications with JMeter, refer to `http://www.youtube.com/watch?v=cudvV12KGiQ` and `https://blogs.oracle.com/onesizedoesntfitall/entry/new_recording_on_using_jmeter`.

Applying configuration performance recommendations

One way of enhancing your application's performance and scalability is by understanding different configuration parameters that you can configure to optimize your application.

In this recipe, we will apply some configuration-tuning tips on an already created application. You can grab this project's recipe by cloning the `ConfigurationsTuning` application from the Git repository.

How to do it...

To know how to apply basic performance-tuning recommendations, perform the following steps.

We will first apply the configuration recommendations:

1. Open the `ConfigurationsTuning` application.

2. Open `web.xml` under the `WEB-NF` folder.

3. Make sure that the **Application** menu is selected from the left sidebar.

4. Expand the **Context Initialization Parameters** section, as shown in the following screenshot:

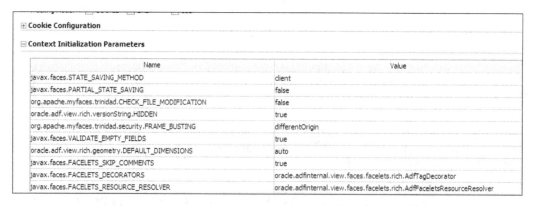

Name	Value
javax.faces.STATE_SAVING_METHOD	client
javax.faces.PARTIAL_STATE_SAVING	false
org.apache.myfaces.trinidad.CHECK_FILE_MODIFICATION	false
oracle.adf.view.rich.versionString.HIDDEN	true
org.apache.myfaces.trinidad.security.FRAME_BUSTING	differentOrigin
javax.faces.VALIDATE_EMPTY_FIELDS	true
oracle.adf.view.rich.geometry.DEFAULT_DIMENSIONS	auto
javax.faces.FACELETS_SKIP_COMMENTS	true
javax.faces.FACELETS_DECORATORS	oracle.adfinternal.view.faces.facelets.rich.AdfTagDecorator
javax.faces.FACELETS_RESOURCE_RESOLVER	oracle.adfinternal.view.faces.facelets.rich.AdfFaceletsResourceResolver

5. Click on the green plus icon to add the following context parameters (if they don't already exist):

Name	Value	Description
`oracle.adf.view.rich.CHECK_FILE_MODIFICATION`	`false`	This setting tells the ADF Faces application to check for the modification of skins and JSP pages at runtime, which slows down the performance due to extra checks. Setting it to `false` is the best way to optimize your application.
`org.apache.myfaces.trinidad.COMPRESS_VIEW_STATE`	`true`	This will decrease the latency as the data state between pages is compressed.
`org.apache.myfaces.trinidad.resource.DEBUG`	`false`	Either remove it or set it to `false` to prevent debugging.
`oracle.adf.view.rich.CLIENT_STATE_METHOD`	`token`	This works when `javax.faces.STATE_SAVING_METHOD` is set to `client` as it specifies the method of saving either by `token` or `all`.
`org.apache.myfaces.trinidad.CLIENT_STATE_MAX_TOKENS`	`2`	Since you are using `token` with your `oracle.adf.view.rich.CLIENT_STATE_METHOD` setting, try to minimize this number based on your analysis as this will save the state for the browser's back button behavior. If you provide a back button inline with your application, decreasing this will reduce the memory per session.
		This should be based on your analysis and can differ by applications. The default value is `15`.
`oracle.adf.view.rich.LOGGER_LEVEL`	`false`	Either remove it or set it to `false` to prevent client-side logging.
`oracle.adf.view.rich.ASSERT_ENABLED`	`false`	Either remove it or set it to `false` to prevent assertions processing on the client side.
`oracle.adf.view.rich.libraryPartitioning.DISABLED`	`false`	This enables library partitioning for ADF components.
`org.apache.myfaces.trinidad.DEBUG_JAVASCRIPT`	`false`	This enables JavaScript obfuscated of ADF JavaScript Libraries.

6. Save everything.

How it works...

In this recipe, we added a couple of configuration settings, which are set inside the `web.xml` file; most of the default values are already tuned.

Using these configuration settings will be beneficial, especially when you have high-availability requirements for your ADF application.

Applying ADF Faces component's attributes recommendations

There are several component-level tuning options that can be applied to the attributes of different components of your page and can increase the performance in a great way.

You'd be amazed by how small attribute changes can make a huge impact on the performance and scalability of your ADF application.

This recipe doesn't require an application as we will discuss those recommendations and elaborate on their importance.

How to do it...

In order to understand different optimizations over a component's attribute, perform the following steps:

1. Use the `immediate` attribute if you don't want to process the data validation.
2. Use the `subform` component if you have a special behavior of grouped components.
3. Use the `rendered` attribute instead of the `visible` attribute to save the component mark up from being written inside the page's DOM.
4. Use the client-side event for relatively simple event handling to speed up the application.
5. Always cancel the server-side event from the client-side event if you don't need it as in the following code snippet:

```
<af:resource>
 function handleClientEvent(event){
   //... your code in here
   event.cancel();
 }
</af:resource>
```

6. Don't use the `clientComponent` attribute unless you need to find the component on the client side.

7. Always consider setting the `childCreation` attribute of a pop up to `deferred`.

8. In the table, set the **EditingMode** field to **clickToEdit** instead of **editAll**:

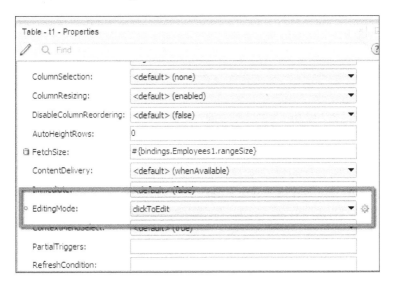

9. Reduce the table's **FetchSize** value whenever possible.

10. Disable the table's column stretching.

11. Consider using the `lazy` delivery instead of the `immediate` delivery for data-enabled components such as tables, trees, and lists.

How it works...

In this recipe, we saw a couple of recommendations to enhance the performance of a component level and in order to understand what each one does, let's take it one-by-one.

Setting the `immediate` attribute to `true` on navigational links or buttons can avoid the processing of data validation on the page and go directly to the next page, which saves processing time; however, always be aware of the lifecycle changes of the `immediate` attribute.

If you have multiple components that have different inputs and buttons for different purposes, a good example is the inline login form or search bar. Putting them in a separate `subform` component can optimize the amount of data being sent back to the server.

Using the `rendered` attribute will allow the ADF lifecycle to write the component's HTML mark up inside the page, which reduces the traffic. If you have a relatively easy action such as changing the value or the visibility, consider using the client-side event instead of the server-side event for this behavior.

Server events occur even if you define a client-side event, so if you don't want to trigger the server-side event, make sure to call `event.cancel()` at the end of your client-side JavaScript function.

Setting the `clientComponent` attribute to **true** will prompt the ADF to create the component's JavaScript object, which will add size to the payload sent to the end user. Setting the `childCreation` attribute of a pop up to **deferred** will make sure that the components inside the pop up are not inserted in the DOM when the page is first rendered and will only be added when the pop up is executed using asynchronous AJAX requests.

Having validation for multiple rows in a table at a time can be a time-consuming process for the server side. Setting the `editingMode` attribute to **clickToEdit** can eliminate that. Having big `fetchSize` implies that more data needs to be processed and fetched from the server and also increases the amount of DOMs displayed to the end user.

Disabling a table's column stretching can decrease the amount of JavaScript added to the page to calculate the amount of size needed to stretch, which means a bigger payload and more waiting time.

Using the `lazy` delivery instead of the `immediate` delivery for data-enabled components such as tables will ensure that the table is first rendered and the data is fetched after that in parallel.

Using Content Delivery Network to load your static resources

When you have multiple static resources in your page such as CSS, JavaScript, and images, it's always beneficial to use a Content Delivery Network (CDN) to parallelize downloading these resources and distribute them across different domain names. Even if you don't have different domain names, you can use the same domain with different sub-domains in order to trick the browser into believing that there are different domain names.

In this recipe, we are going to use a CDN to fetch skin, images, videos, and JavaScript files. You can grab this project's recipe by cloning the `ADFFacesWithCDN` application from the Git repository.

Getting ready

Add an entry of your machine name under your host's file with an entry as follows:

```
127.0.0.1 adffaces js.adffaces.local static.adffaces.local skin.
adffaces.local
```

You can find the `hosts` file at the following locations:

- ▸ `C:\Windows\System32\drivers\etc\hosts` (Windows)
- ▸ `/etc/hosts` (Linux)
- ▸ `/private/etc/hosts` (Mac)

This entry will assign your local IP address to all of the different domain names, which will always reference the same IP address.

How to do it...

To know how to apply a CDN to your ADF application, perform the following steps:

1. Open the `ADFFacesWithCDN` application.
2. Navigate to **Application Resources | Descriptors | ADF META-INF** and double-click on the `adf-config.xml` file.
3. Change to the source mode.
4. Add the following mark up just before the last `</adf-config>` tag:

```
<adf-uri-rewrite-config xmlns="http://xmlns.oracle.com/adf/
rewrite/config">
    <resource-uris>
        <base-resource-uri uri="http://static.adffaces.local:
#{request.serverPort}/" output-context-path="preserve">
            <match-pattern>^.*/(movies|images)/.*\.
(jpg|png|jpeg|gif|mov|mp4)$</match-pattern>
        </base-resource-uri>
        <base-resource-uri uri="http://js.adffaces.local:#{request.
serverPort}/" output-context-path="preserve">
            <match-alias>af:coreScripts</match-alias>
            <match-alias>af:documents</match-alias>
        </base-resource-uri>
        <base-resource-uri uri="http://skin.adffaces.
local:#{request.serverPort}/" output-context-path="preserve">
            <match-alias>af:skins</match-alias>
        </base-resource-uri>
    </resource-uris>
</adf-uri-rewrite-config>
```

5. Save everything, run the `employees.jsf` page, and use any debugging tool to see the difference in loading.

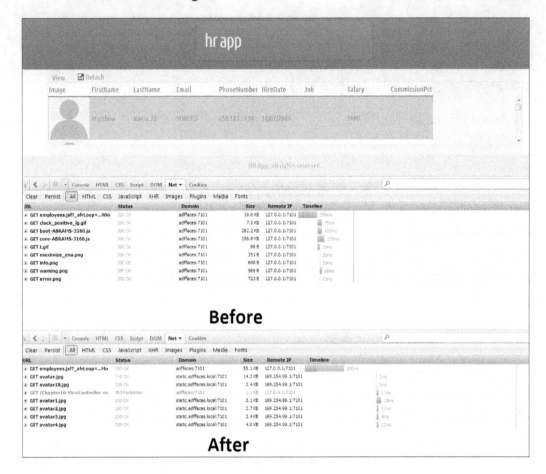

How it works...

When you have a big page with lots of pictures, custom CSS, and JavaScript files, it's always a good practice to have a CDN in place to parallelize the loading of all these files.

In a production environment, these should be different, but in this recipe, you can have the same effect by assigning different domains with the same IP address.

Please note that this technique works best when you have port 80 configured for your application.

In this recipe, we edited the `adf-config.xml` file to give different base URLs for specific relative paths. These are useful since it'll be applied across the entire application, and you can define them in three ways:

- Use the `match-pattern` attribute alone, which will match the pattern and apply the base URL as a prefix to it.

- Use the `match-alias` attribute alone, which will match the component name or feature. The `af:coreScripts` alias refers to the ADF Faces JavaScript core files, such as `af:images`, `af:skins`, or `af:documents`.

- Use a mixture of both if it matches both the URL pattern and component aliases.

See also...

To know more about CDN, check the official documentation at `http://docs.oracle.com/middleware/1212/adf/ADFUI/ap_config.htm#ADFUI13049`.

Using ADF caching to cache and compress static resources

Content delivery network is great to load your static resource in parallel; however, sometimes you might need to cache and compress these resources. Typically, you can use Oracle Web Cache or Oracle Traffic Director, and you can configure these cache rules from your application as well.

Even if you don't have Oracle Web Cache or Oracle Traffic Director, you can cache to the browser directly.

In this recipe, we are going to use ADF Faces caching rule to cache custom CSS files. For this example application, you can continue from the last recipe's `ADFFacesWithCDN` application, or you can grab this project's recipe by cloning the `ADFFacesWithCache` application from the Git repository.

How to do it...

To know how to apply the cache rules on your ADF application, perform the following steps:

1. Open the application.

2. Navigate to **Application Resources | Descriptors | ADF META-INF** and double-click on the `adf-config.xml` file.

3. View the file in the source mode.

4. Add the following mark up just before the last `</adf-config>` tag:

```xml
<adf-faces-config xmlns="http://xmlns.oracle.com/adf/faces/
config">
    <caching-rules xmlns="http://xmlns.oracle.com/adf/faces/rich/
acf">
        <caching-rule id="cssRule">
          <cache>true</cache>
          <duration>5000</duration>
          <agent-caching>true</agent-caching>
          <agent-duration>5000</agent-duration>
          <compress>true</compress>
          <cache-key-pattern>*.css</cache-key-pattern>
        </caching-rule>
      </caching-rules>
    </adf-faces-config>
```

5. Save everything, run the `employees.jsf` page, and use any debugging tool to see that CSS is being loaded from cache, as shown in the following screenshot:

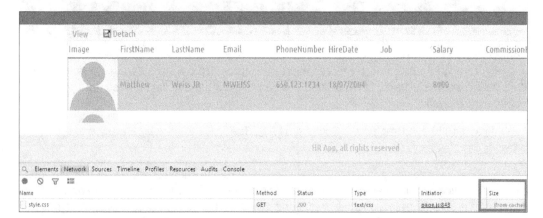

How it works...

Caching works in a similar fashion to CDN; however, if integrated with Oracle Web Cache or Oracle Traffic Director, it'll provide more power and control to the application.

You can have multiple cache rules for your application, images, CSS, JavaScript files, and all of your static resources.

If you don't have Oracle Web Cache or Oracle Traffic Directory, you can save the file to the browser itself by setting the `agent-caching` tag to `true`.

You can also specify the duration of the cache in seconds to specify the cache duration of one of the Oracle cache products of the browser cache.

See also

To know more about ADF Faces caching, refer to the official documentation at `http://docs.oracle.com/middleware/1212/adf/ADFUI/ap_config.htm#ADFUI11661`.

Index

D

data
putting, on maps 190-194
database
application, connecting to 32-34
installing, different options used 14, 15
Database Management Systems (DBMS) 14
date patterns
URL 258
declarative ADF Faces component
creating 302-306
different output components
using 121-126
DimensionFrom attribute 252
Display Label option 53, 54
DisplayMode attribute 185
Don't Repeat Yourself (DRY) 159
Download readme file button 130
drag-and-drop capabilities
adding 237-239
drag-and-drop functionality
URL 240
dynamicComponent
working with 136-138

E

editingMode attribute 326
EmployeesPercentage attribute 183
emptyText attribute 64
escape attribute 126
event response
JavaScript, executing within 229-231
Events attribute 234
Execute attribute 234
Execute function 241, 242
Execute method 242
exportCollectionActionListener tag 129
Expression Language (EL) 45

F

Faces messages experience
enhancing 279-282
fetchSize attribute 64, 70
fileDownloadActionListener tag 129
filterModel attribute 64

flat design techniques
using 172-176
Flat UX
URL 176
footer, page template
layout, adding to 144-147
forms
used, for presenting master-details records
74-77
functionalities
invoking, buttons used 129, 130
invoking, links used 129, 130

G

Gantt charts
tasks, displaying on 200-203
URL 203
gauge component
metrics, displaying with 178-189
URL 189
geographical and thematic maps
URL 194
geographic map 190
getAsObject method 261, 264, 269
getAsString method 264
getClientConversion method 268, 269
getClientId() method 278
getClientLibrarySource method 267, 277
getClientValidation method 279
Git repository
downloading 23-25
URL 23
Go to Bottom button 232
graph component
metrics, displaying with 178-189
URL 189
Group button 53
GroupingUsed attribute 258

H

Halign attribute 144, 145
handleDrop method 238, 240
header, page template
layout, adding to 144-147
headerText attribute 80

Thank you for buying
Oracle ADF Faces Cookbook

About Packt Publishing

Packt, pronounced 'packed', published its first book "*Mastering phpMyAdmin for Effective MySQL Management*" in April 2004 and subsequently continued to specialize in publishing highly focused books on specific technologies and solutions.

Our books and publications share the experiences of your fellow IT professionals in adapting and customizing today's systems, applications, and frameworks. Our solution-based books give you the knowledge and power to customize the software and technologies you're using to get the job done. Packt books are more specific and less general than the IT books you have seen in the past. Our unique business model allows us to bring you more focused information, giving you more of what you need to know, and less of what you don't.

Packt is a modern, yet unique publishing company, which focuses on producing quality, cutting-edge books for communities of developers, administrators, and newbies alike. For more information, please visit our website: www.PacktPub.com.

About Packt Enterprise

In 2010, Packt launched two new brands, Packt Enterprise and Packt Open Source, in order to continue its focus on specialization. This book is part of the Packt Enterprise brand, home to books published on enterprise software – software created by major vendors, including (but not limited to) IBM, Microsoft and Oracle, often for use in other corporations. Its titles will offer information relevant to a range of users of this software, including administrators, developers, architects, and end users.

Writing for Packt

We welcome all inquiries from people who are interested in authoring. Book proposals should be sent to author@packtpub.com. If your book idea is still at an early stage and you would like to discuss it first before writing a formal book proposal, contact us; one of our commissioning editors will get in touch with you.

We're not just looking for published authors; if you have strong technical skills but no writing experience, our experienced editors can help you develop a writing career, or simply get some additional reward for your expertise.

Oracle Application Integration Architecture (AIA) Foundation Pack 11gR1: Essentials

ISBN: 978-1-84968-480-4   Paperback: 274 pages

Develop and deploy your Enterprise Integration Solutions using Oracle AIA

Oracle Application Integration Architecture (AIA) Foundation Pack 11gR1: Essentials

Develop and deploy your Enterprise Integration Solutions using Oracle AIA

Hariharan V. Ganesarethinam

1. Full of illustrations, diagrams, and tips with clear step-by-step instructions and real time examples to develop full-fledged integration processes.

2. Each chapter drives the reader right from architecture to implementation.

3. Understand the important concept of Enterprise Business Objects that play a crucial role in AIA installation and models.

Oracle Fusion Applications Administration Essentials

ISBN: 978-1-84968-686-0   Paperback: 114 pages

Administer, configure, and maintain your Oracle Fusion Applications

Oracle Fusion Applications Administration Essentials

Administer, configure, and maintain your Oracle Fusion Applications

Faisal Ghadially
Kalpit Parikh

1. Provides clear and concise guidance for administering Oracle Fusion Applications.

2. Comprehensively covers all major areas of Oracle Fusion Applications administration.

3. Contains meaningful illustrations that explain basic concepts, followed by detailed instructions on how to implement them.

Please check **www.PacktPub.com** for information on our titles

www.ingramcontent.com/pod-product-compliance
Lightning Source LLC
LaVergne TN
LVHW062304060326
832902LV00013B/2036